York St John
Library and Information Services
Normal Loan

Please see self service receipt for return date.

Fines are payable for late return

Religion and the Politics of Peace and Conflict

Princeton Theological Monograph Series

K. C. Hanson, Charles M. Collier, D. Christopher Spinks,
Series Editors

Recent volumes in the series:

Gale Heide
*System and Story: Narrative Critique
and Construction in Theology*

Jeanne M. Hoeft
*Agency, Culture, and Human Personhood:
Pastoral Thelogy and Intimate Partner Violence*

Lisa E. Dahill
*Reading from the Underside of Selfhood:
Bonhoeffer and Spiritual Formation*

Michael S. Hogue
*The Tangled Bank: Toward an Ecotheological Ethics
of Responsible Participation*

Charles Bellinger
The Trinitarian Self: The Key to the Puzzle of Violence

Philip Ruge-Jones
*Cross in Tensions: Luther's Theology of the Cross
as Theolgico-social Critique*

Mary Clark Moschella
*Living Devotions: Reflections on Immigration, Identity,
and Religious Imagination*

Gabriel Andrew Msoka
*Basic Human Rights and the Humanitarian Crises
in Sub-Saharan Africa: Ethical Reflections*

Religion and the Politics of Peace and Conflict

Edited by
Linda Hogan and Dylan Lee Lehrke

ᗡPICKWICK *Publications* · Eugene, Oregon

RELIGION AND THE POLITICS OF PEACE AND CONFLICT

Princeton Theological Monograph Series 94

Pickwick Publications
A Division of Wipf and Stock Publishers
199 W. 8th Ave., Suite 3
Eugene, OR 97401

www.wipfandstock.com

ISBN 13: 978-1-55635-067-2

Cataloging-in-Publication data:

Religion and the politics of peace and conflict / edited by Linda Hogan and Dylan Lee Lehrke.

xxii + 240 p. ; 23 cm. —Includes bibliographical references.

Princeton Theological Monograph Series 94

ISBN 13: 978-1-55635-067-2

1. Religion and politics. 2. Violence—Religious aspects—Christianity. 3. Violence—Religious aspects—Islam. 4. Violence—Religious aspects—Judaism. I. Hogan, Linda. II. Lehrke, Dylan Lee. III. Title. IV. Series.

BL65.P7 R43270 2009

Manufactured in the U.S.A.

Contents

With gratitude to the Irish School of Ecumenics Trust
for its support of this project

Introduction

Between Legitimation and Refusal: Jewish, Christian, and Islamic Responses to Political Violence

Linda Hogan

> Much of what is narrowly termed politics seems to rest on a longing for certainty even at the cost of honesty; for an analysis that, once given, need not be re-examined. . . .
>
> Truthfulness everywhere means heightened complexity. But it is a movement into evolution.
>
> The politics worth having, the relationships worth having, demand that we delve still deeper.[1]

THE GLOBAL EXPERIENCE OF THE LAST FIVE DECADES PRESENTS US WITH a paradox. On the one hand, when we examine the progress made in particular regions (for example, in Europe), we see that the increasing density of economic and political interdependence creates the sense of a common fate and thus reduces the likelihood of nations resorting to war to settle disputes. Yet on the other hand, one is aware that this process of integration has been accompanied, in Europe, as well as around the world, by rising levels of conflict. Indeed analysts agree that this surge in levels of violence is in part explained by the development of a new type of war in which the boundaries between what would traditionally have been described as "war" (i.e., the violence waged between states or other political actors), and between organized crime and large scale human rights violations have become blurred. Thus it is increasingly difficult to identify the objectives of those engaged in many of

---

1. Rich, *Arts of the Possible*, 39

these new wars, or to establish whether particular conflicts are pursued for political, ethnic, religious, humanitarian, or economic motives. The "global war on terror" embodies many of the characteristics of the new type of war, reflecting the fact that, relatively speaking, although fewer states are in direct conflict with each other, the levels of violence globally are once again on the increase. Humanitarian crises too have become occasions for military intervention, with the oxymoron of the "humanitarian war" occupying a significant place in the current political order. Inevitably, these rising levels of conflict are accompanied by a dramatic increase in annual global military spending.[2] Moreover, as a result of global integration, the trade in arms (both legal and illegal) grows ever more lucrative, more technologically sophisticated, and thus more difficult to control.

That the ethics of war and peace continues to be of concern is, therefore, not surprising. That our conversations quickly turn to religion is not surprising either, given the prominent role that religions continue to play in the ideological, political, and ethical justifications of violence. With respect to the traditions with which this collection is concerned— namely Judaism, Christianity, and Islam—their role in animating and justifying some of the most intractable contemporary conflicts is the subject of global ethical and political debate. Moreover the complex and multi-faceted approaches adopted by the Abrahamic traditions to the matter of political violence are themselves the subject of mutual misunderstanding. Perhaps the most high-profile recent example of this cultural and religious misunderstanding is Pope Benedict XVI's address at the University of Regensburg in September 2006 entitled "Faith, Reason and the University: Memories and Reflections."[3] Both the address itself and its reception illustrate the multiple opportunities for misconception that exist among the religions. Indeed herein we encounter a series of misunderstandings, in terms of perception, of interpretation of history, and in terms of the sensitivities of a community that believes itself to be under attack. Two flash-points emerged as the Pope's comments

2. The Stockholm International Peace Research Institute estimates that the global budget for 2005 was $1 trillion, or 2.6% of global GDP; report available at www.sipri.org/contents/milap/milex/mex_trends.html (accessed November 15, 2006).

3. Benedict XVI, "Faith, Reason and the University: Memories and Reflections," available at http://www.guardian.co.uk/world/2006/sep/15/religion.uk, accessed on May 7, 2008.

were being discussed. The first related to the characterization of the role and status of reason in Islam. The second, intended as an ancillary point to bolster the argument about Islam's putative disregard for reason, related to the use of a quotation from the Emperor Manuel II Paleologus who wrote that the ministry of Muhammad had brought things "only evil and inhuman" and that the Prophet "spread by the sword the faith he preached."[4] The legitimacy of both the historical and moral claims made herein have been the subject of intense scrutiny, and millions of Muslims world-wide have expressed their outrage at what many perceive to be the mischaracterization of the theological foundations of Islam and of its approach to the use of violence. In his perceptive commentary on Pope Benedict's lecture, Rashied Omar draws attention to a difficulty with which all theologians and historians of religion have to contend when they engage in analysis of this kind, namely the difficulty of representing accurately a tradition that is discursive and changeful. Pope Benedict's failure to contend with the discursive nature of Islam, Omar suggests, was one of the central reasons for the offence caused. Thus Omar claims that "using the Paleologus citation as a springboard, Pope Benedict develops an overly-simplistic picture of the complex and diverse Muslim theologies on the nature of God" and that "rather than take account of the diverse and often competing traditions the Pope selectively retrieved from the vast Muslim theological tradition one viewpoint, thereby reducing Islam to one voice of a multi-vocal, centuries-long internal argument."[5] Islam is not a monolithic entity. Theologically, culturally, and historically Islam embodies diverse perspectives on a variety of religious and political concerns. Indeed each of the three traditions with which we are concerned in this collection is a discursive tradition. Judaism and Christianity too can be characterized in terms of being multi-vocal, with many of their core theological tenets also being the subject of "centuries-long internal argument." Despite this however, each of the Abrahamic traditions is frequently miscast as an unchanging, timeless tradition, a tradition, to quote Seamus Heaney, that is

---

4. Ibid.

5. Omar, "Pope Benedict XVI's Comments on Islam in Regensburg: A Muslim Response."

> unshiftably planked in the long long ago, cargoed with
> Its own dumb, tongue-and-groove worthiness';
> 'An un-get-roundable weight[6]

Yet what Omar claims, and what the essays in this collection illustrate, is that on a range of doctrinal and moral issues, and especially on the sensitive matter of justifying violence, the texts, the theologies, and the histories of Judaism, Christianity, and Islam are varied and that mutual misunderstanding will only be overcome if "we delve still deeper."

In fact the connections between religion and violence are complex and multifaceted. From the conflicts in the Middle East and the Balkans to those in Southeast Asia and beyond, religious claims and ideologies frame and legitimate political violence. Moreover in international relations post-9/11, religious language and metaphors have acquired a new political significance. In Israel today the nature and extent of the religious duty to defend or maintain a Jewish presence through "the biblical Land of Israel" is the subject of intense debate,[7] while in the USA and in Britain advocates of the war in Iraq evoke a myriad of arguments from the Christian scriptures and tradition.[8] In a similar vein, though perhaps more controversially, the spokespersons for al-Qa'ida also justify their "Jihad against Jews and Crusaders" in theological terms.[9] Indeed with religious justifications of violence omnipresent in international political discourse it is not surprising that citizens world-wide are increasingly expressing the view that religions are intrinsically violent, that they inevitably incite and intensify political violence, and that politics would be enhanced by the exclusion of religion from the public square.

However such an unambiguous indictment of religious traditions is inaccurate in that it fails to acknowledge the diversity that exists within religions on the issue of whether and under what conditions recourse to violence can be justified. Nor does it acknowledge that pacifism has religious roots. This book seeks to challenge such uninformed views by highlighting the fact that within Judaism, Christianity, and Islam there are analogous ways of engaging with the question of political

6. Heaney, "The Settle Bed," 345.

7. See Solomon, "Ethics of War: Judaism," especially 118–30.

8. The most extensive resource of articles supporting the case for the war in Iraq from a just war perspective can be found at www.ratzingerfanclub.com/justwar/index/html. Authors include George Weigel, Richard Neuhaus, and Michael Novak.

9. Kelsay, "Arguments Concerning Resistance in Contemporary Islam."

violence, so that within each tradition there is a spectrum that ranges from pacifism (or a version thereof) to arguments that specify the strict conditions under which the use of violence may be morally justified. In fact, within each of the Abrahamic traditions there continues a long-standing debate as to whether the "pacifist" or "just war" positions best capture the "essence" of the moral stance of the religion, though it must be conceded that within each tradition pacifist views have always been marginal to the dominant trajectory of legitimation. This collection seeks to highlight the ambivalence of religion vis-à-vis violence by presenting a more complex, variegated account of the internal disputations within each of the three traditions with which we are concerned, there-by contradicting many of the commonly held perceptions about religious responses to political violence.

Traditions of Legitimation and Limits

Recent decades have seen a resurgence of interest in just war and analogous ethical arguments. Titles like *The Return of the Just War*[10] and *The Holy War Idea in Western and Islamic Traditions*[11] are concerned with determining when the use of violence is morally acceptable, under what conditions, and on whose authority. From within the Christian tradition of legitimation a range of authors argue that "properly applied and combined with the subjective virtue of charity, just war doctrine facilitates the assessment of war, and particularly the war on terror in a genuinely moral way."[12] Comparable conversations are also underway within Judaism[13] and Islam.[14] In this collection the essays of George Wilkes and John Kelsay each address the matter of legitimation within a comparative perspective. Wilkes draws comparisons between Jewish and classic Christian just war traditions while examining the difficulties

10. See Aquino and Mieth, *Return of the Just War.*

11. See Johnson, *Holy War Idea in Western and Islamic Traditions.*

12. Johnstone, "War on Terrorism: A Just War?" 40, and "Pope John Paul and the War in Iraq." See also O'Donovan, *Just War Revisited*; Johnstone, "Political Assassination and Tyrannicide: Traditions and Contemporary Conflicts"; van Iersel, "Stopping the Murdering Martyr: Just War Tradition and the Confrontation with Ethical Asymmetry in Warfare"; and Naert, "Impact of the Fight against Terrorism on the *ius ad bellum.*"

13. See for example Bleich, "Preemptive War in Jewish Law"; Halpérin and Levitte, *La conscience juive face à la guerre*; and Niditch, *War in the Hebrew Bible.*

14. See for example Kelsay, *Islam and War;* and Ahmed, *Jihad.*

experienced by Jewish scholars in agreeing on firm principles regulating the conduct of war. He reminds readers that while there is no term in the traditional lexicon of rabbinic religious reflection that translates exactly as "just war," nonetheless it is possible to speak of a significant consensus on key dimensions of the Jewish debate over legitimizing and limiting war. This consensus, Wilkes claims, emerges as a result of the centrality of a series of texts generally considered authoritative, from the Bible, Mishnah, and Talmud to the *Mishneh Torah* of Moses Maimonides, with the authors and editors of successive documents claiming to be faithful interpretations of their predecessors. According to Wilkes the distinction between commanded and permitted wars lies at the core of this continuity, with "just cause" the fundamental building block in traditional calculations of the other features of a legitimate war. Within this consensus however, there is room for divergent interpretations of what is permitted and what is required in relation to war. Indeed Wilkes is adamant that the foundational texts of rabbinic Judaism themselves create the space for divergent interpretations of these obligations, since according to Wilkes their "lapidary declarations" are open to contradictory readings. Additionally, the recognized challenge of applying traditional teachings in very different political and military contexts create further possibilities for a range of positions on the matter of the obligations of Jews in respect of war.

In "Why Should You Not Fight?: The Imperative of War in Islam and Christianity?" John Kelsay too insists that any analysis of religious legitimations of war must be cognizant of the theological and historical contexts of their composition and development. Mindful of this, Kelsay's argument is that both Christian just war and Islamic jihad frameworks are not first and foremost "guides for statecraft" or "violence reduction mechanisms," but rather "frameworks for discerning the commands or guidance of God." This means that the primary issue is never "fighting or not," but rather it is focused on answering the question "what is God leading (a particular community of believers) to do (in a particular context)?" Subsequently, the essay demonstrates how the jihad and the Christian just war frameworks operate first as an historical matter and secondly in the post-September 11, 2001, context. The focus on this latter context involves special attention being given to issues raised by al-Qa'ida's leaders and by the practice of martyrdom operations (in the case of Islam) and to the U.S.-led "war on terror" in the case of the Christian just war.

There is no doubt that the matter of justification is a complex one, and the hazards of idolatry and self-legitimation, particularly of a religious kind, are many. Indeed our history is replete with examples of religious convictions summoned in the service of nationalistic and ethnic ideologies, with religious leaders justifying some of the most brutal and immoral military campaigns on religious grounds. Nor is this hazard consigned to history. Gerhard Beestermöller's "Eurocentricity in the Perception of Wars," and Irina Novikova's "Lessons from the Anatomy of War: Svetlana Alexievich's Zinky Boys," illustrate just how circular and self-perpetuating modern legitimations—whether they be historical, ethnic, or religious—can be.[15] Historical narratives determine assessments of provocation and the requirements of defense. History constructs a version of cause and intention and is crucial in assessments of when political solutions have been exhausted. Moreover these particular constructions of the past are transmitted through families, communities, memorialisations, and often through religious ideologies and iconography. Thus religious leaders especially need to be attentive to the temptations of self-legitimation and ought to seek to guard against the inappropriate use of religion in the construction of the narratives of war. The traditions of legitimation and limits with which we are concerned in this section contain internal mechanisms that are intended to protect the tradition from being usurped and used in the service of military or political ambitions. This is and has long-since been a critical factor in each tradition's concern to distinguish just from unjust uses of violence. Nonetheless the historical record is grim, suggesting that these internal mechanisms are themselves subject to the limitations of culture, time and place.

Traditions of Pacifism and Non-violence

Alongside, and sometimes in opposition to, these traditions of limitations and limits are those of pacifism and non-violence. Indeed within Judaism, Christianity, and Islam there is a spectrum that includes pacifism, though it must be acknowledged that the pacifist perspective is

15. Beestermöller, "Eurocentricity in the Perception of Wars"; and Novikova, "Lessons from the Anatomy of War."

more developed in some traditions than others. The different traditions conceptualize the religious obligation to work for peace in various ways and so no common religious idiom or conceptual apparatus is evident. Moreover, the manner in which the religions hold to this obligation is different, so that within Christianity there is a pacifist strand, exemplified by the peace churches, which denounces any recourse to violence and regards non-violence to be of a non-negotiable religious character. Other religious traditions also include advocates of comparable *a priori* claims, though for the most part the pacifist witness sits alongside the belief that, in certain exceptional circumstances, justice can only be accomplished through the use of violent force. Thus, when we consider the traditions of pacifism and non-violence within Judaism, Christianity, and Islam, we do so in the knowledge that there are no direct comparators here, but rather analogous arguments, histories, and moralities.

In "Imagining Co-Existence in the Face of War: Jewish 'Pacifism' and the State 1917–1948," Mark Levene takes as his starting-point his view that in the decades since the Holocaust and the creation of the state of Israel, the notion of Judaism as a prophetic voice for peace in the world has been almost entirely lost. Replaced in common gentile perceptions by images of Israeli military occupation, violence, and intransigence in Palestine, Levene argues that, against the backdrop of European Jewish destruction, most Jews both within and outside Israel find notions of pacifism or non-violence equally problematic. In this essay Levene's first task is to understand what has happened in the modern Jewish experience to marginalize the ancient prophetic message. Having analyzed the various religious and political factors that explain this marginalization of the irenic tradition, Levene argues that it never went completely away but rather re-emerged in the twentieth century in the challenging surroundings of Palestine, in the ideas and milieu of Brit Shalom (Covenant of Peace) and of its prime and most innovative mover, Martin Buber. In his analysis Levene draws attention to the fact that the development of this remarkable organization embodies two critical paradoxes. The first involves the symbiotic relationship between middle European assimilants (like Buber) as they rediscovered their Jewish roots, and certain Christian theologians attracted to the same reservoir of mystical ideas. Thus it was in a pre-Nazi German environment in which the possibilities of a genuine religious coexistence were richest, not least through common points of enthusiasm, such as that associated with another rediscovery: that of the Jewish Jesus. Secondly, denied the deserved expression of the symbiosis at home in Germany, Buber's Judaism found its greatest challenge, and expression, in the primarily Muslim environment of Palestine, where Brit Shalom, and related organizations, sought political outcomes founded on strictly ethical, bi-national, and hence anti-chauvinist foundations. Levene concludes that in a political climate dominated by concepts of "the clash of civilizations" and fundamentalist exclusivities, Buber's anarchic version of Jewish eschatology is particularly relevant in helping us to confront and overcome humanity's deep and possibly terminal crisis.

The Christian analogue of Jewish "pacifism" is developed in a distinctive manner by Stanley Hauerwas in his "Sacrificing the Sacrifices of War." He argues that the Christian "dis-ease" with war is liturgical and claims that the sacrifices of war are a counter-liturgy to the sacrifice at the altar made possible by Christ. In a far-reaching theological argument, Hauerwas insists that, because Christians believe that Christ is the end of sacrifice—that is, the end of any sacrifice not determined by the sacrifice of the cross—Christians are free of the necessity to secure our existence through sacrificing our and others' lives on the world's altars. He does recognize that the sacrifice that war requires seems to mirror our lives as Christians, making war at once attracting and repelling to Christians. However in an argument that radically contradicts the trajectory of the Christian just war tradition he claims that the Christian alternative to war is worship and that the church is the end of war. This fundamentally different reading of the political significance of the cross of Jesus suggests that through the forgiveness made possible by the cross a people has been created that refuses to resort to the sword so that they and those they love might survive. In this new order, the sacrifices of war are no longer necessary, and humanity can now live free of the necessity of violence and killing. Moreover he argues that if Christians leave the eucharistic table ready to kill one another, then we not only eat and drink judgment on ourselves, but we also rob the world of the witness necessary for it to know that there is an alternative to the sacrifices of war.

In his analysis of the way in which Islam has conceptualized and embodied this pacifist impulse, Muhammad Abdel Haleem argues that the whole character of Islamic teaching tends towards avoiding violence and conflict in all areas of life. The Qur'an makes working to bring about reconciliation between people a highly meritorious act and insists that fighting is permissible only to defend oneself and to protect the oppressed. Thus the normal situation within Islamic teaching is that war is prohibited, although the right to self-defense is given both in terms of permission and in terms of its being a religious obligation. Whereas John Kelsay's essay explores Islamic thinking on the limited contexts in which recourse to violence may be justified, or even required, Haleem's focus is on the religious foundation of the desire for peace. Thus Haleem considers the various components of "the politics of peace in Islam" through a discussion of the significance of particular Qu'ranic texts and historical events. He discusses the treaty of Hudaybiyah from which he draws the conclusion that "God considers this avoidance of war as a victory and reminds them that He sent down His *sakina* on the hearts of the believers, making them calm in the face of provocation on the part of the unbelievers." He argues that this is the essence of pacifism and non-violence within Islam—i.e., "a positive force of spiritual peace, faith, moral resolve and conviction, even love, sent directly from God, has the power to counteract and overcome fear, emotional turmoil and hostility."

Religions and the Gendering of Violence

Having illustrated how this spectrum that ranges from legitimation to pacifism is expressed within each of the Abrahamic traditions, this collection ends by exploring aspects of the ambivalence towards violence as it is enacted in relation to the politics of gender. The purpose here is to indicate how, in each religion, the debates about the permissibility of violence are impacted by, or have an impact on, constructions of gender. There is no attempt to develop a meta-narrative that claims a causal relationship between a religion's approach to political violence and its understanding of gender politics. Rather the essays in this section identify particular manifestations of the three religious cultures through which aspects of the complex dynamic of gender and violence are expressed. Thus in Judaism the discussion revolves around the changing constructions of masculinity evident in Ashkenazic Jewish culture, in Christianity contemporary representations of crucifixion provide the focus for a meditation on the complex manner in which gender and violence intersect in the interpretative apparatus of the tradition, while the discussion of Islam is concerned with the gender-religion-violence nexus as evident in contemporary contestations within that tradition. However prior to considering how the three traditions' respective approaches to gender politics impact on their approach to political violence, the issue of how gender politics and violence intersect is discussed. Mary Condren's essay sets the scene for the discussion of the three Abrahamic traditions by attending to the manner in which gender, religion, anthropology, theology, and psychoanalysis intersect. Thus she treats religion as a complex cultural, social, and psychic phenomenon that shapes and maintains social and gendered relations. Condren points out that whereas psychoanalytic perspectives on war and gender have traditionally focused on the construction of masculinity and been informed by exclusively Freudian perspectives, in recent years, through the work of Melanie Klein, the focus has shifted from the father to the mother. Thus she suggests, the gendering of warfare and the role of religion therein can be better understood through an approach that sees war, not so much a singular event, but rather as a patriarchal culture that enjoys the hegemonic status of naming, interpreting, performing, implementing, and enacting certain social models and worldviews in which the male world (characterized as *public*) takes precedence over that of the female world (characterized as *private* or *domestic*).

Melissa Raphael's analysis of secular and religious male Jewish responses to the Holocaust problematizes Condren's conclusion by illustrating that the gendering of Jewish responses to war and violence is ambivalent, shifting, and multiply determined. Indeed Raphael argues that Ashkenazi (Eastern, Western, and Central European Jewish) men's attitudes to violence unsettles the customary Second Wave feminist assumption that patriarchal religion *either* supports, *or* less commonly protests, regimes of violence. Rather the diaspora ethics and culture of Ashkenazi Judaism complicates the options. In fact there is a spectrum of positions between the prophetic criticism of violence and complicity with violence, reminding one that religious patriarchies do not take one single, universal, and consistently oppressive form. Thus she claims, the fact that a religion is male-dominated does not mean that it always sanctions a macho or warlike stance, that it glorifies violence, or that it offers a clear and direct impetus for a community's defense against violence. Raphael's study of how social violence has been construed in Ashkenazic Jewish culture presents us with a complex and fascinating set of paradoxes indicating that the gendering of Jewish responses to war and violence is plural and variously determined. She concludes her analysis with the observation that, since 1948, Israeli cultural rhetoric and representation have refigured Jewish masculinity so as to erase the humiliating memory of the male Ashkenzic victim of the Holocaust and to encourage and permit what many regard to be the successful defense of the Jewish family and territory.

David Tombs's challenging gendered analysis of Christ's crucifixion argues that the revelations from Abu Ghraib ought to prompt Christians to re-read the story of Christ's crucifixion with attention to the sexual dimension common in torture practices. Reading the gospels with an awareness of how sexual humiliation was used against prisoners at Abu Ghraib highlights aspects of the crucifixion that are otherwise easily passed over. Tombs's textual and cultural analysis makes a persuasive argument that during his passion (when he was flogged naked, when he was subsequently stripped a further two times, and when he was left naked to die in front of a mocking crowd), and particularly at the crucifixion itself, the sexual element of the humiliation suffered by Jesus becomes clear. Yet he notes that it is striking that there is no acknowledgment of this side of Christ's suffering in *The Passion of the Christ*, a movie that, notwithstanding its many limitations, is regarded as offering a graphic and realistic portrayal of crucifixion. According to Tombs, despite its graphic portrayal of physical pain, the movie hides the full cruelty of crucifixion. In answering the question, Why is the sexual component of the humiliation of crucifixion hidden?, Tombs suggests that the behind this discomfort with and avoidance of sexual humiliation is a particular model of masculinity. Thus he concludes that the movie constructs a model of Christ's power, manliness, and sanctity that would be undermined by the possibility that the crucifixion event could be interpreted, in part, as sexual humiliation, as a form of sexual abuse.

In a passionate and angry essay Haleh Afsher argues against the common misconception that Islam is intrinsically violent, and that this finds expression both in world politics and in gender politics. Such discussions, Afsher insists, imagine Muslim women as silent victims hidden in the cloak of the *hijab*, awaiting the return of their men to the home and their brave warriors to the hearth. Such imaginings, according to Afsher, though encouraged by some Muslim men, remain far from the truth, and are best understood in the context of the history of Orientalism. Afsher discusses the pacifist as well as the "just war" strands within Islam and develops her analysis of the Islamic approach to violence focusing more specifically on questions of gender. She challenges the conventional view that "Islam defines itself, 'through disgust for women's bodies.'"[16] Rather, she argues that such beliefs are rooted in a superficial understanding of the faith and an inability to engage with the vibrant discussions initiated by Muslim women who, over the past century and a half, have contested many of the misinterpretations of the Qur'an that had been central to the thirteen centuries of interpretation and instruction by men about the lives of women. Moreover, she insists, at the core of the contestations has been the question of violence against women. Afsher concludes her analysis by discussing some recent struggles of Muslim women who, in the name of their faith, have argued for different pathways to peace.

In her magisterial *Foundations of Violence*, the late Grace Jantzen argues that we will only be able to resist what she calls the "necrophilic *habitus* of modernity," that, unchecked, will continue to bring about violence, death, and destruction, when we have begun to construct alternative political, ethical, and religious discourses[17]—that is, discourses that no longer valorize, sacralize, or justify violence. There is no doubt that religion can and must make a distinctive contribution to the construction of these alternative discourses, not least because they have a long record of complicity in the framing and legitimating of political violence. In a more positive vein, however, one can see from the essays in this collection that the pathways to these alternative discourses are plentiful and the resources from which the Abrahamic traditions can draw in the development of these discourses are many. The story is a complex one, however because, as is evident throughout this collection, these three religions embody and express an ambivalence vis-à-vis religion so that statements about the irenic nature of a particular religion cannot capture fully the discursive and contentious character of these internal conversations. In an attempt to relativize the importance of the question about the doctrinal position of particular religions vis-à-vis violence, the Christian theologian Paul Valadier suggests that we focus

16. Toynbee, *The Guardian*, September 28, 2001.
17. Jantzen, *Foundations of Violence*, 10.

on a different and more fundamental question, namely, whether and how the Christian tradition can enable the kind of dialogue that will ameliorate irrational fears and encourage the different religions to recognize their irreducible complementarity.[18] The essays in this collection suggest that this is a task not only for the Christian tradition, but rather is one that can and ought be shared in by the traditions of Judaism and Islam as well. Moreover our respective traditions are replete with exemplars, both historical and contemporary, who witness to the possibilities for inter-religious dialogue and understanding. For religious persons, undoubtedly, these issues are particularly challenging since they require us to confront the complexities and limitations of our own traditions while also responding to their often-radical demands. Yet in these complexities lie the possibilities for the religions to develop a greater sense of mutual understanding, since it is in these complexities that the commonalities between the religions on the matter of political violence are found.

18. Valadier, "La barbarie dans la civilization," 472

PART ONE

Traditions of Legitimation and Limits

1

Legitimations and Limits of War
in Jewish Tradition

George R. Wilkes

SOMEWHAT CRYPTICALLY, THE *MISHNAH*, A CORE RABBINIC TEXT FINALLY edited at the end of the second century CE, states that "The sword comes into the world for the delay of justice, and for the perversion of justice, and on account of the offence of those who interpret the Torah (the revealed law or teaching) not according to its true sense."[1]

Cryptically, because the practical application of this apparently pacifist statement will be unclear not only to the ear of a Christian unaccustomed to Jewish tradition, but also to a Jewish scholar very well acquainted with Jewish tradition.

What does it mean to say that the sword comes into the world "on account of the offence of those who interpret the Torah not according to its true sense"? Does this mean it is a misinterpretation of the law to advocate armed violence, even in self-defense? Or is armed conflict a divine punishment for other misinterpretations of Torah, perhaps for the consequences of passively relying upon God's protection in the face of armed threat?

I would like to introduce Jewish parallels to just war thinking with a close eye to some of the difficulties that Jewish scholars have in agreeing on firm principles regulating the conduct of war. Some of these difficulties parallel the disagreements between traditionalists and modernists within the Churches, between nationalists and universalists—the different sections of the Jewish community, too, are engaged in a

1. *m. Pirkei Avot* 5:11.

contest over the authority of individuals and religious leaders to define Jewish values, including the notion of "legitimate" military conduct. The room for divergent interpretations is laid by the foundational texts of rabbinic Judaism themselves, texts whose lapidary declarations are, like that quoted above, commonly open to quite contradictory readings. Add to that the changes in historical context since the compilation of the *Mishnah*, particularly in military and political terms, and the challenge of applying traditional teachings today becomes all the greater.

There are some fundamental differences between Jewish and Christian tradition that demand acknowledgement before we can begin to state with clarity the ways in which Jewish and Christian traditions are comparable. There is no term in the traditional lexicon of rabbinic religious reflection that translates exactly as "just war." We shall see in the discussion below of the theological bases for introducing justice in war that this is more than a semantic difference. Similarly, the rabbis of mishnaic and post-mishnaic times have not sought to establish legitimation for "holy war," again a term which is not generally used in rabbinic reflection on armed conflict. Though parallels may be assumed or sought, it would be unhelpful to conflate Jewish just war thinking with the Old Testament "holy war" as it has been represented in the works of scholars in the tradition of Gerhard von Rad and, more recently, Susan Niditch.[2]

As important as biblical texts are in Jewish discussion of war, these texts have been re-interpreted time and again by Jewish commentators. Scholars are still in the early stages of reconstructing the changes wrought in the course of the history of Jewish religious and political thought. Academic overviews of the subject have often simplified the history of Jewish discussion of justice and war so as to suggest that there is a classic approach to legitimating armed response that has changed little from biblical times. In part, this is a response to the common rabbinic practice of drawing authority from the assertion of continuity between the canonical biblical and early rabbinic texts, and then between those texts and subsequent commentaries. Within traditionalist circles, this sense of the need for continuity is heightened by the normative acknowledgement that subsequent writers lack the authority to reject the conclusions of earlier generations, particularly with respect

---

2. Von Rad, *Holy War*; Niditch, *War in the Hebrew Bible*.

to these foundational texts. Thus, as we shall see below, the *Mishnah* already presents its key distinctions between forms of justifiable armed conflict as a commentary on the mandates given for biblical wars, and subsequent commentators have presented their works as commentaries on the text of the *Mishnah*. A strand of Zionist historiography has cemented this idea of a static post-mishnaic law of war further, arguing that Jews, having no effective military power since the failure of the revolts against the Roman occupation of Judea, had no occasion to revisit the topic until the coming of the state of Israel.[3] On closer study, new works can be seen to have changed rabbinic commentary on war—a prominent reality in Jewish experience and a major source of ethical reflection, particularly in biblical commentaries—in every era; at and following the time of Jesus, in the middle ages, in early modern times, and repeatedly in more recent times. Jewish discussion of the topic has thus developed period by period in a comparable fashion to that seen in Christian just war theory, albeit from different bases and with variant effects. This discussion has reopened as the state of Israel has faced new military and political situations in recent decades, but the best efforts of legal codifiers have not closed this debate at any point in Jewish history.

It would therefore be both anachronistic and over-simplistic to treat Jewish just war thinking as a historically less-developed basis for biblically-inspired and monotheistic just war traditions, whether Christian or Muslim. Nevertheless, this very different tradition may be a useful foil against which we can reflect on Christian, Muslim, and secularized Western ideas about justice and war. In some respects, Jewish traditions undercut the notion that it is possible to have a coherent just war theory. In other respects, however, the comparison with Jewish tradition can help us to view Christian and other approaches in sharper relief, underlining that many of the most important resources used in just war theory are not peculiar to one theology but shared across faith boundaries and without necessarily making reference to the historical conditions in which Christian theologians elaborated theories legitimating war.

---

3. Edrei, "Law, Interpretation, And Ideology."

Jewish Understandings of War

Jewish commentary on the application of justice and ethical limitation in armed conflict is divided over the very question, "What is war?" In pre-modern times, Jewish commentators tended to treat war as a fact of life, and lasting peace as an aspiration only for the period following the coming of the Messiah. Before such a time, war, in this view, is by and large governed only by the exercise of force. War is imposed on Jews as part of the world of "the nations." In this situation, some of the earliest post-mishnaic commentaries asserted that "One who has mercy on the cruel will, in the end, be cruel to the merciful."[4] Still today, there is a minority strand within the Orthodox Jewish world open to arguments to the effect that the rules of war do not apply when one's opponent does not follow them. The first Chief Rabbi of the Israeli Defense Force (IDF), Shlomo Goren, is said to have once stirred controversy within the religious Zionist community by arguing that the limitations to justifiable conduct in war imposed by Deuteronomy 20 are only applicable before the outbreak of hostilities—war by nature being wild, lawless, and uncivilized.[5]

By contrast, a majority of commentators through the ages have judged that the nature of our relationship with God and with other human beings means that we are responsible for lawful conduct of war and in war. The first reference to war in the Bible—in Genesis 14—is also the first event after Abraham's entry to the land of Canaan. Here, Abraham is drawn into a conflict between Canaanite kings after Lot is taken captive. According to Samson Raphael Hirsch, one of the most-respected nineteenth-century biblical commentators and a founder of modern Orthodox Judaism, this episode underscored that, from the outset, Abraham's mission was to bring the values associated with ethical monotheism into a gentile world where war and conflict were the norm.[6] It is apparent, in light of this, that Jewish commentators need not believe that justice in warfare is a demand created by natural law. Even in the midst of a natural chaos, the mission and conduct of Abraham

4. *Midrash Tanchuma, Metzorah* 1/*Koheleth Rabbah* 7.

5. Further discussion of texts according to which war is by nature limitless can be found in Tendler, "Exchanging Territories for Peace." By contrast, Edrei notes that Goren's military ethics were elaborate and reflected serious consideration of restraints applicable to military conduct. Edrei, "Divine Spirit and Physical Power," 255–97.

6. Hirsch, *Terumath Zvi*, 68–69.

signaled for later generations of Jews the duty to follow ethical injunctions and to exercise restraint in making war.

Legitimating War in Jewish Traditions

To begin to understand why there is no phrase in pre-modern rabbinic
Judaism that means "just" or "holy" war, we might go back to Adam and
Eve. In Jewish biblical interpretation, Adam and Eve did not experience
the absolute change of state that Christian traditions have described as
"the Fall"—there is no word for "the Fall" in Jewish tradition, nor is there
an original sin that conditions our nature as humans, and from which
we need to justify our salvation. It is true that some more tradition-
ist streams of Judaism, particularly the kabbalistic mystical tendencies,
have incorporated cosmological beliefs that work in somewhat similar
ways. In these traditions, the children of Adam are not responsible for
the original cosmological change that explains the imperfection of the
world as it appears. They are nevertheless charged with the task of redeeming the physical world through their ethical conduct, even, and
perhaps especially, in time of war. Among these traditionalists, it is not
uncommon to find an emphatic embrace for the absence of a military
tradition in rabbinic Judaism. The avowedly traditionalist *Haredi* (God-
fearing) community in the state of Israel makes a quite pragmatic use
of much of the non-militaristic traditions that have historically characterized post-mishnaic Judaism, both in elaborating polemics against
the state of Israel and in justifying refusal to perform military service.[7]
Traditionalist Jews are not ideologically committed to pacifism in all
circumstances, but at times mainstream traditionalist justifications for
a passive acceptance of adversity give birth to a more developed idealistic pacifism than is the norm. To give but one example, the Lithuanian
rabbi Aharon Shmuel Tamrat (1869–1931) deliberately advocated non-
violence as the appropriate response to the persecution faced by Jews
during the east European pogroms.[8] The traditionalist argument for a
passive acceptance of violence as a punishment from God is that the
Jews as a people must face a history of suffering because of the sins of
their forefathers, and particularly because of the sins of the biblical
patriarchs. The view is very much alive among the most enthusiastic

7. E.g., Grossman, "The Danger of Secular Control of Eretz Yisroel."
8. See, e.g., Gendler, "Zionism and Judaism," 87–90.

religious traditionalists today, though it is either not accepted or not seen as sufficient grounds for pacifism by the majority of modernist religious Jews today, whether modern Orthodox, conservative, or liberal.

Even at the traditionalist end of the spectrum of Jewish religious outlooks, many treat war as a fact of life and consequently see armed self-defense as a necessity. The absence of a "Fall" distinguishes rabbinic Jewish notions of justice in such wars from those found historically in Christian thought. Even in the more kabbalistic and mystical Judaisms, the conditions for a just war need not be met for a warrior to be assured of salvation. Nor can salvation, paradise, or the absolution of sins be attained through battle. In time of war, the need for justice is invoked by religious Jews because they are charged to seek to uphold justice in all situations, not because the state of war introduces particular moral challenges. "Justice, justice shalt thou follow," exhorts the writer of Deuteronomy 16:20.[9] In time of war, the need for peace is invoked by religious Jews not because the state of war introduces particular threats to peace, but because, like Aaron, brother of Moses, Jews are enjoined to be the first to seek peace in all situations.[10]

There is, however, a distinctive "state of war" in Jewish tradition, *milchamah*. A biblical word, the Jewish sages of post-mishnaic times related *milchamah* to the Hebrew for "bread," *lechem*. This may well be an inaccurate rendering of the original derivation of the word, given that the sages lived a thousand years after the initial composition of the core biblical texts. Early Jewish debates about the meaning of biblical words as a matter of course display more interest in speculation about the relationship between the meanings of biblical words rather than close analysis of contemporaneous texts, and in this case the connection has allowed rabbinic commentators ever since to render *milchamah* as "a devouring." Thus, one of the most influential twentieth-century Modern Orthodox rabbis, Joseph B. Soloveitchik, explained that *milchamah* refers to a state of uncontrolled instability and crisis.[11] The ethical imperative to try to limit war flies in the face of the nature of war itself, spilling over beyond the original intentions of those who make war as violence

9. Jewish Publication Society Tanakh.

10. *m. Pirkei Avot* 1:2.

11. Soloveitchik, "Insights."

prompts more violence and marks the life of innocent third parties, willy-nilly.[12]

In such a crisis, according to a large majority of exponents of post-mishnaic Jewish tradition, engaging in warfare can be sanctioned religiously if regulated by the laws of war. However, according to this quasi-consensus, even this may not be enough to fully "justify" making war as a norm-shaping dimension of the relationship between Israel and its God. King David was thus deemed by God to be unfit to build the temple because he had blood on his hands (1 Chr 28:3). This is commonly interpreted as being because he was a man of war, not because he breached the rules of battle. At the same time, Jewish tradition does not suggest that David, by taking up arms, has excluded himself from what in Christian terminology might be termed salvation history. The Talmud, the first comprehensive compilation of commentary on the *Mishnah*, also suggests that the messianic age will be initiated by a leader, the *mashiach ben Josef,* who will have to be a warrior, and that only his successor, the *mashiach ben David,* will be fit to re-establish the Temple service and institute a reign of peace.[13] War has a place in history, though its role in fulfilling the purposes of God is a clearly limited one.

Nevertheless, there is a developed Jewish discussion of the conditions in which warfare can be religiously sanctioned. In the earliest rabbinic texts, there is little attempt to systematize the laws relating to warfare, which appear at a number of points in both *Mishnah* and Talmud. Subsequent attempts to codify the laws of war have commonly been indebted to the distinctive interpretations introduced by the twelfth-century legal code of Moses ben Maimon (Maimonides), the *Mishneh Torah* (completed c. 1178 CE). Even the authority widely attributed to Maimonides has done little to reduce the diversity of legal and exegetical commentary on the subject in subsequent centuries. For clarity's sake, this ongoing discussion will be examined here in light of six of the major conditions laid down in Christian texts on just wars, giving enough grounds to highlight some of the distinctive continuities in rabbinic tradition as well as the areas characterized instead by his-

12. See the discussion of *b. Baba Kama* 60a–60b (in the Babylonian Talmud) by Lévinas, "Les dommages causes par le feu."

13. Babylonian Talmud, *b. Sotah* 42a.

torical changes and disagreements between Jewish exponents of ethical conduct in war.

Just Cause

The distinction between different justifications for making war lies at the basis of mishnaic characterizations of religiously-sanctioned warfare. Like many Christian Scholastics a millennium later, the rabbis under Roman and then Byzantine rule distinguished between obligatory and permitted wars. A key to the mishnaic[14] identification of divine laws relating to war was through classifying each biblical war according to whether it was 1) "commanded" or "obligatory" (a *milchemet mitzvah*, or *milchemet hova*), 2) "permitted" (a *milchemet reshut*) or 3) contrary to divine law. One implication that might be read into the mishnaic discussion was that this distinction was made with an eye to limiting the scope for war. It was only the earlier battles for self-defense recorded in the first five books of the Bible that were "commanded" and "obligatory", while the later wars fought by King David to expand his territory were merely "permitted." For the authors of the *Mishnah*, it was only the earlier wars that were commanded by God, and as a result any subsequent wars could not attain the same degree of religious sanction.

In two cases, the *Mishnah* states[15] that the earliest books in the Bible instance a divine command for war without quarter: against the Amalekites, who drew this situation on themselves through uncompromising hatred for the Israelites and by dint of their cruelty in attacking the vulnerable, non-combatant stragglers crossing the desert;[16] and against those Canaanites who refused to make peace with the conquering Israelites.[17] Here, rabbinic tradition recognizes something much like the Semitic "ban," an ordained slaughter of men, women, and children without mercy. However, these instances were classed in mishnaic and post-mishnaic discussions as exceptions that were no longer relevant, the first because the peoples concerned had intermarried to the point that they were no longer distinguishable, and the first and second because God no longer presented his people with direct commands such

14. *m. Sotah* 8.
15. Ibid.
16. Exodus 17:8–16; Deuteronomy 25:17–19.
17. Deuteronomy 20:16.

as these.[18] As to the Romans and other peoples who practiced various forms of idolatry at the time, the editors of the *Mishnah* and Talmud concluded that they need not be seen as idolaters of the most egregious type. Though these peoples might "associate" other deities with the one true God, they also upheld moral codes reflecting a level of religiosity that enabled Jews to interact with them, on a secular and sometimes on a religious level.[19] This common sense of morality was also a basis for the confrontation between Jewish approaches to justice and war and the international laws of war of the day. The mishnaic discussion defines "war" by reference to a situation in which no mercy can be expected from an enemy.[20] The pagan with a moral sensibility or tradition can be turned from a barbaric "enemy" into a potential partner.

The *Mishnah* may be read as implicitly restricting the future scope for a just cause, though many later writers, following Maimonides, have instead read the *Mishnah* as a positive basis for decisions to make war at any point in history. According to Maimonides, the categories of the *Mishnah* could be applied to non-biblical wars when the principles which underlie them are understood: the earlier commanded or obligatory wars are also wars of defense, based on defense of the greatest value of all, religion—they are wars mandated by the defense of religion. This means that a war against the threat of idolatry may be mandated in the present as well. The discussion of the laws of war in Maimonides's *The Laws of Kings*[21] has since become in many practical respects canonical in all sections of the Orthodox community, though Maimonides took an extreme position on legitimate cause for war, which is not widely accepted or understood. Motivated by his extreme position on the spread of "idolatry" in his own day, a position probably already formed in the light of his experience as a young man of the zealous Almohad dynasty in Spain and North Africa, Maimonides blurred the distinction between the defensive commanded war and the merely "permitted" war, which many commentators have argued could only lawfully be pursued

18. These instances are discussed further in the *Mishnah, m. Yadayim* 4:4; *Babylonian Talmud, b. Kiddushin* 5:9; and Maimonides, *Mishneh Torah*, 14/5, *Hilkhot Melakhim*, 5.

19. See Novak, *The Image of the Non-Jew in Judaism*.

20. *m. Sotah* 8.

21. The final section, treatise 5, of the final book, 14, of Maimonides' legal code, the *Mishneh Torah*.

against the aggressive "idolaters" condemned in the *Mishnah*.[22] In his *Guide of the Perplexed* (c. 1198 CE), Maimonides repeatedly asserted that, without reason and religion, man can be expected to act like an animal, and in such instances fully paralleling the war without quarter laid out in the Bible and *Mishnah*, the full panoply of restrictions placed on the making of war do not apply.[23] In the state of Israel in recent decades, this dimension of Maimonides's work has generally been marginalized as mere philosophical reflection, a throwback to Aristotle without practical ramifications. However, some Orthodox Israelis appear less certain. Thus, Rabbi Shlomo Riskin, a leading settler and a "moderate" in a number of senses, but primarily in the sense that he accepts the authority of the democratically elected Israeli government, argued in the wake of the killing of one of his students that, as "idolatry" motivates the suicide bomber to try to erase the image of God in Israeli citizens, this expands the justifiable cause for retaliation against the bombers and their supporters.[24]

This extension of the category of "idolater" was in part a product of Maimonides's own Islamic environment, though his approach also drew on a reading of talmudic precedent. While the *Mishnah* seems to distinguish more clearly between the commanded war of self-defense and the merely permitted war fought to expand territory, the Talmud's commentary on the mishnaic text introduces a further category of wars that lies on the borderline between the *Mishnah*'s types: "wars fought to reduce the number of idolaters that they should not rise up against them."[25] The confusion over the characterization of justification according to cause is already apparent in a debate on the subject reported in the talmudic text. This type of war was, according to the majority viewpoint noted in the Talmud, a situation threatening the defense of the people. By contrast, Rabbi Yehudah was reported to have argued that such a situation fell short of the conditions for a commanded war, thus falling into the category of wars that were simply "permitted." The rabbis cited in the talmudic text concluded that, although this was an

22. Blidstein, "Holy War in Maimonidean Law," 209–20.

23. See, e.g., Maimonides, *Guide of the Perplexed*, Part III, chapters 18, 33, and 41.

24. Riskin, "Shabbat Shalom: Parshiot Acharei Mot—Kedoshim Leviticus 16:1–20:27."

25. *b. Sotah* 44b.

obligatory war of self-defense, a declaration of war still had to precede the onset of initial hostilities by at least three days.

By the twentieth century, the pace of warfare had altered radically, and the interpretation of the text changed with it. Now, the discussion between Rabbi Yehudah and his colleagues was used to suggest grounds for a debate of the permissibility of a pre-emptive attack where the hostile intentions of an enemy made an invasion appear likely, a debate rekindled by the Six Day War in 1967 and again by the state of Israel's campaigns in Lebanon and in the West Bank and Gaza.[26] No text shows the multiple dimensions to the changes in rabbinic discussion of the legitimating of armed conflict more clearly. Empowerment through the state of Israel, which brought on, according to some Zionists and anti-Zionists alike, a radical re-reading of the law, was also only the latest environmental change that occasioned a historical re-evaluation of the ethical dilemmas involved in applying the most authoritative texts to contemporary situations.

Legitimate Authority

In rabbinic tradition, limitations on the power of rulers to make war begin with interpretations of the role of the biblical priest in the preparation for battle (Deut 20:2–20). While only the king is competent to initiate steps to prepare for war, the priest, with the help of an augury comparable to those deployed in Greece and Rome, judges whether the time is ripe and announces the decision to the people who will engage in war. The Talmud replaces the priestly augury with a vote in the Sanhedrin, empowered in some circumstances to evaluate whether or not there is justifiable cause.[27]

For almost two thousand years, there has been no Sanhedrin, and there is thus no universally accepted means to give this ultimate religious sanction to the deployment of a Jewish army. Before the founding of the state of Israel, leading religious Zionists, with the sanction of the Chief Rabbi of Palestine, Abraham Isaac Kook, argued that the rabbinic precedents could now be applied to the Jewish defense efforts there—a controversial move among Orthodox Jews, since, in the absence of a Sanhedrin, it entailed recognizing the legitimacy of the secular Jewish

---

26. Bleich, "Preemptive War in Jewish Law," 3–41.
27. *b. Sanhedrin* 29b.

authorities. Kook's forceful support for Jewish efforts at self-defense, and his fulsome acceptance of the role of the executive in military affairs as a replacement for the king,[28] have continued to sway his followers in the IDF chaplaincy.

There was, however, no automatic equation between religious Zionism and support for unchecked executive pre-eminence in military affairs. In the eyes of many disciples of Kook, the Sanhedrin is effectively a gathering of legal experts ensuring adherence to the law. By contrast, the leading minister from the National Religious Party involved in the drafting of the basic laws at the founding of the state of Israel, Zorach Warhaftig, insisted that the Sanhedrin is in fact a democratic check on the ruler, and that its mantle in the decision-making preceding a war could be assumed by the Israeli parliament, the Knesset.[29] Debate on this point has continued within the religious Zionist community, reviving again in the light of the political tensions in Israel associated with the invasion of Lebanon in 1982[30] and again with the second Intifada.

In a war of self-defense, the normative rabbinic tradition has not insisted upon a legal or democratic check from a Sanhedrin-like body, but the question of legitimate authority nevertheless arises. The biblical account of Abraham giving chase and defeating Lot's captors established a broad precedent for going to war in defense of a third party that has been unjustly attacked.[31] A minority position that persisted into medieval times extended the precedent of Abraham giving chase into a mandate for serving in gentile armies, even as mercenaries. This may also be used as an argument for individuals, motivated by conscience or conviction, to rise in rebellion against unjust rule. The generally accepted position, however, has insisted that the legitimate political authorities are responsible for decisions governing war and peace, not the individual. The more hard-line figures in the Jewish settlements in the West Bank who have rebelled against disengagement plans determined by the Israeli government have had to appeal to religious authorities

28. There is clear precedent for this in the writing of the sixteenth-century commentator Isaac Abravanel. See Kimelman, "Abravanel and the Jewish Republican Ethos," 201–11.

29. Rackman, *Modern Halakhah for Our Time*, 150.

30. See discussion in Zohar, "Morality and War: A Critique of Bleich's Oracular Halakha," 245–58.

31. Horowitz, *Spirit of Jewish Law*, 146–47.

proclaiming withdrawal to be against the law. In 2004, a group of rabbis of this persuasion sought to establish a Sanhedrin, proclaiming that they had the blessing—as was technically necessary—of the leading rabbis of the generation.[32] However, within the more moderate wing of the religious settler movement, committed more thoroughly to the democratic process, even a rabbinic Sanhedrin may not overrule the will of the elected government.

Right Intention

"Right intention" is one of the more difficult of the Christian just war stipulations to translate into Jewish terms. In a Christian theological context, right intention may take on particular significance because of the need to examine whether participation in war making affects the prospects of an individual gaining salvation. We have already seen that salvation is not a central feature of Jewish discourse about justification in making war. A second reason "right intention" does not feature prominently in Jewish debate in this field could be that it is one of the most difficult stipulations to judge, regardless of one's faith tradition. Moreover, intention slips down the list of priorities wherever Jewish commentators focus on the uncontrollable nature of war, which can so easily make the motivation for initial military steps irrelevant once a conflict has escalated. Thus, the powerful kings who initiated the war described in Genesis 14 may not have envisaged that the weaker kings they targeted would overthrow them once Abraham had been drawn into the military equation.

A fourth challenge to the application of the test of "right intention" in a Jewish context is posed by the focus of rabbinic ethical discourse on right practice, which is perceived as the more important factor into which judgments of right intention should be contextualized. Intention, or mental dedication (*kavanah*), is integrated within a wide range of rabbinic discussions, from how to pray to how to solve legal dilemmas, but in the rabbinic discussion of commanded and permitted wars, "intention" is raised less with respect to personal commitment than with respect to ultimate objectives. This is particularly important in light of the need to judge whether or not a permitted war is legitimate.

32. "Potential Sanhedrin." Available from http://www.chayas.com/sanhed.htm #launch.

However, even in the case of a commanded, defensive war, questions about right intention are an integral part of the process of determining war aims, largely because different war aims so often come into conflict with each other. In the state of Israel, the most prominent of the debates over legitimate war aims has turned of the question of whether it is permitted to give up land in exchange for peace. The religious community approaches this in the light of a question deemed to be still more important: whether concessions or abstention from negotiations poses a greater threat to life. Thus the former Chief Rabbi of Britain, Immanuel Jakobovits, a committed exponent of peace and Palestinian rights, nevertheless argued that the executive did not have the power to initiate a dangerous peace.[33] Israeli governments should therefore only be encouraged to sue for peace if it were clear that a peace would be lasting, a common position within the Orthodox Jewish community.[34]

In the wake of the massacre of Arab civilians by IDF troops in the village of Kibiyeh in 1953, retribution for a series of killings of Jewish civilians nearby, a prominent Orthodox intellectual, Yeshayahu Leibowitz, published an article arguing that the attack was unjustifiable. The article highlights the dilemmas posed by the use of right intention as a guide for justification of war. Indeed, the article underlines that right intention is not by itself enough to justify waging war. Leibowitz, instead of focusing on the questionable idea that a strike against innocent civilians can be described as justifiable "retribution," compares the retributive strike in Kibiyeh to the action of the biblical sons of Jacob who attacked the sons of Shechem after the rape of Dinah. Just as they were cursed by Jacob for their application of a notion of "strict justice," so, too, Leibowitz claimed that the strict retribution meted out in Kibiyeh was a travesty of the greater morality expected of the children of God.[35] A response to Leibowitz was published by one of the most influential figures within the National Religious movement, Rabbi Shaul Yisraeli,[36] who offered

33. Cohen, *Dear Chief Rabbi*, 24.

34. See, e.g., Ravitsky, *Messianism, Zionism and Jewish Religious Radicalism*; Tendler, "Exchanging Territories for Peace"; and Groner, "A Response to the Halakhic Ruling against the Return of Territory."

35. "After Kibiyeh", *Beterem*, 1953. Translated in Goldman, *Yeshayahu Leibowitz*, 185–90.

36. "The Kibiyeh Incident in the Light of Halakha," *Ha'Torah Ve'Hamedinah*, 5–6, Tel Aviv, 1954. See also commentary in Fox, *Modern Jewish Ethics, Theory and Practice*, 242.

a qualified defense of both the actions of Jacob's sons and those of the soldiers responsible for Kibiyeh. The problem with hasty judgments of wrong or right intention, according to this latter view, relates to the need to know how to balance competing ends and justifications; long-term security may necessitate harsh and speedy retribution. But while the justification of disproportionate means as effective retribution defines a position well to the right in the Israeli political spectrum, the need to adopt harsh defensive measures is held by religious leaders in Israel across much of the political spectrum.

Reasonable Chance of Success

A fourth condition for the Christian just war is that justifiable military actions should have a reasonable chance of success. In the second century, the leading rabbi of the generation, Rabbi Akiva, announced that the Jewish people should rise up in support of the rebellion against the Romans led by Bar Kochba (132–135 CE), who Akiva is said to have believed to be the Messiah.[37] The failure of the Bar Kochba revolt has marked religious Jewish discourse about rebellion ever since. Far better, in the eyes of the rabbinic mainstream, to accept defeat where victory appears to be beyond reach. When Rabbi Yohanan ben Zakkai escaped from the Roman army the first time it captured Jerusalem (70 CE), he was able to establish the greatest center of Jewish learning seen to that date, providing a model whereby obedience to tyrants could be turned into a self-conscious passive resistance.[38]

The pogroms and then the Holocaust, on the other hand, have played havoc with respect for traditional restraint in conditions where the chances of measurable success are slim. We enter the territory of low-intensity conflicts, into which the civilian is easily drawn and the impact of military action on the achievement of political goals is difficult to measure. We also enter a world in which a violent death is a common prospect, whether a violent response is avoided or not. A considerable portion of the Jewish religious community came to insist that Jews must defend themselves as a testament to Jewish spirit, even without the prospect of effectively countering an enemy action in the

---

37. Discussed, for example, in the Jerusalem Talmud, *y. Taanit* 4:5, 68d.

38. An excellent discussion of the context for the decision to flee is to be found in Tropper, "Yohanan ben Zakkai, Amicus Caesaris," 1–17.

immediate term. "Success" is always difficult to define for a prospective martyr, and though the martyr in Jewish tradition does not gain automatic redemption, he can secure for himself a place in the history of the greater redemption of Israel and the world. The ideology of "Jewish defense," above all other considerations, gained a particular foothold beyond the religious community on the Jewish political right in Eastern Europe.[39] In the state of Israel, the "spirit of Masada" spread across the political spectrum, fostered by army training from the 1950s, but has been particularly strong within the secular majority, not the religious community.[40]

Last Resort

Military action should be conducted as a "last resort"—on this point, the Rabbis appear to be at one with classic Christian just war theory. Though not all of the wars of the biblical patriarchs were explicitly described in the biblical text as being preceded by peace negotiations, the rabbis insisted that they had been. The biblical description of the war against the Canaanites does not explicitly mention it, but even that war, according to rabbinic interpretation, was preceded by peace negotiations.[41] The regulations for war outlined in Deuteronomy 20 insist that a besieging force allow a city's inhabitants to flee at any point in the battle—a suggestive parallel to the medieval Christian ban on the ambush, intolerable because it erased the distinction between warfare conducted by choice and war imposed without regard for the dignity of the individual: it is then, as Michael Walzer notes,[42] a condition in which war easily degenerates into hell.

There are problems, however, problems that are by no means unique to Jewish equivalents of just war theory. How do we know when the last resort has been reached? Modern warfare, conducted at immense speed and therefore often initiated by a pre-emptive strike, has provoked recurrent debate over the conditions laid down for justifiable use of force in rabbinic tradition. In an Israeli context, this debate has,

39. For a particularly good study of the development of the Jewish Right in Eastern Europe, see Shavit, *Jabotinsky and the revisionist movement 1925–1948.*

40. Ben-Yehuda, *The Masada Myth.*

41. Deuteronomy 20, and commentary in *Sifrei* on Deut 20.19.

42. Walzer, *Just and Unjust Wars,* 24.

since at least the 1950s, been prompted by reappraisals of the moral justification for pre-emptive action, forcing religious and secular moralists
alike to examine more closely the meaning of a coherent choice to fight
a war as a "last resort." Ahron Bregman neatly sums up the conclusions
of many of the secularist "post-Zionist" moralists.[43] Israel's wars, which
on a political level are still justified as defensive wars *par excellence*, may
also be broken down into military and diplomatic segments, and each
may be re-examined on the basis of retrospective judgments of their
timing, necessity, and apparent motivation—the assumption that a wise
war can only be a war of last resort permeates this analysis. In the eyes
of Bregman and many of the state of Israel's post-Zionist critics, parts of
the military engagements of 1948, 1967, and 1973 may match the criteria for a fully defensive war, while the State's other military engagements
are in varying ways deplored as in part politically or ideologically-mo-
tivated. The debate over "last resort," particularly in respect to debate
over assessments of the political intentions of the enemy, very easily
slips into a contest over political ideology. In debate among religious
commentators in Israel, this condition—as prominent as it is in early
rabbinic literature on the question—has received less insistent attention
than the need for consideration for civilian life on both sides. Among
Jewish peace activists in the United States and elsewhere, the notion of
the "last resort" is subsumed into broader assessments of the injunction
to seek peace in all situations, including in embarking upon war.

Right Conduct

Finally, the just war in its classic Christian variants implies "right conduct." While the insistence upon moral conduct in warfare is a central
feature of religious Jewish discourse about war, this has historically
proven extremely challenging to define.

In Deuteronomy 21, the Israelite soldier is commanded to respect
the feelings of the wives of their slain enemies and to refrain from having sexual intercourse with captured women; to refrain also from mar-
rying them for one month. While the idea that this constitutes restraint
is somewhat odd by our standards, the so-called "beautiful captive"
passage is nevertheless considered by some to be the most important
example of moral fiber and ethical restraint in the whole Bible: a soldier

43. Bregman, *Israel's Wars, 1948–1993.*

who can restrain himself in the heat of battle and in the face of a "beautiful captive" can restrain himself at any time.[44]

Rabbinic tradition asserts that ethical behavior under wartime conditions underpins ethical commitment in peacetime as well. For this reason, according to one of the leading moderate "settlers," Rabbi Aharon Lichtenstein, the Bible places a specific prohibition on stealing from gentiles (Num 5:5–10; Also covered by the general prohibition on theft already given in Lev 5:20–26) in the midst of a text treating the proper bases for Israel's behavior in a national crisis.[45]

The limitation on justifiable conduct in war is also closely linked to the notions of the "purity of arms" and the professionalism of the soldier. Deuteronomy 20 gives four reasons for which an adult male may refuse to fight, all of which are related to fear—some say to the fear of committing a major sin—and these grounds for conscientious objection have sometimes been used in court cases in the state of Israel where conscripts refuse to fight on grounds of conscience.[46]

The distinction between the commanded and the permitted war is also used as a basis for insisting on a sense of proportionality in justifying conduct in relation to the political cause or objectives of the different categories of war. Thus, a defensive war is often said to justify at least some of the severity described in the earlier books of the Bible, while a war not fought against an immediate threat demands additional limitations on combat.[47] Nevertheless, the majority of commentators, who follow Maimonides with regard to right conduct in wartime, have historically insisted upon compassionate treatment of prisoners and civilians even in a commanded, defensive war.[48]

There is, however, a marginal, extremist strand, outlawed in Israel, for whom such restraints are unethical. Often considered a lunatic fringe in Israel, though prominent among the most radical settlers,

---

44. There are many Hasidic commentaries which highlight this ethical lesson, but for discussions among modernist Jews, see, e.g., Feinstein, "God's Four Questions," and Elman, "Deuteronomy 21," 1.

45. Lichtenstein, "Protecting the Stranger."

46. Sinclair, "Jewish Law in the State of Israel," 262. The four categories are the recently betrothed, new vineyard-tenders, those who had just completed building their homes, and the fearful and faint-hearted.

47. See, e.g., Kimelman, "War," in Katz, *Frontiers of Jewish Thought*, 301–32.

48. *Mishneh Torah, Hilchot Melakhim*, V.

this extreme argues that war is hell, and in hell all laws are suspended. Rabbi Shimeon bar Yochai, living at the time of the Bar Kochba revolt, is recorded as having stated "The best of the Gentiles you shall kill."[49] The vast majority of traditionalist Jews follow interpretative traditions according to which this is not to be taken literally, and for whom the context shows that the literal interpretation has nothing to do with indiscriminate killing—it was a point religious Jews had to explain in response to the accusations made by hostile witnesses at the Beilis Trial in Russia in 1913. However, there is a fringe within the religious right, mainly within the movement that follows the assassinated maverick Meir Kahane, founder of the *Kach* party and the Jewish Defense League, that argues that this is a mandate to kill without discrimination.[50]

One of the keys to biblical restraint on conduct in war is given in Deuteronomy 20, which ends with the injunction not to destroy fruit trees in the pursuit of a military campaign. The sages already extended this mandate to forbid the destruction of food stores, reading the purpose in relation to the impact of war on civilian populations;[51] Josephus claims this was also applied to burning the land and killing domestic animals.[52] Today, an extreme element interested in minimizing such protection for civilian resources makes use of a narrow interpretation of the commentary given by the thirteenth-century Spanish commentator Nachmanides, who took, in some key respects, a more extreme position than Maimonides. While Nachmanides, too, stressed the duty of compassion and the imperative to seek peace, he also argued that restrictions on combat following from the prohibition of the destruction of fruit trees only applied if the sole purpose of such destruction was to inflict needless suffering.[53] Thus, if the destruction of trees (or comparable actions) served a defensive purpose, or even if it was simply a matter of military advantage, Nachmanides concluded that it was permitted. If generalized too far, such a definition would not only reduce the idea of an impermissible "terrorism" to a hypothetical extreme, it would also make just war no more a matter of morality than the most extreme

---

49. *b. Soferim* 15:10; *Mechilta* 14:7.

50. See, e.g., Kahane, "What will the Goyim Say?"

51. *Sifrei* on Deuteronomy 20:19.

52. *Contra Apion*, 2:29.

53. Broyde, "Fighting the War and the Peace."

critics of the idea of military ethics would have it, from Thucydides to Hobbes and Clausewitz.[54]

Jewish Traditions of Legitimizing and Limiting War

It is possible to speak of a large degree of consensus in key dimensions of Jewish debate over legitimizing and limiting war because of the centrality of a series of texts on the subject generally considered authoritative, from the Bible, *Mishnah*, and Talmud to the *Mishneh Torah* of Maimonides. The authors and editors of successive documents, attempting to maintain the continuity, each claim they are faithful interpreters of their predecessors. The distinction between commanded and permitted wars lies at the core of this continuity, just cause being a fundamental building block in traditional calculations of most other features of a legitimate war.

Equally, however, there are major differences between each of these foundational documents, and then again between subsequent commentators, to the extent that there was already an extremely wide range of new uses of the traditional sources for legitimizing and critiquing the resort to force long before the creation of the state of Israel. This diversity is largely a response to the historical transformations of war since biblical times. It is secondarily a response to the practical challenges of applying ancient ethical and medieval teaching in modern states, the paucity of distinctive Jewish political traditions following the Enlightenment exacerbating the peculiar difficulties faced in the formulation of cultures of state-sanctioned violence in the state of Israel.

The diversity of modern Jewish responses to war does not break down into a simple religious-secular divide. There are religious and non-religious pacifists, both engaging with Jewish tradition and contemporary ethical dilemmas in the light of a prior commitment to non-violent means and ends. Similarly, the more extreme elements of the secularist and fundamentalist right wing, inside Israel, the United States, and beyond, derive lessons from Jewish history and tradition that reduce the applicability of ethics in wartime, with a prior commitment to the realist perspective that suggests attempts to limit war are ineffective and in that light unethical.

---

54. Critiqued by Walzer, *Just and Unjust Wars*, esp. 3–33.

The two perspectives represent the extremes at either end of the spectrum of opinion that divides both on realist grounds and on assessments of the values associated with the concept of a secular international law. There is no clear correlation between religious fundamentalism and support for a straightforward application of Maimonides's description of the conditions for a just war, nor between fundamentalist anti-Zionism and a thoroughgoing pacifist rejection of state violence. It is common to seek theological explanations for the divergent prescriptions of Jewish religious groups in relation to Israel's wars, but there is a much more important factor which helps to explain why all political and religious tendencies have divided over the limits of justifiable military conduct in our time: the value attached to international law.

Precedents for the recognition and adoption of international legal standards go back to mishnaic times and to the Bible itself.[55] Jewish legal tradition gives precedent for three broad and divergent responses to developments in secular international law: rejection, either on pragmatic grounds, chiefly relating to perceptions of necessity, or in order to insist on a more idealistic standard; adoption, as long as the resultant standard would be as high as Jewish legal tradition mandates; or adoption, as long as the resultant injunction commands enough respect among parties to a conflict to be practicable.

The impact of different philosophies of law can be as important as real-world forces and theological commitment in interpretation and application of Jewish equivalents of just war criteria. A legal scholar as adept as Ovadia Yosef, spiritual guide of the Sephardi Orthodox party in Israel, *Shas*, can navigate his followers across the spectrum of opinion, revising his judgments of key war and peace issues as the context changed.[56] Just war theories can be a rough and ready tool, easily assimilated to the interests of one or other power in a conflict situation. It is often said that the sages of mishnaic and talmudic renown knew that the exercise of full sovereign power would have played havoc with their high principles. Judah Halevi, an eloquent twelfth-century apologian for a rather immoderate account of Judaism, acknowledged as much in

55. See, e.g., Novak, *Image of the Non-Jew in Judaism*; see also Wilkes, "Judaism and Justice in War," in Robinson, *Just War in Comparative Perspective*, 9–23.

56. Contrast Yosef, "Ceding territory of the Land of Israel in order to save lives," with his more recent positions in Yuchtman-Yaar, "Shas: the Haredi-dovish Image in a Changing Reality," 32–77.

his fictional account of the dialogue between the King of the Khazars and a rabbi, the *Kuzari*. It is the king who says of the Jews, "if you had power you would slay." The Rabbi responds:

> Thou hast touched our weak spot, O King of the Khazars. If the majority of us, as thou sayest, would learn humility towards God and His law from our low station, Providence would not have forced us to bear it (exile, or subjugation) for such a long period. Only the smallest portion thinks thus. Yet the majority may expect a reward, because they bear their degradation partly from necessity, partly of their own free will. For whoever wishes to do so can become the friend and equal of his oppressor by uttering one word, and without any difficulty. Such conduct does not escape the just Judge. If we bear our exile and degradation for God's sake, as is meet, we shall be the pride of the generation which will come with the Messiah, and accelerate the day of the deliverance we hope for.[57]

---

57. Hirschfeld, *Judah Hallevi's Kitab al Khazari*, I, 114–115.

2

And Why Should You Not Fight?:
The Imperative of War in Islam and Christianity

John Kelsay

MY TITLE IS TAKEN FROM QUR'AN 4.75, A VERSE THAT READS IN FULL:
"And why should you not fight in the cause of God and of those who,
being weak, are ill-treated? Men, women, and children, whose cry is
'Our Lord, rescue us from this town, whose people are oppressors, and
raise for us out of your beneficence one who will protect; one who will
help.'"[1] It is an important verse, claimed by many in the history of Islam,
including a number of contemporary militants. The verse is cited, for
example, in the 1998 *Declaration on Armed Struggle against Jews and
Crusaders* signed by Usama bin Ladin and other leaders of the World
Islamic Front. It is similarly important in the argument of *The Neglected
Duty*, a text advertised as the testament of those responsible for the 1981
assassination of Anwar Sadat, and in the *Charter* of Hamas. In these
and other cases, the function of Qur'an 4.75 is to lend weight to the
notion that fighting is an imperative. In the formal language of Islamic
tradition, the argument is that fighting or, if one prefers, "killing"—the
Arabic word *qital* carries either sense—is an "individual obligation."
As the above texts argue, fighting is comparable to fasting or prayer.
Everyone must fulfill his or her obligation; no one can perform the duty
for anyone else.[2]

1. Translations of verses from the Qur'an are my own.

2. The *Declaration* is available in translation at http://www.fas.org/irp/world/para/
docs/980223-fatwa.htm; *The Neglected Duty* in a translation by Johannes J. G. Jansen;
and the *Charter* in a translation by M. Maqdsi.

As any close reading of Qur'an 4.75 indicates, however, all this needs qualification. For it is clear that the overriding issue in this text is *not* fighting. It is, rather, obedience to God and God's Prophet. If we broaden out only a little, say, by setting the individual verse in the context of verses 71–86, we see that the imperative of the query of verse 75 is actually posed in connection with a challenge to those who are wavering, who want to hang back from following the Prophet into battle. These individuals are told that obedience to God's commands, as delivered through the Prophet Muhammad, is the measure of a true believer. In this sense, Qur'an 4.75 is set in the Qur'an's recounting of God's attempts to create a people, an *umma*, that will command good and forbid evil by following the guidance of God. In connection with the career of Muhammad, the story moves from an imperative of nonviolence in Mecca, to the granting of permission to fight for those who have been driven from their homes in the *hijra*, or migration, to Medina, to a claim that war is "prescribed" or "written for" the Muslims (even though they don't like it), to the notion that fighting is an imperative. To put this summarily: The concern of the Qur'an and its Prophet is only secondarily with fighting (or not). The primary concern is always and everywhere with obedience to the divine directives. It is obedience or "submission" which is the measure of the *umma*. Fighting is important only insofar as God commands it. In this regard, it is interesting that Muslim commentators typically suggest that the "waverers" or "hypocrites" addressed in Qur'an 4.75 are actually those who argued with the Prophet at an earlier time. Specifically, we are told that while in Mecca some of Muhammad's associates urged him to authorize armed resistance to the Quraysh, the dominant Meccan tribe. Leading members of the tribe orchestrated a campaign of discrimination and persecution, causing economic and physical suffering for those associated with Muhammad. In that context, Muhammad responded to the would-be Muslim warriors by flatly refusing their request. According to the standard accounts, he indicated God had given only an order to preach. In the absence of a positive command to fight, the Prophet would not— one might as well say, could not—authorize a military response. Those urging military action were distressed by Muhammad's refusal, arguing that the lack of a forceful response would only invite more oppression, as well as make them appear cowardly.[3]

As noted, the Prophet's stance on military force—or the specifics of God's command on that matter—changed with the move to Medina. And, as the story goes, some of the sunshine warriors from the Meccan period became the wallflowers of the Medinan campaign. Ironic, or so the commentators want us to think; their point, as mine, is that the question of fighting is secondary to the question of obedience. The meaning of *al-islam* is "submission," after all. Fighting is only good insofar as it is consistent with the practice of true religion.

This forms the baseline for my reflections. Islam, and with it Christianity, holds that fighting is just, or necessary, or even imperative under certain conditions. Both faiths also hold that fighting is unjust, or unnecessary, or even that there is an imperative of non-violence, under other conditions. The questions are "when?" and "how does one tell?"

Historically these questions are addressed through the frameworks known as *ahkam al-jihad*, or "the judgments pertaining to armed struggle," in Islam, and the just war tradition in Christianity. These are sometimes described as frameworks created by Muslims or Christians for the purpose of limiting violence; insofar as they are concerned with restricting the occasion of and the damage done by war, this characterization is accurate. Similarly, the *ahkam al-jihad* and the just war tradition are sometimes described as theories of statecraft. Insofar as they are presented as characteristic of the practice of wise rulers—as, for example, in the texts known as "mirrors of princes"—this also is fair. My point in this essay is that they are primarily about something quite different, however. They are first and foremost frameworks for discerning the commands or guidance of God.

This becomes clear if we set *ahkam al-jihad* and just war tradition in the wider contexts of *Shari`a* reasoning (typically called "Islamic jurisprudence") and Christian practical reason. For now, let us consider the former. *Shari`a* reasoning is best described as a text-based system of practical reasoning. The aim is to discern or, in the technical language of Islamic tradition, to "comprehend" the *Shari`a* or "path" that leads to refreshment. In the words of the great al-Shafii (d. 820), one of the

---

3. See, among others, Kathir, *Tafsir Ibn Kathir*, 2.511–35; and Qutb, *In the Shade of the Qur'an*, 3.211–52.

greatest of early developers of *Shari`a* reasoning, this is the path that makes for felicity in this world and the next.[4]

Shari`a reasoning rests on the faith that there is such a path, and that God provides guidance with respect to it. In particular, God provides guidance by means of "signs," the most important of which are the texts of the Qur'an and "reports" (*ahadith*) of the *sunna*, or "exemplary practice" of Muhammad.

Shari`a reasoning thus requires attention to these approved texts. It further requires attention to interpretive precedents established by exemplary scholars in the centuries since the time of the Prophet. The idea is to match the guidance revealed in approved texts with one's own circumstances; the judgments of great scholars provide a kind of baseline or set of precedents that guide one in this task.

Historically, this "matching" or "comprehension" of God's guidance was a task for recognized authorities, that is, the `ulama,' or "learned." Trained in the interpretation of Qur'an and *sunna*, these authorities were also knowledgeable regarding the precedents set by exemplary scholars through the centuries. They were thus ready to participate in a kind of transgenerational conversation about the guidance or commands of God, and to deliver opinions (*fatawa*) regarding the duties of their contemporaries. Nowadays, participation in *Shari`a* reasoning must be more broadly construed, as the text-based framework provided by tradition becomes a kind of public philosophy. Muslims with various levels of training in the religious sciences now offer opinions in the newspapers, on television, talk radio, and the Internet. Some would say that this is a problem, creating bands of "irregular `ulama'" offering pronouncements regarding the duties of Muslims.[5] Perhaps that's so. My task, however, is to show how the system of *Shari`a* reasoning works, even in times of stress (now, for example); and to show how the question of fighting is related to the imperative of obedience. In order to show this, I must display an argument among Muslims. Let me first lay out some basic themes of Islamic political thought, then give a very brief account of the modern career of those themes. I'll follow this review with a presentation of four "moments" in an intra-Muslim

---

4. See Risala, *Islamic Jurisprudence.*

5. For more on these developments, see Bulliett, "The Crisis within Islam," 11–19.

argument regarding the tactics of al-Qa'ida, before turning to Christian tradition.

The History of Islamic Political Thought[6]

Classical Themes

Over the course of fourteen centuries, Islamic political thought has centered on two great themes. The first of these emphasizes the importance of establishing a just public order, while the second focuses on notions of honorable combat.

Historically speaking, Muslim scholars held that the establishment of a just public order is an obligation. Some said it was so by God's command; others said this was a dictate of reason. In either case, they usually thought of the phrase "just public order" in terms of a state defined by an Islamic establishment. We would put it this way: a just public order is one in which Islam is the established religion; where the ruler is a Muslim, and consults with recognized Islamic authorities on matters of policy; and finally, where groups committed to other religions could live in safety, being "protected" by the Islamic establishment. This pattern held for many Muslim thinkers from the time of the early Islamic conquests (in the seventh century CE) through the demise of the Ottoman caliphate (in 1924).

Notions of honorable combat developed in connection with reflection on the duty to establish a just public order. The idea was that, under certain conditions, the establishment, maintenance, and defense of justice would require armed force. When such conditions occurred, armed force or combat was to be conducted in accord with norms of honor. For example, resort to combat needed authorization by publicly recognized authorities. Such authorities should make sure that fighting occurred in connection with a just cause, and with the intention of building, maintaining, or protecting public order. The same authorities should consider whether or not fighting would be a proportionate response to perceived injustice, whether Muslim forces were likely to succeed, and whether fighting would serve the end of building the kind of public order that serves peace. Finally, they were to consider

---

6. For more extensive discussion, see Kelsay, *Islam and War: A Study in Comparative Ethics*; idem., "Islam, Politics, and War," 11–19; idem, "Islamic Tradition and the Justice of War," 81–110.

whether combat is the most fitting way to pursue justice considering the circumstances—in other words, are there alternative ways to seek justice that might be more appropriate in a given case?

In addition to these considerations, those fighting for justice were to be governed by the saying attributed to the Prophet Muhammad: "Do not cheat or commit treachery. Do not mutilate anyone, nor should you kill children."[7] Other reports indicate that Muhammad further prohibited the direct and intentional killing of women, the very old, those physically or mentally handicapped, monks, and others. The idea was that honorable combat involved soldiers fighting soldiers and that noncombatants were never to be the direct target of military action. Of course, there are times when combat involves taking aim at a military target, knowing that there is a strong likelihood of indirect harm to civilians (that is, "collateral damage"). In such cases, Muslim scholars debated many issues related to the use of particular weaponry: Should a fighting force make use of mangonels, or hurling machines, for example? The concern in these cases was that certain weapons might cause damage disproportionate or excessive injury to civilians, even though the direct target of the weapon was military in nature.

Modern Tensions

For the last eighty years, the tradition of Islamic political thought has been under stress or under dispute. In itself, this is not unique. Traditions are always susceptible to dispute. That is, they are so for as long as they are *living* traditions. In Arabic, *al-turath* or "tradition" is that which is handed down or bequeathed by one generation to the next. One generation bequeaths to the next a framework for discussion; the new generation tries to establish a "fit" between that which is handed down and its own set of circumstances. That is the nature of tradition. When people stop arguing about a tradition, it is a sign that it is no longer viable.

Thus, Muslim argument is nothing new. Nevertheless, one could say that the last eighty years mark a period of particular stress, in which the most contentious point has been the question "What constitutes a just public order?"[8] In 1924, the new Turkish Republic withdrew sup-

---

7. Cf. among others, Siyar, *The Islamic Law of Nations*, 75–77, where this report of the Prophet's orders is printed.

8. Hourani, *Arabic Thought in the Liberal Age*; and Enayat, *Modern Islamic Political Thought*, are standard references here.

port for the Ottoman ruler. This effectively abolished the last remaining symbol of the great empires of the Middle Period, as well as of the older notions of a universal state governed by an Islamic establishment. In the years following, and indeed for much of the twentieth century, Muslim intellectuals argued about the shape a modern Islamic political order might take. One part of that argument focused (and still focuses) on the sort of legal regime such an order should have. Must a properly Islamic state be governed by divine law only, in the sense that its laws and policies are derived directly from the Qur'an, the example of the Prophet, and interpretive precedents established by the consensus of recognized scholars (the `ulama`)? Or can such a state form its laws and policies based on a more diverse set of sources? For example, can an Islamic state borrow from the legal codes of European nations, or shape its policies based on contemporary international practice? Those holding that an Islamic state must be governed by divine law only are sometimes called "fundamentalists" or "radicals." Those arguing for a more diverse set of sources are sometimes called "moderates." Neither of these terms is adequate. In what follows, I shall employ the more cumbersome, but I believe more accurate terminology of "advocates of divine law governance" and "pluralists."

The focus on the meaning of the phrase "Islamic state" means, in effect, that most modern Islamic political thought is concerned with how one might fulfill the obligation to establish a just public order. More recently, however, attention has turned to the historic notion of honorable combat. We are familiar by now with the "pluralist" side of this debate. Post-9/11, many Muslims argue that, even if the advocates of divine law governance are right and the current state of political order is unjust, there are nevertheless limits on what one may do to affect change. There are some tactics, people say, that violate the Muslim conscience. This is especially true of tactics that make noncombatants or civilians into direct targets of military or paramilitary attacks. The conduct of martyrdom operations in Palestinian resistance to Israel is of concern in this regard. Even more, the use of indiscriminate tactics by al-Qa`ida is of concern.

Pluralist Muslims have been very clear in condemning al-Qa`ida tactics as a violation of Islamic tradition. Less well-covered in American or European media is the fact that some advocates of divine law governance have also been vigorous in this regard. That is, there are those who share with al-Qaʿida a sense that a just public order must be governed by divine law only, yet who think al-Qaʿida's tactics are problematic on Islamic grounds. We can get a sense of this by attending to four moments in an extended conversation between Muslim advocates of divine law governance, beginning in June of 2002.

Recent Discussion of al-Qaʿida Tactics among Advocates of Divine Law Governance[9]

Moment One

The date is June 7, 2002. An al-Qaʿida spokesperson named Sulayman abu Ghayth publishes an article on the internet entitled *In the Shadow of the Lances.*[10] Abu Ghayth (who had become well-known for several statements following 9/11 and the beginning of U.S.-led action in Afghanistan) begins by indicating his purpose, to address the Muslim community and make sure it understands al-Qaʿida's arguments:

> Perhaps the Islamic community is waiting for one al-Qaʿida man to come out and clear up the many questions that accompany any communiqué, message, or picture (concerning 9/11), to know the truth, the motives, and the goals behind conflict with the Great Idol of our generation.

Abu Ghayth's article develops in accord with this purpose. It is a defense of al-Qaʿida's program of fighting against the United States and its allies. He lists a number of reasons that justify such fighting. For example:

> America is the head of heresy in our modern world, and it leads an infidel democratic regime that is based upon separation of religion and state and on ruling the people by the people via legislating laws that contradict the way of God and permit that

---

9. This material appears, in somewhat different form, in several other essays, including Kelsay, "Democratic Virtue, Comparative Ethics, and Contemporary Islam," 697–708; idem., "The New Jihad and Islamic Tradition"; and essays cited *supra*, note 6.

10. Abu Ghayth's article was originally published at www.alneda.com, which at the time was a frequent location for al-Qaʿida-related postings. The website changes URLs frequently, however, so that it is difficult to locate. A convenient translation of portions of the article is available at the website of the Middle East Media Research Institute, www.memri.org, where it is entry No. 388 in the "Special Dispatch Series." I quote from MEMRI's translation, with very slight alterations.

which God has prohibited. This compels the other countries to act in accordance with the same laws in the same ways . . . and punishes any country (that resists) by besieging it, and then by boycotting it. In so doing, (America) seeks to impose on the world a religion that is not God's.

The United States, then, is a prime example of an unjust state, since it is not governed by divine law. Its injustice is compounded by the fact that it seeks to export this form of government. And, as we come to understand, the injustice of the United States is expressed by its willingness to use or to support the use of military force against those who would choose another model for political order. Abu Ghayth lists various places in which this is so: Palestine, Iraq, Afghanistan, Somalia, Sudan, the Philippines, Indonesia, Kashmir, and others. In many of the cases, he cites (as he takes it) the number of innocents killed. This is critical to the argument. For abu Ghayth wants ultimately to justify not only armed resistance to the United States and its allies, but the kind of armed resistance advocated by the leaders of al-Qaʿida and related groups in the 1998 *Declaration on Armed Struggle Against Jews and Crusaders*. In that document, Usama bin Ladin and others argued that fighting against Americans and their allies, "civilians and soldiers," is a duty for each and every Muslim able to do so. In other words, al-Qaʿida's strategy involves deliberate attacks on civilian as well as military targets. Abu Ghayth wants to provide a justification for this:

> God said, "one who attacks you, attack as he attacked you," and also, "The reward of evil is a similar evil," and also "When you are punished, punish as you have been punished."

These Qur'anic citations, as interpreted by recognized religious scholars, establish a right of reciprocal justice. According to this notion, victims of injustice have the right to inflict damage on those responsible for their suffering in a manner proportionate to the harm suffered. According to this line of thought, the numbers of innocents killed by the United States suggests that:

> We (Muslims) have not reached parity with them. We have the right to kill 4 million Americans, 2 million of them children, and to exile twice as many and wound and cripple hundreds of thousands.

It is important to note that abu Ghayth stipulates that the damage inflicted by the United States and its allies is both "direct and indirect." For his purposes, the distinction does not matter. Those who suffer have the right to inflict damage proportionate to their losses. And this, he writes, is the only way to deal with the United States.

> America knows only the language of force. This is the only way to stop it and make it take its hands off the Muslims and their affairs. America does not know the language of dialogue or the language of peaceful coexistence! America is kept at bay by blood alone.

Moment Two

Abu Ghayth's article provides an important defense of al-Qa`ida tactics. Other Muslims are not persuaded, however. And thus I turn to a second moment in recent conversation about Islam and fighting. On July 10, 2002, the television network al-Jazeera interviewed a well-known Saudi religious scholar and dissident, Shaykh Muhsin al-`Awaji.[11] Two other dissidents joined by telephone. All three served time in Saudi prisons for criticism of the royal family and its policies of cooperation with the United States during and especially following Operation Desert Shield and Desert Storm in 1990–91. None of the three are friendly to U.S. policies with respect to historically Muslim states. Indeed, they are in favor of armed resistance to U.S. aggression and approve the use of martyrdom operations.

The conversation then turns to Usama bin Ladin. Since the three scholars agree with al-Qa`ida on the necessity of government by divine law, and further on the justice of resistance to the United States and its allies, it is most interesting that they indicate that, after initial approval of bin Ladin, they and many others have changed their opinion. Shaykh al-`Awaji says:

> In the past, when he was fighting the Russians in Afghanistan, bin Ladin was the greatest of *jihad* warriors, in the eyes of the Saudi people and in the eyes of the Saudi government. He and

11. Again, a convenient translation of portions of the transcript may be found at www.memri.org, Special Dispatch Series, entry number 400. Quotes are from the MEMRI translation.

the others went to Afghanistan with official support, and the support of the learned (the `ulama`).

In some ways, this positive assessment of bin Ladin still holds:

> What the Saudis like best about bin Ladin is his asceticism. When the Saudi compares bin Ladin to any child of wealthy parents, he sees that bin Ladin left behind the pleasures of the hotels for the foxholes of *jihad*, while others compete among themselves for the wealth and palaces of this world.

Nevertheless, according to the dissident scholars, this positive judgment must now be qualified because of al-Qa`ida's tactics. Bin Ladin is guilty of spreading discord among Muslims. He labels people as heretics when he has no proof, and some al-Qa`ida operations bring harm to Muslims. Bin Ladin and his colleagues also violate Islamic norms of honorable combat, and this is an important reason for qualifying earlier, positive assessments.

> . . . he and those with him target innocent people, and I refer to the innocents on the face of the entire earth, of every religion and color, and in every region.

Recalling Islamic tradition on these matters, one cannot help but think of the saying of the Prophet: "Do not cheat or commit treachery. Do not mutilate anyone or kill children (or other noncombatants)." Shaykh al-`Awaji is far from approving of abu Ghayth's (or al-Qa`ida's) notion of reciprocal justice. For him (and for those joining him on the show, since they indicate agreement with all of his points on this matter), Muslims are to fight with honor. This means, among other things, that they are not to engage in direct attacks on noncombatants.

Moment Three

We should not forget that Shaykh al-`Awaji and his colleagues agree with much of al-Qa`ida's program. As I have said, they are not favorably disposed to U.S. policies in the Middle East and elsewhere. The point is that they want to see Muslims fight according to traditional norms.

A different kind of criticism was articulated a few months later by Shaykh `Umar Bakri Muhammad of al-Muhajiroun ("The Emigres"), a fundamentalist group based in the United Kingdom. Shaykh `Umar's tract, *Jihad: The Method for Khilafah?*, appeared at www.almuhajiroun

.com in September 2002.[12] While hardly an elegant piece of work, and thus difficult to read, this tract attempts to evaluate the place of armed struggle in the attempt to found a state governed by divine law. The author then discusses the nature and place of armed resistance in contemporary contexts.

According to Shaykh `Umar, *jihad*, in the sense of "armed struggle," is a term reserved for fighting authorized by an established Islamic government. This is the sense of the reference to *khilafah* in his title. Literally, the term suggests "succession" to the Prophet Muhammad. Shaykh `Umar uses the term as a designation for Islamic government. His discussion reiterates one of the great themes of Islamic political thought, that is, the necessity that justice be embodied in a political order. And, as he indicates, when this political order is in place, it should seek to extend its influence by appropriate means. These can and should include honorable combat.

For the last eighty years, the kind of authority indicated by the term *khilafah* has been absent from political life. This fact sets the context for the rest of Shaykh `Umar's argument. Muslims are required to work to change this situation, and to establish *khilafah*. To that end, may or should they engage in *jihad*? The answer is no, first of all because of the nature of the concept. *Jihad* designates fighting that occurs under the auspices of an established government. By definition, then, fighting that takes place apart from such a government's authorization cannot be *jihad*. To this definitional "no" Shaykh `Umar adds a second reason: Islamic political thought requires that authority be legitimate, in the sense of established through a process of consultation and assent. The submission of Muslims to an authority thus ought not be compelled. Islamic government should be established through persuasion.

Shaykh `Umar indicates the process by which consultation and assent may be conducted in a number of ways. He then moves to a discussion of contemporary resistance among Muslims. In his view, the Muslim community is in a kind of political twilight zone. Without a duly constituted *khilafah*, there can be no fighting worthy of the title *jihad*. Yet Muslims are in need of defense, in Chechnya, Kashmir, and other locations. What are they to do?

12. Muhammad, Shaykh `Umar Bakri, *Jihad: The Method for Khilafah?*

As Shaykh ˋUmar has it, Islam recognizes a right of extended self-defense. Everyone has the right to defend his/her own life, liberty, and property. Everyone also has the right, and in some sense the duty to defend the lives, liberties, and properties of others who are victims of aggression. This kind of fighting is called *qital*, a word that quite literally indicates "fighting" or "killing." Where Muslims are under attack, their co-religionists around the globe may and should come to their defense. When they do, however, they should understand that fighting is delimited, first in terms of its goals. *Qital* is not *jihad*. As such, it is not a proper means of establishing Islamic government. Second, *qital* is limited in its means. Interestingly, in this *qital* and *jihad* are similar, since both are governed by norms of honorable combat, or as Shaykh ˋUmar puts it, by the "pro-life" values of the Prophet Muhammad:

> not killing women and children, not killing the elderly or monks, not targeting the trees or animals . . . foreign forces occupying Muslim lands are legitimate targets and we are obliged to liberate Muslim land from such occupation and to co-operate with each other in the process, and can even target their embassies and military bases. . . .

Tactics that involve direct attacks on noncombatants are ruled out, however.

Moment Four

Shaykh ˋUmar's argument challenges al-Qaˋida's approach at a number of points. Most important for our purposes, however, is the stipulation that even defensive fighting, which almost by definition involves coming to the aid of Muslims in emergency or near emergency conditions, should be governed by norms of honorable combat. It's not surprising, given arguments like this, that the leadership of al-Qaˋida would respond. Thus, in November 2002, Usama bin Ladin, or someone writing in his name, published a *Letter to America* responding to Muslim and non-Muslim criticisms of al-Qaˋida.[13]

The first part of the "Letter" is a list of reasons for fighting against the United States and its allies. The grievances are familiar. On this

13. Translation available at www.observer.co.uk/worldview/story/0,11581,845725, 00.html. Quotes are from this source.

point, the "Letter" restates and extends grievances outlined in earlier documents, not least Sulayman abu Ghayth's internet article (above).

The second part of the text moves to the question of tactics:

> You may then dispute that all the above does not justify aggression against civilians, for crimes they did not commit and offenses in which they did not partake.

The concern here is clearly with arguments that al-Qa'ida tactics violate norms of honorable combat. The author of "Letter" does not accept these. Two counterarguments are cited in justification of a policy of attacking civilians as well as soldiers. First, the United States claims to be a democracy:

> Therefore, the American people are the ones who choose their government by way of their own free will; a choice which stems from their agreement to its policies. . . . The American people have the ability and choice to refuse the policies of their government and even to change it if they want.

Second (and in a way reminiscent of abu Ghayth's argument), the author cites the *lex talionis*:

> God, the Almighty, legislated the permission and the option to take revenge. Thus, if we are attacked, then we have the right to attack back. Whoever has destroyed our villages and towns, then we have the right to destroy their villages and towns. Whoever has stolen our wealth, then we have the right to destroy their economy. And whoever has killed our civilians, then we have the right to kill theirs.

Harm suffered may be avenged by the infliction of damage proportionate to the original harm. Muslims have the right to kill U.S. and other "enemy" civilians, because the United States and its allies engage in actions that kill civilians on the Muslim side.

Christian Practical Reason and the Just War Tradition

In my view, Christian practical reasoning shares a number of features with *Shari'a* reasoning. This may seem surprising. It is true, of course, that not very many working scholars of Christian theology or ethics speak of Christian practical reasoning as "Christian law."[14] However,

---

14. Though the title of Bernard Haring's multi-volume work, *The Law of Christ*, is certainly suggestive.

it does seem right to speak of Christian practical reasoning as a text-based approach, in which the goal is to ascertain God's commands or guidance in particular contexts. Groups of Christians read scripture, in communion with the saints of all ages (i.e., the reading of scripture is informed by "tradition"), and then attempt to "match" this historic guidance (or "precedents") with the facts of a contemporary situation. On this account, the various criteria of the just war tradition may be construed as a kind of interpretive tool (a "framework") for discernment of God's guidance in contexts where the use of military force is at stake.[15]

That said, it is important to note that many interpreters will be uncomfortable with this characterization of Christian practical reason—that groups of Christians read texts in order to ascertain God's commands, or that the just war tradition provides a framework for the discernment of divine guidance. They will be so, first, because of the ways the notion of "divine commands" is understood in contemporary Christian ethics. Let it be said, then, that I do not intend to suggest that Christian ethics should be identified with the type of approach analytic philosophers classify as a "divine command theory."[16] Nor, to keep to matters closer to hand, do I mean to suggest that many Christians would think in ways analogous to those contemporary Muslims advocating what I have described above as "divine law governance, in the strict sense."[17] All I mean to suggest is that, when Christians speak about moral obligation, they typically speak in terms of "doing God's will" or "obeying God's commands." The issue is not the ontological or metaethical status of such language; it is rather that Christian ethics understands agency as a matter of acting in ways consistent with the directives of the God revealed in Jesus, the one who is called Christ.

Nor does the idea that the just war framework enables communal discernment of the commands of God suggest any special notion of

15. I think this description closely resembles the approach outlined by James F. Childress in *Moral Responsibility in Conflicts*. With specific reference to the role of Scripture, see Childress "Scripture and Christian Ethics: Some Reflections on the Role of Scripture in Moral Deliberation and Justification," 371–80.

16. See Idziak, *Divine Command Morality*, among others.

17. Though it would be interesting to compare authors associated with "Christian reconstruction," as for example Rushdoony, *Institutes of Biblical Law*, or in a more popular vein, Falwell, *Listen, America!*

the mode by which Christians apprehend God's directives. The sources of Christian practical reason are often depicted as scripture, tradition, and experience, the last broadly construed as inclusive of wisdom from the natural sciences, the "lessons of history," and the like.[18] Or, if one wants to put this another (and to my mind, more appropriate) way, the source of Christian practical reason is the Word of God, made manifest in Jesus as the Christ, in scripture, and in the preaching of the church. Since these sources clearly suggest that the creation, inclusive of human beings, bears witness to the glory and majesty of God, even this more "word-centered" characterization of the sources of Christian ethics may be construed as indicating that the Christian community should be informed by philosophy, scientific findings, and the like as it attempts to ascertain the command of God in relation to particular questions of practice.[19] With respect to contemporary politics, such a characterization has more in common with Islamic "pluralists" than with the "advocates of divine law governance, in the strict sense," and this provides a partial explanation for the close contemporary association between Christianity and democracy. It also provides a rationale by which Christians can and do collaborate with others who do not share their faith, not least in arguments having to do with the guidance provided by the just war tradition.[20]

A second source of discomfort with my characterization of the just war tradition as the framework by which Christians discern the

18. As, for example, in the works of James M. Gustafson. See his *Theocentric Ethics*.

19. The language deliberately echoes Karl Barth's discussion of the word of God in *Church Dogmatics* I/2. I do not suggest that Barth would be so free with the idea that Christian practical reason should be informed by non-Scriptural sources, although one might make a case for this with respect to the essays collected in *The Humanity of God*. That is a subject for another essay.

20. The language of "natural law" provides an important means of justifying such collaborations. In my view, this language is often misconstrued, particularly when it is taken to signify an way of thinking about practical reasoning which avoids the "particularity" of appeals to divine commands. As a reading of such classic texts as Romans 2.14–16 or Thomas Aquinas' treatise on law (*Summa Theologiae* I/2, q. 90–97) indicates, natural law is the terminology used to designate a mode by which some portion of God's commands or guidance may be apprehended. It does not establish an "independent" source of ethics so much as provide an explanation of how it is that Christians reading agreed upon texts may make common cause with others. However (and as will become clear) it is my view that the making of "common cause" is a critical aspect of religious-moral deliberation, not least because Christian texts are "public domain," read and commented on by others.

commands of God has to do with the common presentation of pacifism as an alternative or even co-equal tradition by which Christians may address questions about fighting. I confess that, on this issue, I am at odds with the majority of scholars of Christian ethics. It is of course true that a variety of Christians believe that discipleship requires opposition to war and/or to Christian participation in war. As John Howard Yoder suggested, such opposition can take multiple forms (one of these being the just war tradition).[21] From my perspective, much depends on the strength and breadth with which Christian pacifists articulate opposition to war and/or to Christian participation in it. If Christian discipleship is, as I believe it must be, a matter of obedience to the directives of the living God, then Christian practical reason cannot presume that the answer to the question "is it right to fight?" must always be "no." This means that certain kinds of pacifism make claims about the necessity of opposition to war that are overly strong and broad. It is also true, of course, that no one thinking in Christian terms should presume that the answer to the question "is it right to fight?" will always be "yes." Here, as in the case of Islam, the prior question is always and everywhere "what does God require?" The issue is not "shall we fight?" but "what is the path of obedience?" Given this, it seems clear that the just war framework provides a means by which Christians may deliberate about the commands of God in relation to particular situations. In some instances, there can be no doubt that deliberation within the just war framework will, or at least should, yield the judgment "do not fight." In others, however, it must be the case that God's directive will be "fight." The strength of this judgment may vary; this would account, on my view, for the way that contemporary interpreters of Christian ethics often speak of war as "permitted" or as "justified," rather than as "just." The last term in particular, would suggest a judgment that war in a particular case is perceived as "right" or even "obligatory." On my account, the variety of judgments associated with the foregoing terms suggests that we think of Christian approaches to war along the lines of a spectrum, whereby the just war framework will sometimes suggest a judgment "do not fight," at other times "it is permissible to fight," and at still other times "fighting is obligatory."

---

21. Here I refer to Yoder's *Nevertheless: The Varieties and Shortcomings of Religious Pacifism*, as well as his *When War Is Unjust: Being Honest in Just-War Thinking*.

Now, how does one tell the difference—that is, how do groups of Christians ascertain the guidance of God with respect to fighting in particular circumstances? As I have been saying throughout this paper, the just war tradition provides a framework by which this question may be answered. This tradition is the result of Christian reflection on and debate concerning the sources of practical reason through the centuries. Its characteristic criteria provide a way of talking about resort to and conduct of war.[22] If one measures success in terms of influence, it seems clear that the just war tradition represents one of the great successes of Christian tradition. Not only is the framework of *jus ad bellum* and *jus in bello* primary in the history of Christian ethics; it has been adapted for general use in modern democratic polities, for example in the United States where Jews and "secular" moralists, as well as Christians, utilize the just war framework as a means of deliberating about the moral dimensions of statecraft. For some, the pluralistic nature of contemporary just war discussion signals a crisis of authority, in the sense that it is often difficult to locate a distinctively Christian voice or consensus in the midst of the general just war debate. Nevertheless, if my characterizations of Christian practical reason are correct, interpreters of Christian ethics ought to expect, and frankly to welcome, such participation as a way of indicating the universal provenance of God.

22. As many note, lists of these criteria vary somewhat, and they do not appear in full until the early modern period. Cf. the historical works of James Turner Johnson, especially *Just War Tradition and the Restraint of War*. Given the obvious fact that the full range of criteria for the *jus ad bellum* and *jus in bello* do not appear in any convenient scriptural text, but are rather the result of Christian reflection through the centuries, the import of my description of Christian practical reason as a practice of reading Scripture in communion with the saints is worthy of note. Then, too, comments on notions of natural law and other modes by which Christian practical reason finds warrants in Scripture sufficient to justify collaborations with non-Christians are important, since it seems clear that Greek and Roman sources, Germanic notions of honorable combat, and other ideas find their way into the just war tradition. As to the criteria themselves, a quick list would include right authority, just cause, right intention, overall proportionality between good and evil, reasonable hope of success, aim of peace, and last or timely resort (i.e., for the *jus ad bellum*), discrimination or non-combatant immunity, and proportionality (here, in the sense of considerations pertaining to particular weapons or tactics and the damage they inflict.)

Just War Tradition and the "War on Terror"

I think this account provides a background against which we may understand just war thinking in the post-September 11, 2001, context. Immediately after the 9/11 attacks, there was a strong consensus among interpreters of just war tradition that military action intended to delimit al-Qaʿida's military capacities would be justified, or perhaps even obligatory. In a noteworthy exchange with the editors of *First Things*, Stanley Hauerwas dissented from this judgment.[23] For most, however, the judgment that military action should be considered just seemed consonant with the just war tradition. Indeed, the declaration *What We're Fighting For*, sponsored by the Institute of American Values and signed by sixty scholars from various faith traditions, might be read as suggesting that, in this case, military action was not only permitted but obligatory:

> At times it becomes necessary for a nation to defend itself through force of arms. . . . We recognize that all war is terrible, representative finally of human political failure. . . . Yet reason and careful moral reflection also teach us that there are times when the first and most important reply to evil is to stop it. There are times when war is not only morally permitted, but morally necessary, as a response to calamitous acts of violence, hatred, and injustice. This is one of those times.[24]

What We're Fighting For insisted that any response to the 9/11 attacks, or more generally to the threat posed by al-Qaʿida, be evaluated in terms of the just war tradition. Interestingly, the document construed the just war tradition, in addition to a number of political and moral judgments consonant with "American values," as "universal," in the sense of "resonant with" judgments that might be supported by various traditions of practical reasoning. Within that framework, one might well argue about the precise scope of a post-9/11 military action: should it, for example, be a matter of deploying special forces with a view toward narrowly designed attacks against al-Qaʿida leaders and training bases located in Afghanistan? Or should it involve a more general military action, with the possible aim of removing the Taliban (here, construed as

23. Hauerwas, "In a Time of War: An Exchange."

24. The text is now conveniently available in Blankenhorn, *The Islam/West Debate*, 21–40. In the interests of full disclosure, I note that I am one of the signatories.

"hosts" for al-Qaʿida) from power? One might further argue about the use of certain weapons (Daisy Cutter and "cluster" bombs, for example) or about the importance of U.N. or Security Council authorization, as opposed to the United States exercising rights of self-defense allowed under the U.N. Charter. The fact is, however, that the consensus in favor of the judgment "in this case, war is just" was broad and deep, including many interpreters of Christian practical reason.

It is interesting here to think further about the reference to war as "necessary," which, if I am correct, characterized not only the argument of *What We're Fighting For*, but much just war discourse following 9/11. It takes us somewhat far afield, but this reference seems to be related to an important shift in recent accounts of the just war framework. In the 1970s and 1980s, many interpreters of just war thinking construed the tradition as built on a "presumption against war," or at least a "presumption against killing (or doing bodily harm)." When the U.S. Conference of Catholic Bishops issued their 1983 pastoral letter *The Challenge of Peace*,[25] for example, they argued that:

> The Church's teaching on war and peace establishes a strong presumption against war which is binding on all; it then examines when this presumption may be overridden, precisely in the name of preserving the kind of peace which protects human dignity and human rights. (section 70)

and:

> The moral theory of the "just-war" or "limited-war" doctrine begins with the presumption which binds all Christians: we should do no harm to our neighbors; how we treat our enemy is the key test of whether we love our neighbor; and the possibility of taking even one human life is a prospect we should consider in fear and trembling. How is it possible to move from these presumptions to the idea of a justifiable use of lethal force? (section 80)

It is this "presumption" or set of presumptions that allows the judgment that "the 'moment' in which we find ourselves sees the just-war teaching and non-violence as distinct but interdependent methods of evaluating warfare . . . they share a common presumption against the

25. National Conference of Catholic Bishops, *The Challenge of Peace: God's Promise and Our Response*.

use of force as a means of settling disputes (section 120)." For some interpreters, this means that even "just" war is best construed as "justified"
or "permitted," rather than "right" or "obligatory." Yet the Bishops reason
differently. For them, the "Christian has no choice but to defend peace,
properly understood, against aggression. This is an inalienable obligation (section 73)." In adopting the language of "inalienable obligation"
(rather than, for example, "inalienable right"), the Bishops leave open the
possibility that fighting might, under certain conditions, be construed
as a duty, at least as a means of fulfilling the command to defend peace
or to resist aggression. The argument is hedged with suggestions that
non-violent resistance is also a legitimate means of defending peace, so
that the logic of the judgment "in this case, war is just" is a bit unclear.
But the Bishops do not invoke descriptions of war itself as "regrettable"
or confine the notion of just war as "war that is permissible, though not
obligatory." Indeed, quoting Pius XII, they suggest that, "Among (the)
goods (of humanity) some are of such importance for society, that it is
perfectly lawful to defend them against unjust aggression. *Their defense
is even an obligation for the nations as a whole, who have a duty not to
abandon a nation that is attacked*" (section 76, emphasis in original).

Even in the midst of an interpretation of just war tradition as
built on a presumption against war, one finds hints of the spectrum
of judgments outlined earlier in this essay. The notion that war might
sometimes be construed as necessary or obligatory becomes even more
pronounced when one considers that such prominent interpreters as
Paul Ramsey and James Turner Johnson never accepted the "presumption against war" or "presumption against killing" account of the just
war framework. In criticizing the U.S. Methodist Bishops' 1986 pastoral
letter *In Defense of Creation*, for example, Ramsey argued that some
construals of the "presumption against war" account should be judged
as incorrect.[26] The "presumption against war" appropriate to just war
reasoning is secondary to the "assumption" that "governments cannot
be denied the right of self-defense,"[27] or that it is morally obligatory to
resist evil, utilizing proportionate means. To put it another way, the "su-
pravalent" presumption of the just war tradition is that it is right to seek

26. Interestingly, he exempted the U.S. Catholic Bishops from this charge. See
Ramsey, *Speak Up for Just War or Pacifism*. Also, see United Methodist Church Council
of Bishops, *In Defense of Creation: The Nuclear Crisis and a Just Peace*.

27. Here, Ramsey was citing *The Challenge of Peace*, section 82.

justice, while an "infravalent" notion demands that one seek justice by proportionate means, or one could say that the basic or essential presupposition of just war reasoning is that one should act so as to limit and/or prevent evil, with the proviso (in the sense of a counsel of prudence) that actions taken based on this presupposition should be non-lethal, insofar as possible. The point would thus be to avoid the consequence of further evil (as in the case of military action that issues in the deaths of noncombatants, even if those deaths are unintended).[28] And Johnson is, if anything, even stronger in his rejection of the "presumption against war" account:

> What Christian just-war doctrine is about, as classically defined (e.g., by Thomas Aquinas), is the use of the authority and force of the rightly-ordered political community (and its sovereign authority as minister of God) to prevent, punish, and rectify injustice. There is, simply put, no presumption against war in it at all.[29]

Having rejected the "presumption against war" account of just war tradition, both Ramsey and Johnson argued that the tradition is really an extension of the notion of good or just governance. Ramsey put this is terms of "in-principled love"; Johnson in terms of wise statecraft acting on the obligation to secure justice. My characterization of a framework by which the Christian community strives to ascertain the commands or guidance of the living God in a particular context provides another way of putting the point, which is that armed force is a necessary and in some sense even obligatory aspect of political service in a fallen world.

In any case, it is this notion of just war as an obligation that explains, I believe, the logic of much just war reasoning after 9/11. The idea was, and remains, that an attempt to delimit the ability of al-Qa`ida and related groups to carry out paramilitary actions should be construed as an obligation of justice.

Of course, the campaign against al-Qa`ida quickly became known as a "war on terror" or, in a slightly more nuanced phrase, a "war against terrorist groups of global reach." The use of such expansive language made some uncomfortable, as did the explicit declaration of a willingness to engage in "preemptive" strikes in the statement on National

28. Ramsey, *Speak Up*, 83–86.
29. Johnson, "The Broken Tradition," 30.

Security Strategy issued by the Bush administration in the fall of 2002.[30] Such discomfort came to the fore in just war argument concerning the possibility of a war to accomplish regime change in Iraq. Insofar as such fighting was depicted by the President and other administration officials as connected with the "war on terror" (for example, in the claims of associations between al-Qa`ida and the regime of Saddam), one might have expected a continuation of the judgments articulated in *What We're Fighting For*, that is, that war intended to delimit al-Qa`ida's military capacities is obligatory. As it turns out that was not the case, and the reasons for that are of interest in a discussion of Christian practical reason and the just war tradition.

Much depends then on the facts of a particular situation. As just war argument with respect to Iraq demonstrates, agreement on the facts can be hard to come by. One sign of this was that, when the Institute for American Values attempted to follow its February 2002 statement with one on *Pre-Emption, Just War, and Iraq*, it could only rally nine of those who signed the earlier statement. Further, the language of the "Pre-Emption" statement, issued in November 2002, suggested that judgment concerning resort to war in Iraq was a difficult proposition. Some arguments for fighting aimed at the deposition of Saddam Hussein seemed right, particularly those focused on Iraq's "material breach" of Security Council Resolutions passed in 1991. Were Iraq to fail "to comply with demands for a renewed and unencumbered program of arms inspections by a near-term date," the statement suggested, then "the use of force to compel compliance would be both justified and necessary." At the same time, "if Iraq does comply, the (Bush) Administration should take 'yes' for an answer . . . (because arms inspections) are morally preferable to a full-scale U.S. military action."[31]

Similarly, an October 2002 panel convened under the auspices of the Pew Forum on Religion and Public Life, and co-sponsored by the Institute for American Values, showed deep disagreements with respect to the guidance offered by just war tradition with respect to fighting in Iraq.[32] Focusing on issues of right authority, Michael Walzer and

---

30. See http://www.whitehouse.gov/nsc/nss.html for the document.

31. For the full statement, cf. Blankenhorn, *The Islam/West Debate*, 239–44. Again, in the interests of full disclosure, I note that I am one of the signatories.

32. "Iraq and Just War: A Symposium"; transcript available at http://pewforum.org/events/index.php?EventID=36.

William Galston argued that any use of force against Iraq, or aimed at the deposition of Saddam Hussein, must necessarily be sponsored by the Security Council. In the absence of such authorization, a war led by the United States, even with coalition partners, would be in violation of the U.N. Charter and thus illegal and immoral.

Turning to the statement on National Security Strategy issued by the Bush administration, Gerald Bradley of the University of Notre Dame argued rather differently. As a Roman Catholic, Bradley noted that the most troubling aspect of the statement, and correlatively of the discussion of fighting in Iraq, was the reference to pre-emptive strikes. Here, Bradley had in mind the U.S. Bishops' argument that only wars of defense, or on occasion wars characterized in terms of humanitarian intervention, should be considered just. Arguing that wars to pre-empt imminent attacks should be considered an extension of defense, Bradley maintained that, in cases presenting a well-founded fear that weapons of mass destruction might fall into the hands of groups dedicated to terrorism, the category of pre-emption should be extended so as to justify attacks "while there is still time." Thus, even if Iraq under Saddam Hussein did not pose an imminent threat to the United States and its allies, its possession of weapons of mass destruction and history of collaboration with terrorist groups might suggest the justice of a pre-emptive strike by the United States.

My own contribution to the panel differed from those offered by Galston and Walzer, as well as by Bradley. Given that the United States had been engaged in a low-grade military conflict with Iraq ever since the "first" Gulf War ended in 1991, particularly in connection with the "no-fly" zones in North and South Iraq, I could not see the point of describing action to enforce Security Council resolutions or to depose Saddam as "pre-emptive." Nor could I see the argument for requiring Security Council authorization in 2002–03, at least not in the sense articulated by Galston and Walzer. While one could argue for Security Council support as an important indicator of international support, and thus as a factor in calculating the likely costs and possibility of success in a military venture, it did (and still does) seem difficult to take the high road of restricting legal and moral authority to the U.N. After all, despite its many virtues, the U.N. lacks most of the attributes of sovereignty envisioned in the just war tradition; as well, its dependence on the willingness of member states to cooperate suggests a weakness well-displayed by failures to respond promptly to genocidal or near-genocidal circumstances in the former Yugoslavia, Rwanda/Burundi, and numerous other instances during the 1990s.[33]

From the just war point of view, authority to make war resides with the head or governing body of a particular political community. Thus, when champions of the Bush administration said that the President and other U.S. policymakers would make decisions based on the fact they were elected and sworn to serve the people of the United States, they had a point.

From the just war point of view, the notion of right authority goes even further. As Johnson argues, those charged with governance of a particular political community are obligated, in connection with their duty to defend against injustice, to consider the state of the international community. When a ruler poses a sufficient threat to the common good so that he or she may be described as a tyrant, it is the duty of other rulers to consider the question of deposition by force. That does not suggest that a decision to carry through with deposition is already made; it simply suggests that the duty to consider, and if necessary to carry through, belongs with the governing bodies of particular political communities.[34]

Given this, my own view was and remains that one could make a reasonable just war case that the United States, in conjunction with others, had the right to use military force aimed at circumscribing or even deposing the regime of Saddam Hussein in 2002–03. From my point of view, the growing uncertainty regarding the resolve of members of the Security Council to carry through on the three-fold policy of weapons inspections, no-fly zones, and economic sanctions put in place following the Gulf War was important in this regard. Then, too, one had to consider the enormous suffering of the Iraqi people in connection with Saddam's evident ability to manipulate "oil for food" and other programs intended to ensure that the civilian population of Iraq did not suffer excessively from the sanctions. By 2002, the situation in southern

---

33. Not to mention the current impasse with respect to the Darfur region in Sudan.

34. For Johnson's views, see *Morality and Contemporary Warfare*; idem., "Aquinas and Luther on War and Peace: Sovereign Authority and the Use of Armed Force," 3–22; idem., *The War to Oust Saddam Hussein*.

Iraq reached crisis proportions, with reports of severe deprivation and high rates of infant mortality.

Even with this right to make war, however, it was not—and still is not—evident to me that the United States would be wise to act. In the Pew Forum, I put this in terms of the maxim that one might have a right to act in a certain way, yet still ask whether it would be wise to exercise this right. I can explain as follows: the just war criteria, as is well known, point not only to considerations of right authority, just cause, and right intention. They also include considerations of the likely balance between goods and evils that will occur as a result of a military action. They suggest a conscientious attempt to weight the possibilities of success, and a good-faith estimate of the likely political situation that will follow from war. In his most recent studies, Johnson speaks of these as the "prudential" or "teleological" criteria of the just war tradition.[35] I should say that these are aspects of the just war tradition that must be considered when one asks whether or not war is prudent or wise, in the sense of serving the cause of justice. Thus, in writing about the deposition of a tyrant, Thomas Aquinas argues that those who see the rightness or justice in such change must nevertheless ask whether it may bring about more harm than good. One can, in other words, have a right to depose a tyrant, but find it unwise or imprudent to exercise that right.[36]

With respect to military action in Iraq, it seemed clear in 2002–03 that one should at least worry about the likely balance of costs and benefits, to the United States, to the people of Iraq, and to the world. One should also worry about the likelihood of ethnic and religious strife following the removal of Saddam, as well as about the probabilities of success in building a relatively just political order. These were and remain very difficult issues to adjudicate—even in the fall of 2005, as I write these lines, success in Iraq remains an open question. For now, though, it is enough to show the movement of just war discourse post-9/11, and to note that here, as with Christian practical reason in general, much depends on judgments people make as they try to match approved sources with the facts of particular contexts.

---

35. Johnson, "Aquinas and Luther on War and Peace."

36. *Summa Theologiae* II-II, q. 42.

Conclusion

Our description of the historic and contemporary trajectories of Islamic and Christian discourse related to war indicates a number of shared interests. With respect to Muslim argument related to the standing of al-Qa`ida's program, the concern to discriminate between combatant and noncombatant targets stands out, and that is certainly a notion with which just war thinkers can identify. With respect to Christian argument related to the "war on terror," the clarification of justice as the presupposition of just war reasoning, of right authority as belonging to particular political communities, and the drive to emphasize the prudential criteria of the *jus ad bellum* are certainly points on which Muslims will have views, particularly with respect to historic aspects of Islamic tradition.

The overarching problem of Islamic and Christian ethics, or more particularly of the just war and *jihad* frameworks, is not resort to and limitation of war, however. As presented in this essay, at least, these frameworks serve to enable communities of believers to discern the command or guidance of the living God. One part of this "divine command problematic" has to do with reading approved texts; another part has to do with ascertaining a "fit" between textual precedents and contemporary situations. Muslims debating the tactics advocated by al-Qa`ida appeal to texts, and specifically to precedents established by successive generations engaged in the practice of *Shari`a* reasoning. But they also debate the "fit" of those precedents with current circumstances—at least, that constitutes an important dimension of the argument advanced by al-Qa`ida spokespersons, viz., that the nature of the U.S. polity and its behavior suggests that standard restrictions on warriors do not hold. Similarly, Christian attempts to ascertain the guidance of God in the context of a "war on terror" suggest disagreements on matters of "fundamentals," and also on the facts relevant to judgment, particularly in the case of the war to depose Saddam Hussein. In both cases, disagreement stands out, and one might suppose this suggests the difficulty of the task set by the traditions: that is, they are attempting nothing less than an apprehension of the command of the living God, who by the testimony of both traditions is in important ways beyond human comprehension. Consider:

> O the depth of the riches and wisdom and knowledge of God! How unsearchable are God's judgments and how inscrutable God's ways! (Rom 11:33 NRSV)

> Say: He is God, the One, God, the Eternal. He does not beget, and He is not begotten. No one is comparable to God. (*Surat al-Ikhlas* or 112)

Or, to cite a text that is in some ways the root from which both traditions spring, "I am who I am (Ex 3:14)."

In describing *Shari`a* reasoning, I noted that for much of Islamic tradition, the point—that is, in terms of the activity for which believers may receive praise or blame—is the effort to discern God's guidance. One might say that virtue is connected with conscientiousness, more than with rightness of judgment. Christian tradition does not often speak in this way, though the nature of Christian practical reason suggests such a statement might well be apt. In both traditions, the requirement of matching textual precedents with contemporary circumstances creates the occasion for disagreement. Faithfulness lies, in some sense, in participation in an argument by which one expresses the intention to follow in God's way. If some are able to actually arrive at right judgment, then that is a wonder, worthy of praise—or, since we are dealing with traditions that affirm that ultimately, all good things come from God, the wonder of right judgment suggests the giving of thanks to the One from whom all things come, and unto whom all things will return.

Of course, no good Muslim or Christian will be content with the notion that the *jihad* or just war traditions are "merely" about argument. Arguments lead to judgments, and judgments inform actions. And yet, there is much to suggest that the problematic of discerning divine guidance should engender a sense of humility in terms of human beings ability to interpret the signs given by God. The difficulty of the task is such that it requires virtues of prudence, justice, wisdom, and fortitude. Indeed, it may ultimately require more than these; practical judgment may require faith, hope, and charity.

In any case, the struggle of Islam and Christianity with the imperatives of justice, and particularly the justice of war, might well suggest the need to widen the circle of argument. The frameworks of *jihad* and just war traditions were developed for use by groups of Muslims and Christians, respectively. To this point, their history largely runs on parallel tracks. Even in those "middle centuries" where the two traditions developed a parallel or analogous interest in Aristotelian notions of justice, their advocates seldom operated as conversation partners. Rather, each tradition developed its own mode of dealing with Aristotle and, if Muslim or Christian interpreters might be viewed as somehow responding to one another in this regard, it was as rivals, while Islamicate and Christian polities engaged one another in intellectual, political, and military combat.

We are now at a point when parallel development is no longer sufficient. So I argue, at least. While there is much to suggest that the conflict between Western and Islamic civilizations is a contemporary reprise of earlier contests between the polities of Christendom and the Islamicate empires, I do not believe this can be all there is to our current encounter. For we—Muslims, Christians, and also Jews and others— are no longer located in discrete geographical and political contexts. In Europe, North America, parts of South and East Asia, the Philippines, and elsewhere, we live and move and have our being in interactions with one another. We are at a point when we are called to read and comment on one another's texts, and even to participate in one another's arguments. To put this another way, we are at a point when it is necessary for Muslims, Christians, and others to see their respective traditions as one long intercommunal argument about the meaning of responsibility to God, the Creator, Governor, and Redeemer of the world. Responsibility can no longer be a matter for "insiders" who claim the prerogative to interpret their respective sources. It must be a matter of public concern, in which anyone willing to put forth the effort and participate deserves a hearing.

How shall we begin? I suggest we take a text, and ask about its relevance for our situation. We need not start "from scratch." The course of intra-Muslim and intra-Christian argument charts our course. We may begin "on either end," but let me suggest we take up Qur'an 2.190:

> Fight in God's cause against those who fight you, but do not overstep the limits: God does not approve those who overstep the limits.

I think this text, or more generally, the notion suggested therein, should be of interest to Muslims, Christians, Jews, believers and non-believers alike—to all those wishing to claim the mantle of justice, in the service of peace.

PART TWO

Traditions of Pacifism
and Non-violence

3

Imagining Peace and Co-existence in the Face of Catastrophe: The Prophetic Jewish Voice and the State, 1917–1948

Mark Levene

I will never forget when in 1987, I was giving a lecture on rabbinic sources on peace at one of the most prominent universities in the United States. An old Israeli orthodox man and his wife were sitting in the front row; he was a well-known scientist. I was expounding on a particular talmudic passage, which reflected on the relationship between peace and compassion, and I heard from this educated scientist, muttered in low tones, words that I will never forget: "He sounds like a Christian." My Orthodox rabbinic credentials did not matter; my fluency with talmudic text did not matter. What mattered was that the texts were too universal and too benign in their relationship to the outside world. And I knew then, I think for the first time, that rational discussion of shared values between Jews and gentiles was a waste of time for many people, no matter how educated. Something else, something dramatically different than logic and reason, would be necessary to heal the wounds of the past.[1]

THUS RECOUNTS MARK GOPIN IN HIS WONDERFULLY THOUGHT-PROVOKING and inspiring book, *Between Eden and Armageddon.* For this author, there are many resonances in Gopin's reflections, though I must hasten to confess at the outset of this piece a singular lack of talmudic knowledge or theological credentials. What attracted me to Gopin's lines rather was his foregrounding of a universal "peace" message as if this

1. Gopin, *Between Eden and Armageddon,* 170.

were intrinsic to Judaism. Again, this may sound somewhat paradoxical given that while, as a historian, I have written on the modern Jewish experience, religious convictions or practice have not been a motivating force, which again is not surprising given a certainly culturally Jewish but otherwise very secular upbringing.

However, issues of violence and non-violence have been much closer to home, many of my more youthful adult years being devoted not to ivory-tower pursuits but to a full-time role as an activist peace campaigner; one in which I incidentally found myself—just as in the environmental movement—repeatedly encountering other very similarly secular Jews. Now, admittedly, as a general rule, none of these good people made a point about their Jewishness as a goad to, or explanation for their thoughts or actions. Or, perhaps, simply, there was no pressing need to do so. By contrast, Marc Bloch, the great historian, and otherwise wholly secular French resistance leader, faced with the imminence of execution by a Nazi firing squad in June 1944, committed to his testament these words:

> In a world assailed by the most appalling barbarism, is not that generous tradition of the Hebrew prophets, which Christianity and its highest and noblest took over and expanded, one of the best justifications we have for living, believing and fighting?[2]

Again, shades of the later Gopin. But also the further telling inference that Bloch's fount of inspiration was to be found not so much in talmudic commentary—something he probably never read—but in the entirely more accessible, if sacred Ur-texts of the Tanach—for Christians, that is, the Old Testament—above all, in a passage such as this:

> And he shall judge among the nations and shall rebuke many people: and they shall beat their swords into ploughshares and their spears into pruning hooks: nation shall not lift up sword against nation, neither shall they learn war any more.[3]

These famous, not to say, quite extraordinary lines from Isaiah seem to sum up Judaic prophecy at its most irenic. Here we have a message, not simply to the Hebrews, but to the entire peoples of the

---

2. Marc Bloch quoted in Bartov, *Mirrors of Destruction*, 145.

3. Isa 2:4 (King James Version).

planet. In the message is a promise of a world to come, yet at the same time restored to its original harmony. Indeed, one upon which the later rabbinic commentators, so profoundly steeped in the books of *Nebi'im* (Prophets) could in turn set their talmudic seal. "By three things is the world sustained," proposed Rabbi Shimon ben Gamliel, "truth, justice and peace."[4] To which Rav Muna, in a further mishnaic commentary, could only add, "These things are one."[5] Is it this essential wisdom, somehow, which lies behind all those "Jews beyond Judaism" who have struggled so fervently in the peace and other progressive movements of modern times? Indeed, is the awareness that peace is achievable only through paths of righteousness and justice so deeply ingrained in the Jewish psyche that it might be operative, even where its proponents have been unaware of its textual origins?

The answers to such questions necessarily lie in the realms of mystery. All I can confirm, albeit on the basis of my rather untutored research on the matter, is a profound linkage between Judaism, peace, and non-violence. Thus, as to Judaic purpose, as provided in a succinctly authoritative if suitably awesome summary:

> Israel is a proleptic community, established by God in the midst
> of time to represent the harmony which was intended by God
> in creation, and which will in the end be the whole human case,
> "when the knowledge of God shall cover the earth as the waters
> cover the sea." (Habbakuk 2:14)[6]

Or, if I can put it slightly more prosaically, the very notion of a Jewish covenant with God, while it entails shared responsibilities of practice binding individual Jews together into a special community, also ultimately involves them in a collective Godly purpose with a prophetic embrace of all humanity.[7] As to peace and non-violence, while these may be enmeshed with messianic promises of a salvation informed by justice, they are more exactly grounded in everyday Jewish practice around obligations associated with *piku'ah nefesh*, the absolute sacred value of human life, the negation of which, in multitudinous talmudic injunctions, would represent not simply an annihilation of a fellow

---

4. Tractate *Avot* 1.18
5. Tractate *Derech Eretz Zuta*, Perek Hashalom, 2.
6. Bowker, *Oxford Dictionary of World Religions*, 513.
7. Isa 42:6; 49:6.

human being created in the image of God,[8] but, over and beyond that, the desecration of God's holiness in the world. "Whoever destroys a single life is considered by scripture as if he had destroyed the entire world," intones the Mishnah Sanhedrin, just as an equally famous passage reads, "He who saves a single life, saves the whole world."[9]

None of this exposition is intended either to blot out some of the more thoroughly warlike not to say atrocity-laden texts that are so central to the narrative of Hebrew "holy war" and conquest of Canaan, nor to pretend that these have no relevance to the latter-day evolution of Judaism. The promise of a redemptive future of eternal peace for all humankind clearly has to be set against a wholly more complex and eristic textual framework that speaks of the violence out of which ancient Israel was borne. If the simple point here, following Gopin's lead, is that the irenic message ultimately became crucial to Judaism as a thought-system and thus to rabbinic self-understanding of the Jewish role in the wider world, the equal problem we, as Gopin, must face is why this has become so remote from mainstream articulations of Jewish, including rabbinic, discourse in the contemporary world.

Why is it, indeed, when we think of those who attempt to meld words of peace and compassion with actual practice that we tend almost never, nowadays, to consider the community whose forbears arguably dreamt up the whole notion in the first place, but instead think of Quakers, Mennonites, or the Baha'i? Or, perhaps of a Martin Luther King, unashamedly recalling Deutero-Isaiah, in his famous 1963 "I have a dream" speech. When was the last time, by comparison, that we can recall a leading *Jewish* figure intoning Isaiah's great imagining of peace when the wolf would lie down with the lamb, the leopard with the kid, and the little child leading them?[10] Why, indeed, when we specifically think of religious Jewish people in Israel today, do we not, as a rule, readily make a connection between them and those ancient wise men of the ilk of rabbis' Hillel, Akiva, or Yohanan ben Zakai, each of whom pronounced that the highest calling of Judaism is love of every human being—a first tangible consequence of which would be both

8. Gen 9:6.
9. Mishnah Sanhedrin 4.5, 4.9.
10. Isa 11:6. See also Wittenberg, "Hope amid flames."

recognition of, and welcome to, the stranger.[11] Instead, we are more likely to conceive of them as utterly uncompromising and venomous in their attitudes towards their Arab neighbors, or even fellow Jews who evince weakness on the "other's" behalf?

The outside image of Israel may have become a vile parody of the truth, monolithic and oblivious to all those Israelis who have stood steadfast for reconciliation and compromise, but the fact that 59 percent of Europeans in a 2003 poll commissioned by the European Commission think that Israel poses the "biggest threat to world peace," cannot be founded on complete moonshine.[12] A little more than a year later a more specifically British poll found that respondents considered Israel the country in the world least beautiful or deserving of their respect, not to say one they would least like to holiday or live in.[13] One can only shudder at what, in the wake of Israel's 2006 Lebanon invasion, or, for that matter the massacre at Beit Hanun, a new round of poll findings might elicit.

We have, in short, a quite extraordinary and glaring dichotomy here. On the one hand, a biblical narrative that posits a people chosen by God, under covenant, to act as a light unto the nations—for which one might presume gentile gratitude—on the other, an image of present-day Israel, and actually, whether we like it or not, by extension, *Klal Israel*—all Jewry—as an entity that arouses in significant swathes of the world community considerable distaste, censure, even obloquy. I propose that simply pronouncing that this is *all* a consequence of anti-Semitism, while it may tell us a great many things, is ultimately insufficient to the task. The contradiction, at least between the Judaic message of peace and the present-day image of Israel as warlike, brutal, and merciless, needs to be answered.

However, my purpose here is not to mount a full-scale explication of the conundrum. Rather, my interest is in that part of the modern Jewish thinking that, I pose, has been true to the non-violence implicit in the language of Isaiah and the other prophets, but paradoxically until quite recently has been largely sidelined if not entirely blanked out from mainstream Jewish self-awareness or response. This, I would

11. Sifra to Leviticus 19:18. See also Gopin, *Between Eden*, 6–7, 9, 29; Kimelman, "Non-Violence in the Talmud," 316–34.

12. Beaumont, "Israel outraged as EU poll names it a threat to peace."

13. Scodie, "Israel is 'least beautiful country.'"

argue, in itself makes the program, in particular emanating from the small group of visionaries around Martin Buber and Judah Magnes, all the more remarkable and extraordinary. Even more so, perhaps, given that some eighty years on from first public enunciations, the peace and co-existence message of these latter-day prophets, both in the Middle East, and beyond, is beginning to return to *political* discourse.

This proposed focus, suggests to me a two-part discussion. The first deals with factors within the Jewish experience, which have competed with and to a significant extent have stifled the irenic voice within modern Judaism. The second, the antidote so to speak, looks exactly to an understanding of the irenic tendency but with the added implication that, while fully grounded in the Judaic, a critical clue to its latter-day renewal lies in a conception of Judaism not in some fixed and hermetically sealed container but rather in an evolving response to the outside world, and, not least, in a form of dialectical engagement with other religions and cultures. I seek to develop this argument not by further forays into Jewish theology but instead by reverting to my more familiar historical hat to consider the Jewish *experience*, particularly between 1917 and 1948. This period surely represents the climacteric in this experience since the time of the ancient world. At one end of it are the Balfour Declaration and the revolutions in Russia; at the other, the Holocaust and the creation of the state of Israel. Necessarily, these events framed the most dramatic possibilities and potentialities in Jewry's diasporic and conceived national existence. In their wake, however, their legacy also seemed to harden into a template for communal understandings of relations between Jews and fellow Jews, as with gentiles, which have remained the dominant, even hegemonic, norm ever since.

The Realities of Jewish Minority Status in Diaspora and Beyond

The implication that the Jewish tendency *against* the irenic is primarily a feature of the experience or interpretation of the recent past necessarily requires some broader contextualization. However, given both the gamut, not to say complexity of Jewish history, this can involve reference only to the most critical contours.

Since the Roman destruction of the temple in year 70 CE and the final liquidation of political resistance in *Eretz Israel* to foreign occupation two generations later, Jewish society has been primarily diasporic, ubiquitous, yet always politically and demographically of a minority nature. For the most part non-evangelizing, it has also been, until the eighteenth or early nineteenth centuries, largely dependent for its internal cohesion and social and religious practice on rabbinic guidance as handed down in halakhic law, itself derived from the Talmud. Equally, however, from third century CE origins, it has conformed to the principle of *dina de-malkhuta-dina*: "the law of the land is law."[14]

This last piece of information is particularly important to this study because it reminds us of the normative diasporic relationship to sovereign power of thousands of Jewish communities across time and space. Though the degree of Jewish powerlessness was usually very far from absolute and hence subject to much recent historiographical debate,[15] without territory, a military, bureaucracy, or a fixed resource base, Jewish society or rather societies—though in terms of self-administration usually autonomous—were *always* politically subordinate to the dominant non-Jewish authority. Again, to assume that this translated into what, in the 1920s, Salo Baron famously referred to as the lachrymose (i.e., tearful) view of Jewish history,[16] is now generally dismissed by serious historical scholarship. That said, for much of the Jewish world, looking back from 1917, the notion of being at the mercy of relentless and entirely antagonistic state and popular social forces would have seemed blindingly obvious; particularly from what had become the primary Ashkenazi Jewish heartlands in the Russian empire, where turn-of-the-century pogroms were the most tangible evidence of Jewish vulnerability. Indeed, it must have reinforced what in Gopin's view was a deep grain of traditional rabbinic pessimism in which the ancient tribal adversary, Amalek, or, alternatively, the character of Esau, became symbolic of an entire gentile world intent on persecuting and even exterminating Jewry.[17]

Whether this really represents a *general* Jewish view is more arguable. The Ashkenazi rabbis of the middle ages certainly had advocated

14. Bowker, *Oxford Dictionary of World Religions*, 284.

15. For contrasting views, see Bauer, *Jewish Emergence from Powerlessness*; Biale, *Power and Powerlessness in Jewish History*.

16. Baron, "Ghetto and Emancipation, Shall we revise the traditional view?" 513–26.

17. Gopin, *Between Eden*, 69, 109.

passive martyrdom in the face of rampaging crusaders and fellow travelers, as the ultimate expression of *Kiddush Hashem*—glorification of God and sanctification of his name.[18] But in western and central Europe, where these intense traumas had occurred, such notions proved almost entirely redundant in an Enlightenment and post-Enlightenment milieu where the demands on Jews were less of an obliterating and more of an acculturating kind; even though that in itself could be viewed as deeply threatening to the social fabric, cohesion, and well-being of traditional Jewry. In the Muslim world, by contrast, neither such existential threats, nor demands, as a general rule, applied.[19] It was in eastern Europe that the strain of Jewish pessimism in the face of early modern and then more contemporary anti-Jewish violence most persisted, culminating with strong resonances of the *Kiddush Hashem* tendency amongst many Orthodox communities during the Holocaust. Yet equally, this passivity received an almost violent repudiation and approbation by new, secular, and increasingly strident Jewish voices. Especially within a Zionism that came to be the dominant political ideology of Jewry from the time of the Holocaust, the behavior of the Orthodox—not to say the great bulk of European Jewry, for (allegedly) having gone to their collective destruction as "lambs to the slaughter"—was evidence of the bankruptcy of a traditional interface with the gentile world, which, in the process, had turned European Jews into "worthless" people.[20]

Of course, we need to be cautious here before making sweeping statements. How often, indeed, does one need to repeat that Jews, no more, nor less than any other group, are not and never have been a monolithic community, or had a single voice. That said, we have to weigh against that the entirely radical rupture with the Jewish past, which began to crystallize with the events of 1917 before being brought to an apparent post-catastrophe apotheosis with the creation of the Jewish state. The acute existential threats to the totality of Jewish existence of this

---

18. Bowker, *The Oxford Dictionary of World Religions*, 547.

19. One can be over-celebratory on this score. See, for instance, Brann, *Power in the Portrayal, Representations of Jews and Muslims in Eleventh and Twelfth-Century Islamic Spain*, for a powerful critique of writers such as S. D. Goitein who, from an earlier generation, tended to overstate the notion of Muslim-Jewish symbiosis. Nevertheless, one general rule holds: traditional Islam was more tolerant and amenable to Jewish existence than Western Christianity. See Cohen, *Under Crescent and Cross*.

20. Segev, *The Seventh Million*, 183.

period thus certainly did promote and accelerate some common Jewish responses. In particular, these included the search for a self-image and identity that was proactive, rather than reactive; muscular if not overtly militaristic as opposed to passive; self-liberating and heroic rather than weak and dependent; the culmination of which was the myth of the new Jewish man and woman, whether in the face of impossible odds as in Warsaw ghetto uprisings, or in the armed struggle for the state of Israel. This new self-image did not necessarily embrace *all* Jewry. Again, the ultra-Orthodox in particular remained notably introverted in post-Holocaust years. But the attempted recasting of mainstream Jewish life—whether in the diaspora or Israel itself—around the idea and practice of an autonomous nation did rather reinforce a general Jewish, as opposed to specifically Judaic, post-Holocaust topos that as the world did not give a damn abut their fate, Jews could only look to their own as guarantor of their collective survival. Not only thus was Israel "the few against the many" but with gentile antipathy or indifference as backdrop, *its* avoidance of another Holocaust became predicated on a self-understanding of absolute, undivided, and unflinching strength, both military and political.[21]

Which rather begs the question as to the existence of Jewish protagonists of peace, let alone Jews who might style themselves as "pacifists." When all is said and done, pacifism is predicated on a worldview that rejects the worst in favor of what is best in humankind. It may entail retreat from the world but is more likely to be founded on an essential assurance that communication and understanding *is* possible, not only with one's own kind but across cultural and social boundaries with very different peoples and creeds. This would hardly make pacifism passive but on the contrary rather active. Thus, in Jewish, or even, for that matter, Judaic terms, it would seem to be dependent on conditions in which a historic suspicion of the world beyond *Klal Israel* could be demonstrated to be either non-proven, or, at least, in abeyance, or retreat.

Interestingly, one place where Gopin has suggested some early modern forerunners of this possible tendency is in nineteenth century Risorgimento and post-Risorgimento Italy: that is, in a society where Jewish–non-Jewish relations were notably, and, in some ways, unusually

21. Gertz, *Myths in Israeli Culture*, chapters 1 and 2.

color-blind, optimistic, and intellectually open.[22] Here, the Orthodox theologians David Luzzatto and Elijah Benamorzegh developed halakhically-grounded interpretations of traditional texts that, albeit in different ways, strongly emphasized not only the universal rather than the particular in Judaism but also a specifically Jewish role in making the world a better place.

For Luzzatto this revolved around a recasting of the Jewish conception of *hemlah*, or compassion in the world; indeed, through this source, a common ground could be found between Jews and all peoples, even polytheists, as members of a single human family.[23] If Judaism's specific role in this was to promote God's oneness, Benamozegh would strikingly add: "Humanity cannot discern the essential principles on which society must rest until it meets with Israel. But Israel cannot plumb the depths of its own national and religious tradition until it meets with humanity."[24] Thus, while Benamozegh saw in the Torah a reflection of a single divine wisdom, lost in ancient times, refinding that unity for all humankind demanded both a kabbalistic-like recognition that parts of that unity were to be found in the multiplicity of faiths and that Jewry's specific role in this universal quest was to act, among the nations, as ambassadors, intermediaries, and peacemakers. Strikingly both writers, but most particularly Benamozegh, were formidably well versed and receptive not just to Jewish but also to particularly Christian, Oriental, as well as Enlightenment texts.[25] On all accounts, therefore, they have much in common with our German and Czech Jewish group of exemplars. However, like them, it also has to be said, they rather stand out as isolated examples of a *religiously* grounded Jewish peace orientation.

Paradoxically, in the context of World War I—the Great War— Jewish *secular* opposition to war, *is* evident. In Britain, for instance, a sizeable section of men of Russian-Jewish birth or origin attempted to refuse or avoid military conscription, not a few of them as so-called "fly boys," seeking refuge in Dublin, where compulsory military service as throughout British-ruled Ireland, until very late in the war, did not

22. For a partial explanation of this phenomenon, see Segre, "The Emancipation of Jews in Italy," 227–37.

23. Gopin, *Between Eden*, 89–97.

24. Bowker, *The Oxford Dictionary of World Religions*, 134.

25. Gopin, *Between Eden*, 97–109.

apply.[26] There is little to suggest, however, a Jewish religious motivation for their dissent, or even a penetration of essentially gentile ideas of conscientious objection. Avoidance of conscription came not because they were pacifists *per se* but more simply—and honestly—because they did not want to fight. This was motivated in considerable part by aware-ness of what their fathers and brothers had endured in the Russian army, and in lesser part by straightforward economic factors—the war provided a steady supply of welcome work (primarily in the mak-ing of military uniforms) for the otherwise impoverished yet heavily tailoring-focused Jewish communities of the big British cities. The fact that Britain's Russian ally was also the anti-Semitic state of the era, *par excellence,* certainly helped to dampen any lingering enthusiasm to take the King's shilling and, for some of the avoiders, this combined with socialist objections against the war.[27]

Again, there is a further set of paradoxes here. There is no doubt that in the radical socialist, anti-militarist arena, large numbers of secular Jews across Europe, during the war years and beyond, were strident and prominent: though, like comparable latter-day European and American peace campaigners, on universalist, not particularist grounds. This, cut no ice with anti-Semites who very often charged ideological opposition to the war as a case of a specifically international *Jewish* conspiracy to sabotage national morale, to the point where, in Germany in particular, it became a stock-in-trade accusation made not only by proto-Nazis but practically the entirety of the nationalist spectrum.[28] The only pertinence of this for our discussion, lies in the degree to which an undoubted, in part notably "Jewish," anti-war resistance was genuinely grounded in an irenic desire for dialogue and the minimization of human suffering, or, rather on a pragmatic assessment of power relations between the war-fighting polities and their potentially revolutionary adversaries. Most of the evidence would point to the latter conclusion. Even the Russian-Jewish anarchist and anti-war campaigner, Emma Goldman, who was particularly famed for her anti-militarist denunciations, for instance,

---

26. See Levene, "Going against the Grain," 96–101.

27. Kadish, *Bolsheviks and British Jews,* chapter 5.

28. For the classic study, see Cohn, *Warrant for Genocide,* chapter 6.

fell short of a position of absolute non-violence when it came to the class struggle or the opportunity to overthrow the state.[29]

Perhaps the key point, is that such internationalist anti-war activists, whether they were consciously or unconsciously responding to Jewish traditions, remained a distinct *minority* in terms of European Jewish responses to the war. Much more mainstream, especially in western and central Europe was identification, not to say patriotic loyalty, to the state of one's birth or domicile, combined with an entirely duty-bound Great War participation of Jewish youth in their respective armies. Moreover, given repeated nineteenth-century gentile aspersions as to an avowed Jewish inability to be good soldiers,[30] with racial innuendoes to this effect an added early twentieth-century stock-in-trade,[31] it was often taken to be little short of a point of honor for Jews to serve and in so doing prove the accusations false. To have done otherwise, and "unreservedly sponsor pacifism or ethical politics among the European peoples" as the acolyte of Buber, historian and genuine Jewish pacifist Hans Kohn, might have wished, would, he acknowledged, have left them open to the charge of being "aliens and traitors."[32] Perhaps Kohn could have taken heart from what some compatriot German Jews were observing as soldiers and administrators in the occupied, often densely Jewish populated regions to the Russian east, during the course of the war. One, Arnold Zweig, in his disillusionment with German military rule in the Lithuanian region, for instance, was sufficiently impressed by what he saw as an Orthodox Jewish repudiation of "illusions of temporal authority" that he surmised that behind this lay a religious reality anchored in notions of divine and universal justice.[33] Yet nowhere in the Europe of 1914, not even in anti-Semitic Russia, did official Jewish leaderships do anything other than very publicly rally to the cause of *union sacrée*: national unity in war.

As for Zionism, the very quest for what it perceived as the normalization of the Jewish condition through nation-statehood, both

29. See Goldman, "Preparedness: The Road to Universal Slaughter," 277–281.

30. For an extract from the Seminal Paulus-Riesser debate (1831) on the subject, see Mendes-Flohr and Reinharz, *The Jew in the Modern World*.

31. For key analyses, see Gilman, *The Jew's Body*; idem, *Franz Kafka: The Jewish Patient*.

32. Mendes-Flohr, *A Land of Two Peoples*, 97.

33. Liulevicius, *War Land on the Eastern Front*, 28.

determined its course towards and ultimately legitimated the military imperative—the resort to force—as necessary, realistic, and modern.[34] First Prime Minister David Ben-Gurion, in declaring the sovereignty of the Israeli state in May 1948, may have pronounced it as "based on the precepts of liberty, justice, and peace taught by the Hebrew Prophets,"[35] but surely uppermost in his mind at that moment were more palpable concerns associated with the urgency to achieve a monopoly of violence within the putative state's notional boundaries: not least given the then clear and present danger of outright conflict with its Arab subjects, neighbors, and surrounding polities.

One might wish to emphasize here that there is no shocking revelation in this inference. All modern states assume a monopoly of violence.[36] And all reserve to themselves the right to use it as instrument for the achievement of domestic and foreign policy ends, not only to ensure their own integrity, but also—as a general rule—for the security and well being of at least the compact majority of their citizens. The only sense in which this reality was startlingly different for the Jewish state was in the simple fact that there had not been one for the best part of two thousands years. Political Zionism thus represented a definitive rupture with a Jewish dependency on the diasporic condition. Even then, one can overstate the case. There were both biblical and talmudic concepts of just war: albeit in the latter case, developed in the exilic realm of abstraction.[37] One might blithely argue that from 1948, the only Judaic issue at stake was whether these dictums were to be somehow updated and adapted to the strikingly new circumstances of Israel's real but perilous existence, or, alternatively, jettisoned in favor of an entirely secularized political science or jurisprudence.

Except, one might rhetorically ask, what had any of this got to do with either Judaism or even the Jewish relationship to the land—*Eretz Israel*—itself? Of course, in mainstream Zionism there has always been a tension, a dichotomy, between the biblical, God-given, covenantally-tied basis upon which Jews claimed entitlement to the land, on the one hand, and the creation of a modern, internationally recognized, yet

34. See Shapira, *Land and Power, The Zionist Resort to Force, 1881–1948*.

35. "Proclamation of the State of Israel," in Mendes-Flohr and Reinharz, *The Jew in the Modern World*, 480.

36. See Giddens, *The Nation-State and Violence*.

37. For detailed exploration, see Gopin, *Between Eden*, 65–74.

self-empowering political entity, on the other. To take this line of questioning further, one might ask if the two could operate in tandem at all—except, that is, by violence—given that Zionist state-building could only proceed, in the first instance, by large-scale Jewish immigration and settlement to a country *already* peopled. Or is the point, rather, that the very project of Palestinocentric Jewish national formation by *standard* political methods—that is in defiance of, or obliviousness to, the existence of the country's mostly non-Jewish, indigenous population—ensured that Jews *qua* would-be or actual Israelis would not only cast themselves adrift from the prophetic injunctions upon them but equally make for conditions in the Holy Land that would wreck any hope that they might live in peace with their neighbors?

We have already suggested that the very existence of a small circle of prescient Jewish visionaries who understood and struggled with exactly this dilemma is itself significant. With Buber as guiding light, it was closely associated with *Brit Shalom* (Covenant of Peace) in the early years of the British mandate in Palestine, though more accurately, it formed its radical intellectual wing.[38] Later, members of what I will call the "Buber circle" were involved in the League for Arab-Jewish rapprochement, formed just before World War II, while, finally, Buber himself, along with Magnes, were instrumental in the formation of *Ihud* (Unity), which was created as an overtly political party in 1942.[39] However, throughout, core members of the circle remained essentially the same, as did their agenda—that is, on the one hand seeking to further *cultural* Zionism, while on the other consistently rejecting Jewish political sovereignty or majority in Palestine, in favor of bi-nationalism, which is to say a single political community comprising two nations: Arabs and Jews. It is to this circle which we devote the second part of our analysis.

38. For the distinction, see Ratzabi, *Between Zionism and Judaism.* Also, for further commentary on the backgrounds and attitudes of Weltsch, Kohn, and other Buber followers, see Lavsky, *Before Catastrophe: The Distinctive Path of German Zionism*, chapter 9.

39. For the *Ihud* manifesto, see Mendes-Flohr, *A Land of Two Peoples,* 148–49. Also Miller, "J. L. Magnes and the Promotion of Bi-nationalism in Palestine," 50–68; and for further background, see Hattis, *The Bi-national Idea in Palestine During Mandatory Times.*

Martin Buber and Friends, and the Struggle for a Prophetic Peace

The key paradox of the position of the Buber circle, is that while their agenda was formulated as a conscious bridge over which modern Zionism might re-find a genuinely Judaic purpose, the actual gap between the visionaries and the Zionist mainstream only grew wider and more unbridgeable as the possibility of statehood grew stronger. Openly espoused as an explicit goal in the pre-World War II *Yishuv* (the collective name for the Palestinian Jewish community) only by the so-called revisionist wing under Vladimir Jabotinsky, the 1942 enunciation of the Biltmore Program by the dominant movement effectively made the drive for sovereignty the avowed aspiration of all self-respecting Zionists. What with the public utterance of the necessity of autonomous military force—again previously the preserve of the revisionists—embraced by all sections of the mainstream, *Ihud*'s open *political* declaration for bi-nationalism in opposition to Biltmore marked more than simply a rupture with the main thrust of Zionist thought and action. Henceforth, the circle was not simply marginalized by the mainstream but increasingly vilified, primarily on the grounds that their overtly moralistic position endangered the needs of *practical* politics.[40]

The grouping, however, had its own consistent riposte, regularly declaring that the assumption that morality and politics could be placed into two separate compartments was itself deeply flawed, not to say hubristic. "Peace is possible, because it is necessary"—a statement originally derived from the Christian pacifist Mortiz von Egidy, though popularized by Buber's non-Zionist, Jewish anarchist mentor, Gustav Landauer—was one Buber himself often quoted.[41] In spite of the increasingly violent nature of the Arab resistance to Zionist immigration and settlement in this period, and some notable defections or simply flights to safer havens—not least Hans Kohn to the United States—the core grouping continued to eschew any notion of Arab subordination to Jews. There could be no "Gibeonite hewers of wood, or drawers of water," stated Buber in an imaginary dialogue on the Biltmore Program

---

40. For the increasingly fraught polemic between *Ihud* and its detractors, see Mendes-Flohr, *A Land of Two Peoples*, 150–78.

41. Ibid., 32–33, n.68. See also the chapter devoted to Landauer in Buber, *Paths in Utopia*.

in 1944.[42] On the contrary, the only way to the genuine achievement of peace in Palestine was through a humanistic relationship with the Other, which demanded not simply living alongside—the formula of the mainstream—but together *with* Arabs. Ongoing dialogue (Buber's favorite topos) and responsiveness, not least on the Jewish part with Islam, Arab language, and culture, and on the basis of absolute equality, mutual respect, and goodwill, thus, were as essential to the circle's strivings for the creation of a common homeland as was the insistence that only political compromise would achieve this goal.[43]

So who, then, were the founding spirits of these ideas, and, perhaps more to the point, what was it that impelled them not only to articulate a position at such complete odds with the compact majority of the *Yishuv* but to the extent of being practically anathematized for it? In terms of numbers, one can certainly say that the grouping was tiny. *Brit Shalom* itself, between its inception in 1925 and its terminus in 1933, had a grand total of 60 members in Palestine and 13 abroad, with some 80 further sympathizers worldwide.[44] The Buber circle represented only a fraction even of this whole. However, what they lacked in weight, they undoubtedly made up for in terms of intellect. In addition to Buber, the group included Robert Weltsch, Ernst Simon, Gershom Scholem, Hugo Bergmann, and Hans Kohn; a little galaxy, of some of the most brilliant and luminous of twentieth-century thinkers. However, the fact that they shared a tranche of views about the connection between Judaism and the larger world may owe not a little to the very specific central European, more specifically German Jewish cultural milieu from which the vast majority hailed—the only notable exception being the American-born Judah Magnes.[45]

---

42. Buber, "Dialogue on the Biltmore Programme," in Mendes-Flohr, *A Land of Two Peoples*, 161. One should perhaps add that this was not the first time this trope was famously used; Lord Curzon in his October 26, 1917, oppositional memorandum to the imminent British government Balfour Declaration used exactly this biblical reference. See George, *The Truth about the Peace Treaties*, Vol. II, 1129.

43. Buber, "The National Home and National Policy in Palestine," in Mendes-Flohr, *A Land of Two Peoples*, 82–91.

44. See Weiss, "Central European Ethnonationalism and Zionist Binationalism," 94.

45. Magnes, though a founder of *Ihud*, was not actually a member of the earlier *Brit Shalom* grouping. Nevertheless, the German debt is also clear; Magnes studied at the universities of Berlin and Heidleberg. See Goren, *Dissenter in Zion: From the Writings of Judah L. Magnes*.

A critical source here is Michael Löwy's *Redemption and Utopia: Jewish Libertarian Thought in Central Europe*, also provocatively subtitled *A study in elective affinity.*[46] Löwy's remit actually embraces a somewhat broader range of Jewish intellectuals, both Zionist and non-Zionist, the commonality lying in that all came from a generation of highly educated and acculturated middle-European, German-speaking Jewry, born in the late 1870s or 1880s: Buber, for instance, was born in 1878. Each, argues Löwy, was also strongly influenced by not only German traditions but the thought processes and ideals of their immediate milieu inspiring them, again quite distinctively, to join the poetry-infused, German neo-romantic reaction against what was perceived as the then-dominance of a functional, sterile modernity. As Löwy provocatively puts it, if these Jews beat an ultimate path to the prophet Isaiah it was "by way of Novalis, Holderin, and Schelling."[47] One might also note, that this meant, superficially at least, they also had something in common with those non-Jews from their generation who might have turned to the German ultra-nationalist right.[48]

In fact, all of Löwy's group turned sharply to the radical libertarian left, the only distinction lying not in whether this involved an embrace of anarchism, socialism, or communism, but whether, like Buber, this led as well to a commitment to Zionism; Löwy's sample, for instance, also including the non-Zionists Gustav Landauer, Walter Benjamin, George Lukacs, and Franz Rosenzweig. The ideological positions of these intellectuals, thus, were very diverse and sometimes prone to change. What Löwy, however, very convincingly argues is that there was something about the specific constellation of historical, cultural, and social factors that predisposed *all* these figures towards a particular strain of *Jewish* thinking.

Again this may sound odd, or even counter-intuitive, when one poses that many of them proclaimed an overt atheism. Even then, however, many were quite willing to consider themselves, *á la* Lukacs, as religious atheists, or even more provocatively, as in the case of Scholem,

---

46. Löwy, *Redemption and Utopia.*

47. Ibid., 35.

48. See Shapira, "Buber's Attachment to Herder and German 'Volkism,'" 1–30; also Mosse, *Germans and Jews: The Right, the Left, and the Search for a "Third Force" in Pre-Nazi Germany,* 85–94.

as a "religious anarchist."[49] What drew them to the Judaic, above all, Löwy argues, was the notion of messianic redemption, or as Buber put it Judaism's "most profoundly original idea."[50] This yearning for an absolute future that transcends all reality of past and present, as the true and perfect life, and in which the world would be delivered from evil, not only chimed in with their neo-romantic rejection of tight-laced, urban-orientated bourgeois values; it also had a very tangible consonance with possibilities for actual, revolutionary change in a political world whose first immediate culmination was the Great War, and the revolutionary sequence which followed. The fact that this "generation was the defeated of history"[51] cannot thus detract from the originality of their interpretation of these events, or their varying prescriptions for what amounted to the possibility of a terrestrial utopia.

What is interesting most specifically about the Buber circle is not only the way Judaic prophecy is enlisted to this end but how it actually absorbs and melds other traditions, including modern Christian thought and scholarship in the process. Certainly the consequent thought patterns would appear to be almost entirely unique to this group. Russian Jewish intelligentsia of the period, whether Zionist-orientated or more obviously of an internationalist revolutionary hue, were almost all notable for the degree to which they ran away from Jewish religiosity, to the point—and clearly there was a reaction here against the traditional straight-jacketed authority of the rabbis—where they became profoundly anti-clerical.[52] As for Orthodox Judaism itself, where one can discern a messianic tendency—most obviously in the Hasidic movement—it is of a highly internalized kind. The world may be fractured, and hence the task of Jewry to restore to it its holiness. But the route to that restoration lies through a quietist emphasis on prayer and repentance strictly within the confines of Jewry and the maintenance of *Halakha*: talmudic law.[53]

---

49. Löwy, *Redemption and Utopia*, 26, 66. Löwy notes that many Israeli teachers were scandalized by Scholem's 1971 admission.

50. Ibid., 51.

51. Ibid., 2.

52. Ibid., 40–46.

53. Both Buber and Scholem, the greatest scholar of Hasidism, were, from different perspectives, seminal figures in bringing the messianic tendencies in the movement into wider public view and understanding. However, the essentially very closed nature

For Buber's circle, and perhaps most insistently in the writing and speeches of Buber himself, the need for redemption, reparation, and restoration—or perhaps to use that more all-encompassing kabbalistic term for healing, *tikkun*—is equally crucial and messianic. However, it is also something that is achievable in the here and now through humanity's self-willed yet direct collaboration with God. Buber's messianism has been described as an open eschatology.[54] It is also why, paradoxically, he is like Scholem and others in his circle, another religious anarchist. His famous 1949 book is not called "Paths towards Utopia" but *Paths in Utopia*, implying that the ideal society—or put another way by Buber himself, the Kingdom of God—is not something to be put off to the indefinite future.[55] All of his circle, especially Scholem and Kohn, were fascinated by the Jewish eschatological notion of *Et Ketz* (end time)—a messianic-led end of days, replete with images from Isaiah in which radical but universal change will establish (or *re-establish*) "an age of harmony between man and God, between man and nature, and among men."[56] However, crucially for Buber, re-finding the essential elements of biblical prophecy also provided a human potential for its imminent arrival.

Buber's eschatology, thus, is unusual in the intensity of its humanism. And so too in its relationship to Palestine for ends which have little or nothing to do with a specific self-centered Jewish polity. Indeed, this is perhaps why Buber is so vehemently opposed to the idea of a specifically Jewish state, even going head-to-head in a much publicized encounter with Prime Minister Ben-Gurion in 1957 to denounce the latter's own secular-based claim to be redeeming Israel as a false prophecy of "Quasi-Zionism" founded on "an exaggerated politicization" that "keeps men from hearing the voice of the living God."[57] True Zionism, by contrast, here as in so many of his pre-1948 epistles, Buber argued, was founded in the Jews' unique prophetic calling. As such, it did not

---

of most Hasidic groups continues to lend to the complexity of scholarly interpretation. See Rapoport-Adler, *Hasidism Reappraised*.

54. Löwy, *Redemption and Utopia*, 53.

55. Ibid., 54–55. For further interpretation, also with reference to Buber's anarchism, see Doubrawa, "Martin Buber, the Anarchist."

56. Löwy, *Redemption and Utopia*, 19.

57. Quoted in Keren, *Ben-Gurion and the Intellectuals: Power, Knowledge, and Charisma*, 77–78.

deny Jewish nationhood but carried with it a supranational quality, the entry of which into world history required of the House of Jacob a form of service—that is as a religiously motivated community—which through its summons "to walk before them in the light of the Lord" signaled a redemption for *all* nations.[58]

This relationship, between *community* and morality, just as more famously, his existential exposition of social relations in the idea of "I-thou" is thus fundamental to the Buberian strain of Zionism.[59] The purpose of messianic prophecy, he proposed as early as 1925, is "not for the emancipation of a people but the redemption of the world; the emancipation of a people is but a sign and pathway to the emancipation of the world."[60] Nine years later, still living in Germany in the face of Nazism in total power, Buber was still expounding to Jewish audiences the same message:

> Israel's function is to encourage the nations to change their inner structure and their relations to one another. By maintaining such relations with the nations and being involved in the development of humanity, Israel may attain its unimperiled existence, its true security.[61]

Even more vociferously, in 1942, at the time of Biltmore and, of course, at the very height of the "final solution," Buber dared to openly challenge the path of political Zionism as the very antithesis of his proposed route to redemption:

> By opposing Hebrew humanism to a nationalism which is nothing but empty self-assertion, I wish to indicate that, at this juncture, the Zionist movement must decide either for national egoism or national humanism. If it decides in favour of national egoism, it too will suffer the fate which will soon befall all shallow nationalism i.e., nationalism which does not set the nation a true supranational task. If it decides in favour of Hebrew humanism, it will be strong and effective long after shallow na-

58. Ibid., 78. For further classic statements of the Buber argument see "Hebrew Humanism," in Buber, *Israel and the World*, 240–52. And in summation, idem, *On Zion, The History of an Idea.*

59. Buber, *I and Thou.* For wide-ranging analysis of Buber's oeuvre, see also Schilpp and Friedman, *Philosophy of Martin Buber.*

60. Quoted in Löwy, *Redemption and Utopia*, 57.

61. Buber, "Jew in the World," 170.

tionalism has lost all meaning and justification, for it will have something to say and bring to mankind.[62]

Assessing Buberian Irenism, Then and Now

What then can one conclude about the Buber circle, their place in history, or their relevance to the current situation in the Middle East? Can the prophetic injunction from Isaiah, "Zion will be redeemed with justice"[63] really be the touchstone for Jewish *political* engagement as the grouping believed? Or is the fate of people who articulate such messages always to be denigrated as dangerous meddlers who frankly would do best to leave well alone. In 1945, for instance, *Ihud* was openly attacked in a wall poster campaign by *Herut* (Freedom), the political wing of the overtly terroristic Irgun movement, as a group of "omniscient" professors from *Har Ha-tzofim*—literally, the Mount of Observers, or Beholders. The charge was sarcastic but clever. Buber, Magnes, and many of the leading *Ihud* lights were professors, in Magnes's case president, of Jerusalem's Hebrew University, whose home was indeed Mount Scopus (*Har Ha-tzofim* in Hebrew). Above it all, in their refined tranquility, and, as the *Herut* poster insinuated, "on the heights of a moral Olympus,"[64] what practical hands-on utility could *Ihud* really offer in a time of both Jewish catastrophe and ongoing crisis?

Buber's response was as one might expect: "Sometimes it is harder to speak the truth, than to lose control, lash out, and call upon others to do the same."[65] But underlying the rebuke remained the hard core of the Buberian vision: the *creative* search "not for a "fictitious" peace . . . but a true peace with the neighboring peoples which alone can render possible a common development of this portion of the earth."[66] More practically, it should be emphasized, that *Ihud*'s bi-national route to this goal might have been marginal but far from implausible in the context of Palestine in the twilight of the Mandate. The concept of a multinational state as a modern alternative to a standard nation-statism had its roots in middle-European theories of state and society, which to the key

62. Idem., "Hebrew Humanism," 248.

63. Isaiah 1:27.

64. Mendes-Flohr, *A Land of Two Peoples,* 174.

65. Buber, "Our Reply," 176.

66. Ibid., 178.

protagonists of *Ihud* were practically second nature, though it has been consciously not part of this contribution to pursue the associated political theorization here.[67] Nevertheless, it is to be remembered that when, in 1946, Buber and Magnes presented the *Ihud* program for a bi-national polity—one state, two peoples—to the Anglo-American Committee of Inquiry on the future of Palestine, their proposals received an entirely positive welcome, to the point where this was actually the Committee's recommendation for the country's post-Mandate governance.[68]

Elements of the wider *Yishuv* also supported these proposals, not least the majority of the kibbutz movement, the very experimental socialist, collective farms throughout Palestine that Buber extolled as the very basis for his notion of a decentralized federal commonwealth—"a community of communities"[69]—founded upon and living together through social justice. Nor did one necessarily have to embrace the messianism to accept that what Buber, or Magnes, were saying was a logical and reasoned response to the lack of prescience on the part of the mainstream leadership in its single-minded drive to sovereignty. As early as 1930, Magnes had warned that if Zionism followed the route towards "the *Wille zur Macht,* the state, the army, the frontiers," thus denying the other community its just aims, "we must not be surprised if we are attacked, and what is worse, if moral degeneration sets in amongst us."[70] How prophetic he was. With absolutely no other viable route out of the current impasse—save for more extreme violence—is it any wonder, despite the immense paradox involved, that bi-nationalism, as if it were indeed *practical* politics, is being discussed and espoused again not only by Israeli and other Jewish dissenters but by some of the more farsighted Palestinian peace activists and political thinkers too.[71]

There certainly is a striking irony as well as tragedy, here. Part of the problem for Magnes and Buber, at the time of *Ihud,* was not only the intransigence and ideological tunnel vision of the Zionist leadership, it

67. For wide-ranging treatment, see Weiss, "Central European Ethnonationalism." Also, for the Austro-Marxist theory of the multi-ethnic state, see Hanf, "Reducing conflict through cultural autonomy: Karl Renner's contribution," 33–52.

68. Magnes, *Arab-Jewish Unity.*

69. Buber, *Paths in Utopia,* 137.

70. Hertzberg, *The Zionist Idea,* 447.

71. See amongst others, Abu-Odeh, "The Case for Binationalism."; Khalidi, "A One-State Solution"; Judt, "Israel: The Alternative."; Lazare, "The One-State Solution."

was also the complete lack of partners to be had in the Palestinian Arab camp. Those who were willing at this critical juncture to make even tentative moves towards them, such as Fawzi Darwish al Husseini, or the labor leader, Sami Taha, were immediately branded as traitors and cut down by Palestinian "patriots."[72] *Ihud's* program thus continued to remain marginal in principle part because by 1947–48 nobody much on either side of the divide was listening, which itself is indicative of the fact that to have done so would have required of Jewish and Arab political leaders alike a responsibility to implement a logic that they knew to be counter to their *separate* national interests. In other words, even if the Buberian prescience about the consequences of failure was absolute, could it equally be that what the visionaries were saying most perfectly belonged if not to a different time, then to a different space?

As we have already noted, the Buber circle largely came out of a middle-European milieu. Buber himself was thoroughly immersed in the German intellectual world and did not finally leave for Palestine until 1938, when he was already sixty. His formative years, long before the Nazis, moreover, were spent grappling with currents in German neo-romantic scholarship hardly peculiar to a student of Jewish background. His discovery and then engagement with the mystical in Hasidic thought was actually preceded by his turn-of-the-century doctoral studies on the thirteenth-century German-Christian mystic, Meister Eckhart, and the more theosophically-inclined sixteenth-century Jacob Böhme.[73] Buber was hardly alone in these enthusiasms; Landauer and Lukacs were two in particular who shared it.[74] To say that they arrived at an absorption in mystical Judaism by way of a mystical Christianity may be stretching the point just a little. After all, most of Löwy's key figures were rather taken with Spinoza too. However, one has to remember something else about these individuals. Whereas with their parents' generation the whole purpose of life had been to assimilate to being "good" Germans, an effort that involved consciously distancing themselves from traditional *Yiddishkeit*, for those of Buber's, the result was that many of them were literally "cut off for the most part from the Jewish tradition." Their

72. In the case of Fawzi Darwish al-Husseini, from the most prominent Palestinian family, by a rival family faction. See Lappin, "Israel/Palestine: Is There a Case for Binationalism?"

73. See Friedman, "Martin Buber's Encounter with Mysticism," 43–81.

74. Löwy, *Redemption and Utopia*, 35, 132–33, 139.

re-finding it, as Shalom Ratzabi points out, was a "radical process."[75] But it was arguably also a quite emotionally complex and painful one, entailing as it did a twofold rejection both of the Kantian or neo-Kantian rationalism with which they had been imbued, as well as—in so far as this was still part of their cultural background—the equally rationalist bedrock of traditional central European Judaism itself.

The result, however, was not just what Löwy refers to as a partial *dis-assimilation*; and implicitly hence, a form of intellectual cultural revolt "against their parent's assimilation" in order "to save the Jewish religious culture of the past from oblivion";[76] it also quite strangely meant that these German Jewish libertarians were coming at *their* Judaism in a fresh way, almost as if they were beholding it *for the first time*. The result was an immediacy of engagement with what they imagined to be a primal Judaism—an *Urjudentum*—that necessarily was at variance with much of the more recent rabbinic tradition.[77] It is immaterial, in so far as this discussion goes, whether they really had struck at some authentic core. The point is that through their explorations they were able to glean something profoundly humanistic and universal from within it, which had otherwise been lost, just as in this same process of self-discovery they were able to read into their re-exposition of what Buber called "subterranean Judaism" role models and heroes who included not only Isaiah, Jeremiah, and indeed Spinoza but also the Essenically-orientated early Christians and, above all, that other great prophet of, and for humanity, who they duly reclaimed as one of their own: Jesus.[78]

Here then, is our final irony. What the Buber circle attempted to do against the odds in Palestine was actually, in a critical sense, a displacement of something which, under different circumstances, might have been entirely plausible in Germany: a symbiotic coming together of Jews and Christians through a common recognition of shared historic religious roots and contemporary humanistic potentialities. Of course, such assertions have to come with some serious caveats and reservations. Previous generations of Jewish reformers had sought and failed to find genuine partners in dialogue, leading Scholem to

75. Ratzabi, *Between Zionism and Judaism*, 24.

76. Löwy, *Redemption and Utopia*, 35.

77. See Mendes-Flohr, *A Land of Two Peoples*, 17.

78. Löwy, *Redemption and Utopia*, 57, 133, 160.

ultimately dismiss the whole notion of German-Jewish dialogue as a myth.[79] Moreover, the circle's arrival at their own irenic position was anything but simple; Buber, we ought to recall, began the Great War as one of its enthusiastic supporters, believing the experience would usher in a greater communal consciousness. Only under Landauer's influence did he move to an outright oppositional stance.[80] Similarly, while Buber in particular may have broken with centuries of Jewish anathema against Jesus, this hardly amounted to some notion of convergence, or reconcilability between the two religions, much to the chagrin of some of his Christian interpreters.[81]

All that said, and quite in contradiction to the famous (or infamous) Daniel Goldhagen thesis, which more or less slates all pre-1945 Germans as anti-Semites,[82] Buber and his group undoubtedly did have potential partners from across the Jewish-Christian divide. These notably included religious socialists of the ilk of Paul Tillich, Leonard Ragaz, and Eugen Rosenstock-Huessy, who shared not only much of the philosophical foundations of the Buber circle but also the deep desire to translate these foundations into actual humanitarian realities.[83] This potential synergy, moreover, with Christians whom the Buber circle would have counted as friends, also began to emerge at the time of the Weimar Republic, when Jewish and Judaic expression in Germany really was beginning to transcend the apologetics of previous generations.[84] The Holocaust may have put paid to that specific potentiality in middle Europe, just as it tragically may have reinforced mainstream Jewish tendencies to view any theological and actual cross-connections to Christianity—or for that matter, Islam—with suspicion; Buber, after all, is much more revered today in Christian circles than he is in Jewish ones.[85]

79. See Weise, "Struggling for Normality," 98.

80. See Flohr, "The Road to 'I and Thou,'" 201–25.

81. See, for instance, von Balthasar, *Martin Buber and Christianity: A Dialogue between Israel and the Church.*

82. Goldhagen, *Hitler's Willing Executioners: Ordinary Germans and the Holocaust.*

83. See for instance, Novak, "Buber and Tillich," 159–74.

84. See Brenner, *The Renaissance of Jewish Culture in Weimar Germany.*

85. For a notably acerbic portrayal of Buber's 'un-Jewish' theology, see Weiss-Rosmarin, "Martin Buber," 3–5.

Nevertheless, what Buber, and those like him, had to say surely cannot be measured only by their success. "We Jews," said Buber, "we of the blood of Amos and Jeremiah, of Jesus and Spinoza and all the earth shatterers who, when they died, were unsuccessful, we know of a different world from this one which subscribes only to success."[86]

It is exactly against this grain—represented in our actual world through a hegemonic globalization whose consequence, in the form of an accelerating human-made climate change, is heading us towards an apocalypse of self-destruction—which is the very reason why the Buberian message, and with it that of the biblically prescient, needs so urgently now to be heeded. Both implicitly and explicitly it carries with it a core Judaic teaching about the purpose of non-violence in our current so perilous situation: not just in Israel-Palestine but across the entire face of the planet. Said Hillel, the great first-century Jewish sage: "That which is hateful to you, do not do to others. That is the whole of the Torah. All the rest is commentary."[87]

86. Quoted in Bowker, *Oxford Dictionary of World Religions*, 168.

87. Tractate *Shabbat* 31. The dictum translates into the latter-day case for a global equity per person in terms of carbon emissions, as conceived in Aubrey Meyer's visionary "Contraction and Convergence" framework for combating anthropogenic climate change, available from http://www.gci.org.uk.

4

Sacrificing the Sacrifices of War

Stanley Hauerwas

The Moral Practice Called War

WAR IS A MORAL PRACTICE. BY CALLING WAR A MORAL PRACTICE I AM NOT necessarily suggesting that I believe war to be "a good thing." Drawing appreciatively on Alisdair MacIntyre's understanding of practices, James McClendon quite rightly argued that powerful practices can be narrated through the New Testament understanding of "principalities and powers." McClendon, moreover, is surely right to suggest that such powers are all the more dangerous because they can be perversions of God's good creation.[1]

Yet more importantly, I use the phrase "the practice of war" to try to think through the ethics of war in a different manner than beginning with positions such as pacifism and/or just war. I do not want to be misunderstood. I think the kind of work done to clarify how pacifism or just war is necessary is invaluable if it helps us to better understand how Christians should respond to war.[2] But I am also impressed by the reality that no matter how hard we work to understand either the moral limits or the form war should take in terms of the pacifist or just war options, it makes very little difference for the actual practice of war.

---

1. McClendon, *Systematic Theology*, 170–77.

2. In his fine book *Arguing about War*, Michael Walzer characterizes pacifists as those who deny that war is sometimes justifiable because they believe war is a criminal act. I should like to think this paper suggests that the pacifist position can appreciate the complex moral character of war. Walzer, *Arguing about War*, ix.

That pacifism or just war reflection have little effect is not, I think, because some people perversely think war is a good thing or even a conspiracy of the military-industrial complex. I certainly do not need to suggest, as the current war in Iraq amply demonstrates, that for many war turns out to be a great economic boon. But surely something deeper is going on. Everyone confesses, "war is horrible," yet we continue to have war. Sentimental appeals to peace too often turn out to be the grounds to justify the judgment that even if war is horrible and/or terrifying, sometimes we must be willing to go to war.

In the past, I have argued that war continues to seem necessary because we have found no way to tell the stories of our lives in which war does not play a role.[3] We cannot get rid of war because war has captured the habits of our imaginations. We quite simply cannot comprehend a world without war. This is as true of the pacifist as it is of the just warrior. What would the pacifists do if they actually got the world they say they want? In an odd way, pacifists can be as dependent on the existence of war to make their world intelligible as those who think that war at the very least must be tragically accepted. That is why I have argued that pacifism and nonviolence are inadequate descriptions for the disavowal of violence required by being a disciple of Jesus. Peace is a deeper reality than violence.[4] But if that is true, then we need to locate the peaceful practices that constitute our lives that too often fail to be named as such.

Yet to say that war is a habit of our imaginations does not tell us enough. Enda McDonagh and I have called for the abolition of war, but in order to appreciate why war is such a stubborn reality, I think we need to know better why war remains so morally compelling.[5] War is

3. Hauerwas, "Should War Be Eliminated?" 169–208; idem, "Can a Pacifist Think About War?" 116–135.

4. This was, of course, at the heart of Yoder's account of the peace made possible by Christ. For my explicit reflections on the issue, see Hauerwas, *Performing the Faith*, 169–83.

5. For more on our *Appeal to Abolish War*, see Hauerwas, "Reflections on the 'Appeal to Abolish War' or What Being a Friend of Enda's Got Me Into," 135–47.

I recently discovered a remarkable passage in John Keegan's *A Brief History of Warfare: Past, Present, Future*. Keegan says, "War is now avoidable; war is no longer necessary. The poor may fight, but the right rule. It is with their weapons that the mad ideologies of peasant countries tread the path of blood . . . at the threshold of a new era in history, can we but seize the opportunity, on the threshold of a genuinely new world order. We can stop now if we only choose, by a simple economic decision of the

not only morally compelling, it is also quite fascinating, if not beautiful.[6] I want therefore to offer some suggestions about the very character of war as a practice, the loss of which would make the lives of many less full.

My strategy is not unlike that of William James in his famous essay, "The Moral Equivalent of War."[7] James argued that, in spite of his pacifism, if war is to be abolished we must find a moral equivalent to war.[8]

---

governments of the rich states not to make more arms than they need for their own purposes, and not to supply any surplus that remains to the poor, the have-nots. . . . The time has come to end war." Keegan, *Brief History of Warfare*, 8.

I discovered this quote in Black, *War: Past, Present, and Future*. Black used the quote to exemplify what he took to be a great silliness. I believe debates among between military historians concerning how the history of war can or should be written to be quite important for those wanting to write about the morality of war.

6. J. Glen Gray observes, "What are these secret attractions of war, the ones that have persisted in the West despite revolutionary changes in methods of warfare? I believe that they are: the delight in seeing, the delight in comradeship, the delight in destruction . . . That war is a spectacle, as something to see, ought never to be underestimated . . . There is a popular conviction that war and battle are the sphere of ugliness, and, since aesthetic delight is associated with the beautiful, it may be concluded that war is the natural enemy of the aesthetic. I fear that this is in large part an illusion. It is, first of all wrong to believe that only beauty can give us aesthetic delight; the ugly can please us too, as every artist knows. And furthermore, beauty in various guises is hardly foreign to scenes of battle . . . If we think of beauty and ugliness without their usual moral overtones, there is often a weird but genuine beauty in the sight of massed men and weapons in combat. Reputedly, it was the sight of advancing columns of men under fire that impelled General Robert E. Lee to remark to one of his staff: 'It is well that war is so terrible—we would grow too fond of it.'" Gray, *Warriors: Reflections on Men In Battle*, 28–31.

7. James, "The Moral Equivalent of War," 3–16.

8. The war to which James sought to find an equivalent was surely the Civil War. One of James's brothers had been wounded in that war and in many ways never recovered. In his *The Metaphysical Club: A Story of Idea in America*, Louis Menand discusses the effects of the war on Oliver Wendell Holmes. Menand wonderfully observes that Holmes had gone off to fight because of his moral beliefs, but the experience of the war "did more than make him lose those beliefs. It made him lose his belief in beliefs." Menand, *Metaphysical Club*, 4. According to Menand, Holmes concluded from his experience of the war that certitude leads to violence. He was determined to avoid certitude about anything. Holmes assumed, of course, that we could not live if there were not some things we are certain about. Truth is, therefore, just the "name for what it is impossible for a person to doubt" (ibid., 63). Though not a philosopher, I think Menand rightly presents Holmes as the embodiment of the spirit that led to American pragmatism. James did not lose his belief in belief, but then neither did James experience the combat that shaped Holmes's life.

According to James, war was the institution that "is the great preserver of our ideals of hardihood, and human life with no use for hardihood would be contemptible. Without risks or prizes for the darer, history would be insipid indeed; and there is a type of military character which every one feels that the race should never cease to breed, for everyone is sensitive to its superiority."[9] Therefore, "war is a permanent human *obligation*" we abolish to our detriment.[10]

James thought that war could not be eliminated unless some alternative were found to preserve the virtues war requires. He thought this particularly important in developing bourgeois social orders and what he quite wonderfully called "the pleasure economies" of such societies. James proposed that:

> If now there were instead of military conscription a conscription of the whole youthful population to form for a certain number of years a part of the army enlisted against *Nature*, the injustice would tend to be evened out, and numerous other goods to the commonwealth would follow. The military ideals of hardihood and discipline would be wrought into the growing fibre [sic] of people; no one would remain blind as the luxurious classes now are blind to man's relations to the globe he lives on, and to the permanently sour and hard foundations of his higher life.[11]

The line of reflection I take in this paper is analogous to James's suggestion, but I hope it will become obvious that I think James's understanding of war is inadequate. He failed to see that war is a sacrificial system and any alternative to war must be one that sacrifices the sacrifices of war. Indeed, I will argue that the greatest sacrifice of war is

9. James, "The Moral Equivalent of War," 7.

10. Ibid., 8.

11. Ibid., 13. James's was the epitome of the ethos of the Victorian male. Every life should be the strenuous life; so testing oneself in "nature" was essential to being "manly." That "nature" was to be "tamed" was, therefore, a given. The significance of "The Moral Equivalent of War" for understanding James's position has seldom been developed. In his recent book, *William James: On Radical Empiricism and Religion*, Hunter Brown sees, rightly, I think, the continuity between this essay and James's *The Varieties of Religious Experience*. Brown notes, "Material self-abdication through the voluntary adoption of poverty is the strenuous life, James says; it is the 'moral equivalent of war' which transforms the ideal of selfless heroism, traditionally associated with military risk and self-sacrifice, into a strenuous heroism of ascetic identification with the disenfranchised through the personal abdication of one's material privileges." Brown, *William James: On Radical Empiricism and Religion*, 98.

not the sacrifice of life, great as such a sacrifice may be, but rather the sacrifice of our unwillingness to kill. That sacrifice—that is, the sacrifice of our unwillingness to kill—is why war is at once so morally compelling and morally perverse.

By calling attention to the sacrificial character of war, I hope to show that the Christian "disease" with war is liturgical. The sacrifices of war are a counter-liturgy to the sacrifice at the altar made possible by Christ. Because Christians believe that Christ is the end of sacrifice— that is, any sacrifice that is not determined by the sacrifice of the cross— we are free of the necessity to secure our existence through sacrificing our and others' lives on the world's altars. However, the sacrifice that war requires seems to mirror our lives as Christians, making war at once attracting and repelling to Christians.[12] A large claim to be sure, but one I hope to show is not without reason.

The Moral Logic of the Sacrifice of War

In his extraordinary book *War Is a Force That Gives Us Meaning*, Chris Hedges, a war correspondent, tries to explain why he became so addicted to war that he could not live without being in a war. War had quite simply captured his imagination, making it impossible for him to live "normally." Hedges observes:

> I learned early on that war forms its own culture. The rush of battle is a potent and often lethal addiction, for war is a drug, one I ingested for many years. It is peddled by myth makers— historians, war correspondents, film makers, novelists, and the state—all of whom endow it with qualities it often does

12. The grammar of this sentence gives the impression that war is a constant running through history. I think that presumption is problematic. The kind of war constitutive of the modern nation-state system is quite different than the wars fought between "kingdoms." "War" is a contested concept that requires analogical display. I continue to wonder, however, if a history of war can be written that does justice to the disanalogies between different kinds of conflicts. Moreover, I continue to think that just war theorists owe us an answer to the question, "If a war is unjust, is it still a war?" That people continue to describe an unjust war as war still seems to suggest that war can be distinguished from systematic killing and, therefore, in some sense be "legitimate." Thus the assumption: "I had to kill X or Y, but that I had to do so is legitimate because it was war." That is the assumption that I think must be challenged. The need to describe unjust war as nonetheless war, rather than state-sponsored murder, seems analogous to the need to describe the American treatment of prisoners as "abuse" rather than torture. I owe this observation to Charlie Collier.

possess: excitement, exoticism, power, chances to rise above our
small stations in life and a bizarre and fantastic universe that
has a grotesque and dark beauty. It dominates culture, distorts
memory, corrupts language, and infects everything around it,
even humor, which becomes preoccupied with the grim per-
versities of smut and death. Fundamental questions about the
meaning, or meaninglessness, of our place on the planet are laid
bare when we watch those around us sink to the lowest depths.
War exposes the capacity for evil that lurks not far below the
surface within all of us. And this is why for many war is so hard
to discuss once it is over.

The enduring attraction of war is this: Even with its destruction and carnage it can give us what we long for in life. It can
give us purpose, meaning, a reason for living. Only when we are
in the midst of conflict does the shallowness and vapidness of
much of our lives become apparent. Trivia dominates our conversations and increasingly our airways. And war is an enticing
elixir. It gives us resolve, a cause. It allows us to be noble.[13]

According to Hedges, war makes the world coherent and under-
standable because in war the world is construed as black and white,
them and us. Moreover, echoing J. Glen Grey's account in *The Warriors*,
Hedges notes that war creates a bond between combatants found almost nowhere else in our lives. War does so because soldiers at war
are bound by suffering for the pursuit of a higher good. Through war
we discover that though we may seek happiness, far more important is
meaning.[14] "And tragically war is sometimes the most powerful way in
human society to achieve meaning."[15]

The meaning often assumed to be given by participation in war,
particularly in the West, draws on the close identification of the sacrifice required by war and the sacrifice of Christ. Allen Frantzen calls
attention to the continuing influence of the ideal of chivalry for how

13. Hedges, *War is a Force That Give Us Meaning*, 3. Hedges argues that war cor-
respondents are crucial for the legitimation of war. The story of a war, a story that often
belies the anarchy of battle, becomes the way war is legitimated. So newspapers and
magazines are essential parts of the war machine.

14. Interestingly enough, often the anti-war efforts function in a similar way for
participants, that is, the anti-war movement needs an enemy if it is to have some common purpose.

15. Hedges, *War is a Force*, 10. Hedges book has been rightly celebrated as an honest and insightful account of war, but in many ways Grey's book remains the classical
description of the moral power war has over our imaginations.

English and German soldiers in World War I understood their roles. He notes that development of chivalry depended on the sacralization of violence so that the apparent conflict between piety and predatoriness simply disappeared. Instead, the great manuals of chivalry "closed the gap between piety—which required self-abnegation and self-sacrifice— and violence rooted in revenge. The most important presupposition of chivalry became the belief that one bloody death—Christ's—must be compensated by others like it."[16] Drawing on pictorial evidence, Frantzen helps us see that the connection between Christ's death and those that die in war is at the heart of how the sacrifice of the English, Germans, and Americans who died in World War I was understood.

Moreover, the language of sacrifice continues to play a central role in how war is understood, not only in World War II but also in the current Iraq war. I think the language of sacrifice is particularly important for societies like the United States in which war remains our most determinative common experience,[17] because states like the United States depend on the story of our wars for our ability to narrate our history as a unified story.[18] World War I was particularly important to the extent

16. Frantzen, *Bloody Good*, 24. Frantzen's use of pictorial evidence to sustain his argument is overwhelming. After reading his book, war monuments become much less innocent than we normally assume.

It was only after I finished this essay that I discovered Ivan Strenski's extraordinary book, *Contesting Sacrifice: Religion, Nationalism, and Social Thought in France*. Strenski argues that Catholic eucharistic theology of sacrifice, a theology in reaction to Protestant denial of the centrality of the Eucharist, provided the discourse for the French understanding of sacrifice for the nation and, in particular, for war. Strenski's story is a fascinating account of how the language of sacrifice worked for the way World War I and the Dreyfus affair were understood. His book is as good a documentation as I could want for the argument of this essay.

17. In his article "How to Get Out of Iraq," Peter Galbraith quotes the historian J. W. Chambers, who maintains that war has been "central to the way the United States has developed as a nation and a society" from the very beginning. Galbraith continues, "The conquest of Indian lands, the expulsion of first the French and then the British Empires, western expansion, the preservation of the Union, and America's accession to global power status after 1914 were all accompanied by, and in part accomplished through military exertion" (Galbraith, "How to Get Out of Iraq," 41).

But what has changed is American spending on the military. Before 1939, American spending was comparable to the standards of other great powers, but because of its wealth American can now budget for guns on a vast scale while still allowing most of its citizens to enjoy a high standard of living. (I have to say, this may be changing.)

18. Recent American war fighting strategy—that is, the use of massive force to eliminate the need for American soldiers to be killed—has created a moral crisis in

that it represented the reintegration of the American South into the union called the United States.[19]

Whatever one may think of Carl Schmitt's argument that all the legitimating concepts of the modern state—a state according to Schmitt that gains its moral intelligibility from war—are secularized theological concepts, I certainly think his analysis helps us understand much about America.[20] For example, Carolyn Marvin and David Ingle begin their book, *Blood Sacrifice and the Nation: Totem Rituals and the American Flag*, asking:

> What binds the nation together? How vulnerable to ethnic and religious antagonism is our sense of nationhood? What is the source of the malaise we have felt for so much of the post-World War II period? Above all, what moves citizens to put group interests ahead of their own, even to surrendering their lives? No strictly economic explanations, no great-man theory of history, no imminent group threat fully accounts for why members of enduring groups such as nations consent to sacrifice their immediate well being and that of their children to the group. Whatever does, tells us a great deal about what makes nation-states enduring and viable. This book argues that violent blood sacrifice makes enduring groups cohere, even though such a

the American military and society. Michael Walzer critiques American war strategy in Kosovo by reminding us of Camus' dictum: "You can't kill unless you are prepared to die." This at the very least requires that American generals be prepared to risk the lives of their soldiers. See Walzer, *Arguing about War*, 101–2.

I suspect the American unwillingness to sacrifice our troops has everything to do with the ethos that currently grips the American people. Russell Baker, for example, observes that a kind of sterility has crept into American politics. He continues, "In this atmosphere history has a dreamlike quality. A war is said to be in progress, and the President describes himself as a 'war president,' but, except for military professionals, no one is asked to fight or sacrifice or even, as in World War II, to save waste fats and grease. We are asked only to shop with a generous hand, to accept a tax cut, and to be scared" (Baker, "In Bush's Washington," 25). One of the great divides in America is the increasing gulf between the moral commitments constitutive of the armed services and the general ethos of American society.

19. In *Women and War*, Jean Bethke Elshtain observes that nation states can exist on paper before they exist in fact. Accordingly, she argues that the United States was an historical construction that visibly came into being as a cause and consequence of the "Great War." Prior to that war, America was a federation of strong local and regional identities in which the centralized federal government was fairly limited. World War I reintegrated not only the South into the Union, but also the immigrants who had flooded into America in the nineteenth century. Elshtain, *Women and War*, 106–20.

20. Schmitt, *Roman Catholicism and Political Form*.

claim challenges our most deeply held notions of civilized behavior. The sacrificial system that binds American citizens has
a sacred flag at its center. Patriotic rituals revere it as the embodiment of a bloodthirsty totem god who organizes killing
energy.[21]

Marvin and Ingle argue that self-sacrifice is the central theme of
the American civil religion of patriotism and that nowhere is that better exemplified than in the American fetish of the flag. They provide
extraordinarily rich and diverse iconographic and textual evidence to
sustain their argument. For example, they call attention to a quote from
Dwight D. Eisenhower's published account of his induction into West
Point. Eisenhower begins by describing the rough first day of initiation
into West Point at the end of which he confesses to being weary and
resentful. Eisenhower writes, however, "toward evening we assembled
outdoors and, with the American flag floating majestically above us,
were sworn in as cadets of the United States Military Academy. It was an
impressive ceremony. As I looked up at our national colors and swore
my allegiance, I realized humbly that *now I belonged to the flag*. It is a
moment I have never forgotten."[22]

21. Marvin and Ingle, *Blood Sacrifice and the Nation*, 1. Marvin and Ingle's argument draws heavily on Durkheim, whose general account of religion I find quite un-
persuasive, but it works quite well for their purposes.
    I think Marvin's and Ingle's book lends some support to my contention that one of
the reasons war has become a habit is that future generations feel the need to sacrifice
their young to show that they are worthy to represent those who sacrificed their youth
to give the present life. It does not matter what the past war was about or what the
present war concerns. What is important is that the sacrifice be repeated to show we are
rightful heirs of the sacrifices that we believe have been made on our behalf. Think of
the oft-made sentiment about those who have died in past wars: "We cannot let them
have died in vain."
    22. Ibid., 135. Marvin and Ingle quite rightly focus on the importance of the flag,
but their case could have been made stronger if they had attended to the confusion in
American churches between the cross and the flag. It is not uncommon for the flag to
appear on church bulletins, particularly on the Fourth of July. There is even an anthem
entitled the "Statue of Liberty." The lyrics read: "In New York harbor stands a lady with a
torch raised to the sky, and all who see her know she stands for liberty for you and me.
I'm so proud to be called an American, to be named with the brave and the free! I will
honor our flag and trust in God, and the Statue of Liberty. On lonely Golgotha stood a
cross with my Lord raised to the sky; and all who kneel there live forever as all the saved
can testify, I'm so glad to be called a Christian, to be named with the ransomed and
whole! As the statue liberates the citizen, so the Cross liberates the soul. Oh, the Cross
is my Statue of Liberty. It was there that my soul was set free. Unashamed I'll proclaim
that a rugged cross is my Statue of Liberty, my liberty." "Statue of Liberty," (song) 1974.

The crudity that often accompanies the identification of the flag with the sacrifice of war should not be used to dismiss sentiments like that expressed by Eisenhower, because I think there is something profoundly right that the flag should embody the moral logic of the sacrifice of war. The battle for Pork Chop Hill in the Korean War nicely illustrates the moral logic at the heart of war. Pork Chop Hill was a strategic point that controlled access to the Inchon valley. In the course of the war, Pork Chop Hill had changed hands many times. Late in the war, the hill had been retaken by American troops, but at a terrible cost. By the end of the battle, fewer than a dozen Americans were left on the top of the hill.

This was in the last stages of the peace talks, and the Americans were afraid if they withdrew the dozen men left on Pork Chop Hill, such a retreat could be interpreted as a loss of the will to fight and could, therefore, prolong the war. They were sure the enemy would counterattack and the dozen left would be killed. Yet if the Americans reinforced the men left at the top of the hill, more than the twelve would be killed. There was a debate at division headquarters with the result that the twelve were reinforced. The justification for the decision to reinforce was if they had not done so, it would have dishonored the memory of all the men who had died on Pork Chop Hill. The more sacrificed to honor past sacrifices, the more the moral stakes for which the war (or battle) has been fought often must be raised.[23]

23. The necessity to raise the stakes for which a war is fought in order to do justice to the sacrifices made in the war is a troubling phenomenon for those committed to just war reflection. How do you keep war limited when it seems necessary to justify war using moral descriptions that can only make the war unlimited. This strikes me as particularly troubling for democratic societies in which the "real" reasons for going to war must be put in terms to justify citizen soldiers going to war.

In his extraordinary memoir of the war in the Pacific, William Manchester observes, "The longer the casualty lists—the vaster the investment in blood—the greater the need to justify the slain" (Manchester, *Goodbye, Darkness*, 242).

For a poignant, novelistic account of the need to prevent civilian populations from knowing of the horror of war in order to guard the sacrifice of the ordinary soldier, see Perry, *Shoulder the Sky*.

There has been insufficient investigation of the relation between democratic societies and just war requirements. George Weigel has recently called for the development of a "Catholic international relations theory" that is surely a step in the right direction. Weigel argues that such a theory must accept the "enduring reality of the nation-state system" and argues that the acceptance of such a system will not necessarily commit Catholics, and he also says American foreign policy, to a "realist" account of interna-

In *He Came Preaching Peace*, John Howard Yoder wonders why it is so hard for political leaders to admit mistakes, to confess they were wrong. He asks, for instance, if it was necessary to withdraw American soldiers from Vietnam in 1975, or from Beirut in 1983, "Why can it not be admitted that it was wrong to send them there in the first place? Why can the statesman not afford to advocate peace without saying it must be 'with honor?' Why must the willingness to end the war be dulled or perhaps even denied by the demand that we must still seem to have won it?"[24] I think the answer to Yoder's perfectly sensible questions is quite simple: to acknowledge a policy or a strategy was mistaken is thought to betray the sacrifices made by those who as a result of the policy died.

It is often observed that the first casualty of war is truth, but how do you tell the truth without betraying the sacrifice of those who accepted the terms of battle?[25] War is a sacrificial system that creates its own justification. Hedges is right that war creates its own culture, but that it does so indicates the moral power of war. No doubt war creates a comradeship seldom found in other forms of life, but it does so because war subjects lives to sacrifices otherwise unavailable. That is the moral practice and power that war is.

---

tional relationships. And Weigel calls pacifists "naive" (Weigel, "World Order: What Catholics Forgot," 31–38).

24. Yoder, *He Came Preaching Peace*, 138.

25. In a lecture at the Church of Ireland General Synod, Rowan Williams observed, "But if we want to ask others to repent and search this past, we must do the same, and try to understand how we are seen and why we are hated and feared. It is a challenge addressed to us all, and it is the hardest word that Christ can speak to us. We so long to be only the innocent victim; we shrink from seeing that in different degrees we are all involved both in receiving and in causing suffering." www.archbishopofcanterbury.org/1172 consulted October 10 2008.

In an extraordinary essay, "The War on People—and on the Truth—in Croatia," Slavenka Draculic observes that though his father fought as a Partisan in World War II, he never talked about his involvement in that struggle. His father's silence was but an instance of the silence around the war, making possible the manipulation of images to support the Croatian war. Draculic observes, "The more I think about it, the more I am convinced that the contribution of his silence and the official version of the historical events of 1939–45 made this latest war possible" (Draculic, "The War on People—and on the Truth—in Croatia," B6). This leads Draculic to conclude, "Yet if the truth is not established about the war for the homeland, the next generation will one day find itself in exactly the same situation as my post-World War II generation. All they will have to rely upon will be dusty images and bloody stories" (ibid., B7).

The Sacrifice of the Refusal to Kill

I think it is a mistake, however, to focus only on the sacrifice of life that war requires. War also requires that we sacrifice our normal unwillingness to kill. It may seem odd to call the sacrifice of our unwillingness to kill "a sacrifice," but I want to show that this sacrifice often renders the lives of those who make it unintelligible. The sacrifice of our unwillingness to kill is but the dark side of the willingness in war to be killed. Of course I am not suggesting that every person who has killed in war suffers from having killed.[26] But I do believe that those who have killed without the killing troubling their lives should not have been in the business of killing in the first place.

In *On Killing: The Psychological Cost of Learning to Kill in War and Society*, Lt. Col. Dave Grossman reports on General S. L. A. Marshall's study of men in battle in World War II. Marshall discovered that of every hundred men along a line of fire during a battle, only 15 to 20 would take part by firing their weapons. This led Marshall to conclude that the average or healthy individual—that is, the person who could endure combat—"still has such an inner and usually unrealized resistance toward killing a fellow man that he will not of his own volition take life if it is possible to turn away from that responsibility."[27]

Grossman observes that to study killing in combat is very much like the study of sex. "Killing is a private, intimate occurrence of tremendous intensity, in which the destructive act becomes psychologically very much like the procreative act."[28] What, therefore, leads men to

26. It is equally true that those who return from war who have not killed may be deeply wounded both literally and figuratively. See, for example, Corbett, "The Permanent Scars of Iraq," 34–66.

27. Quoted in Grossman, *On Killing*, 1. Grossman has a chapter that deals with those who are "natural soldiers," that is, those who have the predisposition of a killer. He estimates that "those who like to kill" comprise no more than 2 percent of the military. He concludes, "Whether called sociopaths, sheepdogs, warriors, or heroes, they are there, they are a distinct minority, and in times of danger a nation needs them desperately" (ibid., 185).

28. Ibid., 2. William Manchester reflects on his returning to battle on Okinawa even though he had been wounded. He observes his irrational act "was an act of love. Those men on the line were my family, my home. They were closer to me than I can say, closer than any friends had been or would be. They had never let me down. And I couldn't do it to them. I had to be with them, rather than let them die and me live with the knowledge that I might have saved them. Men, I now know, do not fight for flag or country, for the Marine Corps or glory or any other abstraction. They fight for one another. Any

kill? Grossman suggests that what leads soldiers to kill is not the force of self-preservation but the power of another form of intimacy, that is, the accountability they feel with their comrades. Thus Richard Gabriel observes, "in military writings on unit cohesion, one consistently finds the assertion that the bonds combat soldiers form with one another are stronger than the bonds most men have with their wives."[29]

As a result, Grossman found it was very difficult to get soldiers to talk about having killed. Many would take refuge in the impersonality of modern war, attributing most deaths to artillery or bombing. The same process seems to be working in the attempt to depersonalize the enemy. Soldiers are often criticized for denying the humanity of the enemy by calling the enemy names such as "kraut," "jap," "reb," "gook," "yank," "dink," "slant," "slope," or "hajji." Moreover, the enemy is not "killed" but "knocked over," "wasted," "greased," "taken out," "mopped up," or "lit up." But surely these attempts to depersonalize the enemy as well as rename the process of killing should be understood as a desperate attempt to preserve the humanity of those that must kill. As Grossman observes, the dead take their misery with them, but the man who killed another must forever live and die with the one he killed. "The lesson becomes

man in combat who lacks comrades who will die for him, or for whom he is willing to die is not a man at all. He is truly an animal" (Manchester, *Goodbye Darkness*, 391).

In an extraordinary letter commenting on this paper, my friend Fritz Oehlschlaeger observes: "I suppose I wonder if it's as difficult for us to sacrifice our unwillingness to kill as you suggest. I found those quotes from General Marshall and Lt. Col. Grossman fascinating. If what they suggest is right, though, why, then, should war be so compelling? How does it square with the generally Darwinian image of ourselves we're almost inevitably disposed to adopt today—i.e., where we must, as successful survivors, view ourselves as the offspring of the apparently most efficient survivors (killers?) of the past? I notice all the accounts here of killing do stress its "private and intimate" quality (Grossman, Manchester, the powerful story of Harry Steward, etc.). But I wonder if that's the whole of the story; I wonder if the compelling quality of war resides precisely in the release from all that private inhibition. So that, in all the kinds of cases you cite, there is a tremendous psychological barrier to killing (it causes revulsion, etc.), but it's the giving up of these internal restraints, the loss of oneself in the mass movement of force, the freedom to kill justifiably (or perhaps in some realm of war beyond good and evil where justifications no longer matter) that is the real source of the fascination and compelling quality of war." I have no doubt that Fritz is right about this, at least for some soldiers.

29. Quoted in Grossman, *On Killing*, 149. The analogy between killing and sex invites the thought that mass killing in war is comparable to pornography. For if one of the conditions of pornography is its anonymous character, it is exactly the same kind of anonymity that characterizes much of the killing in modern war.

increasingly clear: Killing is what war is all about, and killing in combat, by its very nature, causes deep wounds of pain and guilt. The language of war helps us to deny what war is really about, and in doing so it makes war more palatable."[30]

Grossman's book reports conversations and interviews he has had with veterans who have killed. Often these reports include at first a euphoria that they have survived followed by an overwhelming guilt at what has happened—that is, they have killed another human being. Often this guilt is so strong that the one who has killed is wracked by physical revulsion and vomiting.[31] For example, William Manchester, the novelist and World War II veteran, describes his assault on a sniper in a fishing shack who was one-by-one picking off the Marines in his company. Manchester was terrified by fear, but he broke into the shack and found himself in an empty room. There was a door to another room he also broke down, although he feared in doing so the sniper would kill him. But it turned out the sniper was in a harness so he could not turn around fast enough. "He was entangled in the harness so I shot him with a 45 and I felt remorse and shame. I can remember whispering foolishly, 'I'm sorry' and then just throwing up. . . . I threw up all over myself. It was a betrayal of what I'd been taught since a child."[32]

Particularly agonizing are the occasions when the enemy has been shot but does not instantly die. Harry Steward, a Ranger and U.S. Army master sergeant, tells of a remarkable incident during the Tet offensive in 1968. He and his men suddenly found themselves confronted by a "guy" firing right at them. Steward was wounded in the arm, but the men on each side of him were killed. Steward charged with his M-16, mortally wounding the enemy. He was still alive but would soon die. Steward reports he could still see the wounded man's eyes looking at him with hate. Later as the flies were beginning to swarm over the dying man, Steward covered him with a blanket and rubbed water onto his lips. The hard stare started to leave his eyes. He tried to talk, but he was too far-gone. "I lit a cigarette, took a few puffs, and put it to his lips. He

30. Ibid., 93.

31. Ibid., 115–16.

32. In *Goodbye Darkness*, Manchester describes why he had to write: "Abruptly the poker of memory stirs the ashes of recollection and uncovers a forgotten ember, still smoldering down there, still hot, still glowing, still red as red." Manchester, *Goodbye Darkness*, 3–7.

could barely puff. We each had a few drags and that hard look had left his eyes before he died."[33]

The pathos of such reports is how the very character of what is told isolates the teller. Killing creates a world of silence isolating those who have killed. One of the most poignant conversations Grossman reports took place in a Veterans of Foreign Wars hall in Florida in 1989. A Vietnam vet named Roger was talking about his experience. It was early in the afternoon, but down the bar an older woman began to attack him:

> "You got no right to snivel about your little piss-ant war. World War Two was a real war. Were you even alive then? *Huh*? I lost a brother in World War Two."
>
> We tried to ignore her; she was only a local character. But finally Roger had had enough. He looked at her and calmly, coldly said: "Have you ever had to kill anyone?"
>
> "Well no!" she answered belligerently.
>
> "Then what right have *you* got to tell *me* anything?"
>
> There was a long, painful silence throughout the VFW hall, as would occur in a home where a guest had just witnessed an embarrassing family argument.
>
> Then I asked quietly, "Roger, when you got pushed just now, you came back with the fact that you had to kill in Vietnam. Was that the worst of it for you?"
>
> "Yah," he said. "That's half of it."
>
> I waited for a very long time, but he didn't go on. He only stared into his beer. Finally I had to ask, "What was the other half?"
>
> "The other half was that when we got home, nobody understood."[34]

Grossman observes that if soldiers like Roger are to regain some sense of normality they need to be reintegrated into society. Rituals of reentry, therefore, become extremely important. Grossman suggests that those who have killed need to have constant praise and assurance from peers and superiors that they did the right thing. Awarding of medals becomes particularly important. Medals gesture to the soldier that what he did was right and the community for which he fought is grateful.

33. Grossman, *On Killing*, 116–17.
34. Ibid., 249–50.

Medals mark that his community of sane and normal people, people who do not normally kill, welcome him back into "normality."[35]

Grossman calls attention to Richard Gabriel's observation that "primitive societies" often require soldiers to perform purification rights before letting them rejoin the community.[36] Such rites often involve washing or other forms of cleaning. Gabriel suggest the long voyage home on troop ships in World War II served to give soldiers time to tell to one another their stories and to receive support from one another. This process was reinforced by their being welcomed home by parades

35. Ibid., 272.

36. Of course one of those "primitive societies" was the church. Once even soldiers who had fought in "just wars" still had to confess and do penance before being allowed to partake of the Eucharist. In the same letter referred to above, Fritz Oehlschlaeger observes: "Something you comment upon on p. 22 [of the draft of this chapter] reminds me of the (to me) most terrible moments of *The Iliad*. It concerns the observation by Richard Gabriel that primitive societies require soldiers to perform purification rites before rejoining the community. In Book X of *The Iliad*, Diomedes and Odysseus go on a mission in the night to discover what's going on in the Trojan camp and they run into a man, Dolon, who has been sent by Hektor to find out whether the Greek ships are guarded. Odysseus captures Dolon, who supplicates him; Odysseus, as I remember it, assures him he need not fear and then gets information from him about the camp, including some about splendid horses belonging to the Thracians who are sleeping nearby. Odysseus then kills Dolon, and he and Diomedes proceed to the Thracian camp, where Diomedes kills twelve of the men in their sleep, the resourceful Odysseus being careful to drag each out of the way as they're killed so that the horses do not step on the corpses after Diomedes and Odysseus take them. Diomedes kills the Thracian king, and they leave just as the remaining Thracians are being aroused from sleep. After this particularly grisly and arguably not very honorable episode, Homer says of the two: 'And the men themselves waded into the sea and washed off the dense sweat from shin and shoulder and thigh. Afterwards when the surf of the sea had rinsed the dense-running sweat away from all their skin, and the inward heart had been cooled to refreshment, they stepped into the bathtubs smooth-polished, and bathed there, and after they had bathed and anointed themselves with olive oil they sat down to dine, and from the full mixing-bowl drawing the sweet-hearted wine poured out an offering to Athena.'" Homer, *The Iliad*, Book X.

I must say this always causes a visceral reaction in me. I've never actually vomited in response to it but that's distinctly the basic feeling I have. How are we to regard this? Is what's to be washed away merely sweat? What is the inward heart of Odysseus? What is it capable of? Does this ritual enable the killing they've just completed? How can they so easily be refreshed? How can they even consider eating? How can these apparently "civilized" practices (those "bathtubs smooth-polished") be related to, or integrated with, or dependent on, what has just occurred? What is a human being that he can resourcefully draw aside the dead as his companion kills them in their sleep and then sit down to dinner and wine?

and other forms of celebration. Yet soldiers returning from Vietnam were flown home often within days and sometimes hours of their last combat. There were no fellow soldiers to greet them. There was no one to convince them of their own sanity. Unable to purge their guilt or to be assured they had acted rightly, they turned their emotions inward.[37]

I think it is a well-attested fact that war veterans seldom want to talk about the experience of battle. No doubt the complex emotions of fear, the exhilaration danger produces, and the bonding between comrades make speaking of battle difficult. But how do you explain to another human being that you have killed? No doubt there are mechanisms that allow some to create an emotional distance between themselves and what they have done; but, at least if Grossman is right, men often remain haunted by their experience of having killed in a manner that can have—sometimes years later—destructive results.[38]

37. Grossman, *On Killing*, 272–73. Manchester notes that navy nurses were rare in the Pacific, which resulted in the scuttlebutt that the navy thought depraved Marines might rape them. He observed the Marines "believed the story. We knew from our pony editions (small versions of American magazines) that there was some concern at home over how to handle trained killers like us when the war ended. One prominent New York clubwoman suggested that we be sent to a reorientation camp outside the States (she suggested the Panama Canal zone), and that when we were released there, we be required to wear an identification patch warning of our lethal instincts, like a yellow star." Manchester, *Goodbye Darkness*, 273.

38. Grossman's *On Killing* has a number of chapters in his book dealing with descriptions that allow the soldier to "explain" what they have had to do—e.g., "I was following orders," "He was killed by the group," "I was just doing my job." A recent letter reproduced by Deacon Stan Grenn in *Jesus Journal* 88 makes poignant reading:

Dear Sir,

For twenty-two years I have carried your picture in my wallet. I was only eighteen years old that day that we faced one another on that trail in Chu Lai, Vietnam. Why you did not take my life I'll never know. You stared at me for so long armed with your AK-47 and yet you did not fire. Forgive me for taking your life. I was reacting just the way I was trained, to kill V.C. or gooks, hell you weren't even considered a human, just a gook/target, one and the same.

Since that day in 1967 I have grown a great deal and have a great deal of respect for life and other peoples of the world. So many times over the years I have stared at your picture and your daughter, I suspect. Each time my heart and guts would burn with the pain of guilt. I have two daughters myself now. One is twenty. The other one is twenty-two and has blessed me with two granddaughters, ages one and four.

Today I visit the Vietnam Veterans Memorial in D.C. I have wanted to come here for several years now to say goodbye to many of my former comrades. Somehow I hope and believe they will know I'm here. I truly loved many of

To kill, in war or in any circumstance, creates a silence. It is right that silence should surround the taking of life. After all, the life taken is not ours to take. Those who kill, even when such killing is assumed to be legitimate, bear the burden that what they have done makes them "different." How do you tell the story of having killed? Killing shatters speech, ends communication, isolating us into different worlds whose difference we cannot even acknowledge. No sacrifice is more dramatic than the sacrifice asked of those sent to war, that is, the sacrifice of their unwillingness to kill. Even more cruelly, we expect those who have killed to return to "normality."[39]

The Sacrifice of Christ and the Sacrifices of War

In *Blood Sacrifice and the Nation*, Marvin and Ingle assert that their book is about religion—specifically the religion of American patriotism. They acknowledge that nationalism is not usually considered a religion, but

---

them, as I am sure you loved many of your former comrades.

As of today we are no longer enemies. I perceive you as a brave soldier defending his homeland. Above all else, I can now respect the importance that life held for you. I suppose that is why I am able to be here today.

As I leave here today I leave your picture and this letter. It is time for me to continue the life process and release my pain and guilt. Forgive me Sir. I shall try to live my life to the fullest, an opportunity that you and many others were denied.

I'll sign off now Sir, so until we chance to meet again in another time and place, rest in peace.

39. Manchester suffered a head wound, which means "you are never going to get the shattered pieces of remembrance just right. In addition I have repressed what war memories I do have for so long that I have no way of knowing how distorted they are now" (Manchester, *Goodbye Darkness*, 194). Later, Manchester says, "it was somewhere on the slopes of that hill (Sugar Loaf on Okinawa) where I confronted the dark underside of battle, the passion died between me and the Marine Corps. The silver cord had been loosed, the golden bowl broken, the pitcher broken at the fountain, the wheel broken at the cistern. Half the evil in the world, I thought, is done in the name of honor. I now caught the jarring notes of the 'Marine's Hymn'—which, after all, was a melody lifted from an obscure Offenbach operetta—and the tacky appeals to patriotism which lay behind the mass butchery on the islands. On Sugar Loaf, in short, I realized something within me, long ailing, had expired. Although I would continue to do the job, performing as the hired gun, I now knew that banners and words, ruffles and flourishes, bugles and drums, the whole rigmarole, eventually ended in squalor" (ibid., 381–82).

This is why we so desperately need witnesses like Manchester. We are just beginning to have those who have been in Iraq provide similar accounts. See, for example, Galloway, "Combat in Iraq: What's it really like?" A13.

they claim that nationalism shares with sectarian religions the worship of a killing authority, which they argue is central to religious practice and belief. According to Marvin and Ingle, that is why religions flourish when they are powerless and persecuted. The authors then observe:

> In the religiously plural society of the United States, sectarian faith is optional for citizens, as everyone knows. Americans have rarely bled, sacrificed or died for Christianity or any other sectarian faith. Americans have often bled, sacrificed and died for their country. This fact is an important clue to its religious power. Though denominations are permitted to exist in the United States, they are not permitted to kill, for their beliefs are not officially true. What is really true in any society is what is worth killing for, and what citizens may be compelled to sacrifice their lives for.[40]

This is a sobering judgment, but one that cannot be ignored if Christians are to speak truthfully to ourselves and our neighbors about war. I think, however, that Christians must insist that what is true is not what a society thinks is worth killing for, but rather that for which they think it worth dying. Indeed, I sometimes think that Christians became such energetic killers because we were first so willing to die rather than betray our faith. Yet the value of Marvin and Ingle's claim that truth is to be found in that for which you are willing to kill is how it helps us see that the Christian alternative to war is not to have a more adequate "ethic" for conducting war.

No, the Christian alternative to war is worship. I am well known for the claim that the first task of the church is not to make the world more just, but to make the world the world. That claim is but a correlate of the assertion that the church does not have a social ethic. Rather the church is a social ethic. I am quite aware that such claims can lead to misunderstandings, but I think they are particularly useful in this context. The church does not so much as have a plan or a policy to make war less horrible or to end war. Rather the church is the alternative to the sacrifice of war in a war-weary world. The church is the end of war.

For example, consider these words from Augustine:

> It is we ourselves—we, his City—who are his best, his most glorious sacrifice. The mystic symbol of this sacrifice is celebrated in our oblations, familiar to the faithful. . . . It follows that justice

40. Marvin and Ingle, *Blood Sacrifice and the Nation*, 9.

is found where God, the one supreme God, rules an obedient City according to his grace, forbidding sacrifice to any being save himself alone; and where in consequence the soul rules the body in all men who belong to this City and obey God, and the reason faithfully rules the vices in a lawful system of subordination so that just as the individual righteous man lives on the basis of faith which is active in love, so the association, or people, of righteous men lives on the same basis of faith, active in love, the love with which a man loves God as God ought to be loved, and loves his neighbor as himself. But where this justice does not exist, there is certainly no "association of men united by a common sense of right and by a community of interest." Therefore there is no commonwealth; for where there is no "people," there is no "weal of the people."[41]

The sacrifices of war are undeniable. But in the cross of Christ, the Father has forever ended our attempts to sacrifice to God in terms set by the city of man. We (that is, we Christians) have now been incorporated into Christ's sacrifice for the world so that the world no longer needs to make sacrifices for tribe or state, or even humanity. Constituted by the body and blood of Christ, we participate in God's Kingdom so that the world may know that we, the church of Jesus Christ, are the end of sacrifice.[42] If Christians leave the eucharistic table ready to kill one another, we not only eat and drink judgment on ourselves, but we rob the world of the witness necessary for the world to know there is an alternative to the sacrifices of war.

The silence that surrounds the taking of life in war is surely an indication, a judgment, that we were created to be at peace with one an-

41. Augustine *City of God* 19.23 (Bettenson, 889–90). Augustine's claims make clear that the aforementioned unity made possible by the spectacle of war (and anti-war) is really a false unity because it is founded on the injustice of community constituted by false sacrifices.

42. For those readers who may suspect that I am underwriting a satisfaction theory of atonement, I need to say that that is the last thing I should want to do. Not only do I think there are deep difficulties with satisfaction theories (and it is disputable whether Anselm is appropriately associated with such theories), but also, and even more importantly, I think such "theories" wrongly separate the person and work of Christ. I am simply not convinced that Christians need an "atonement theory." For my reflection on these matters, see Hauerwas, *Cross-Shattered Christ*. It is interesting that the view of the eucharistic sacrifice that Strenski suggests Catholics developed after the Reformation imitates in many ways Protestant versions of sacrificial accounts of the atonement. See Strenski, *Contesting Sacrifice*, 12–51.

other and God. We were not created to kill one another. We were created to be in communion with one another. There is no more basic natural law than the prohibition against killing. When we kill, even when we kill in a just war, our bodies rebel. Yet that rebellion is a marker of hope. Christ has shattered the silence that surrounds those who have killed, because we believe that the sacrifice of the Son makes possible the over-whelming of our killing that we might be restored to a life of peace. Indeed, we believe that it remains possible for those who have killed to be reconciled with those they have killed. This is no sentimental bond-ing represented by the comradeship of battle, but rather the reconcilia-tion made possible by the hard wood of the cross.

War is a mighty practice, a power that destroys those ennobled by the force of war.[43] We are fated to kill and be killed because we know no other way to live. But through the forgiveness made possible by the cross of Jesus we are no longer condemned to kill. A people have been created who refuse to resort to the sword that they and those they love might survive. They seek not to survive, but to live in the light of Christ's resurrection. The sacrifices of war are no longer necessary. We are now free to live free of the necessity of violence and killing. War and the sacrifices of war have come to an end. War has been abolished.[44]

43. This sentence echoes Simone Weil's extraordinary essay, "The Iliad or the Poem of Force." Weil says, "Violence obliterates anybody who feels its touch. It comes to seem just as external to its employer as to its victim. And from this springs the idea of a destiny before which executioner and victim stand equally innocent, before which conquered and conqueror are brothers in the same distress. The conquered brings misfortune to the conqueror, and vice versa." Weil, "The Iliad or the Poem of Force," 234.

44. John Howard Yoder observes that the gospel does not only imply an ethic of peacemaking nor does it merely lead to a nonviolent life-style. Rather, the gospel pro-claims a reconciled view of the world. Yoder calls attention to Phillips's translation of Ephesians 2:14–17, which reads: "Then he came and told both of you who were far from God (the outsiders, the Gentiles) and us who were near (the insiders, the Jews) that the war was over." Yoder comments: "That is the gospel—not that war is sin. That also is true, but alone it would not be the gospel. The gospel is that the war is over. Not merely that you ought to love your enemy. Not merely that if you have a 'born again experience,' some of your hateful feelings will go away and you maybe can love. Not merely that if you deal with your enemies lovingly enough, some of them will become friendly. All of that is true, but it is not the gospel. The gospel is that everyone being loved by God must be my beloved too, even if they consider me their enemy, even if their interests clash with mine." Yoder, *He Came Preaching Peace*, 54–55.

Dr. Alex Sider and Charlie Collier made invaluable criticisms and suggestions that have made this a better essay.

5

The Politics of Peace in Islam

Muhammed A. S. Abdel Haleem

The Politics of Peace in Islam

In Islam—as in any system, be it philosophical, religious, or political—the politics of peace normally stems from the general philosophy or worldview of that system. The religion of Islam preached by the Prophet Muhammad is not named after an individual or a nation like many other religions, but is defined as devotion and submission to God: the word *islam* means worship of God alone and acceptance of His commandments; God, who is in Islam *rabb al-'alamin*, the Caring Lord of all the worlds, including all human beings, not only the Lord of Muslims. This Caring Lord of all placed human beings on earth to multiply and thrive in it,[1] not to spread corruption or cause strife and war.[2] In the Qur'an all prophets before Muhammad emphasise this sense of *islam* as their own religion.

The Qur'an defines God's intention in creating people as different nations and tribes, as not to war against each other but "to get to know each other":

> People, We created you all from a single man and a single woman, and made you into nations and tribes so that you should get to know one another. In God's eyes, the most honoured of you are the ones most aware of Him: God is all knowing, all aware.[3]

1. Qur'an 11:161.
2. 2:105.
3. 49:13.

The phrase used in this verse, *'li ta'arafu'* (to get to know one another), is a reciprocal form of the Arabic verb. This reciprocity occurs in the Qur'an in its discussion of crucial situations, particularly in relation to the avoidance of conflict, within the family, the nation, and between different nations, and in relation to mutual cooperation. The diversity of languages and races on Earth is a sign of the great power of God, placed next to His power to create the heavens and the earth,[4] just as the diversity of religions is part of His scheme.[5]

Sources of Islamic Law

In talking about the politics of peace in Islam or indeed any aspect of the Islamic faith, it is important to begin by explaining that it was the revelation of the Qur'an in the seventh century that made Muhammad a prophet, and brought about the Islamic religion and civilization. The Qur'an is the supreme authority in Islam. It is the fundamental and paramount source of the creed, rituals, ethics, and laws of the Islamic religion. It is the book that "differentiates" between right and wrong, so that nowadays, when the Muslim world is dealing with such universal issues as globalization, the environment, combating terrorism and drugs, issues of medical ethics, and feminism, evidence to support the various arguments is sought in the Qur'an. This supreme status stems from the belief that the Qur'an is the word of God, revealed to the Prophet Muhammad via the archangel Gabriel, and intended for all times and all places.

Of secondary status to the Qur'an is the Hadith: the records of the sayings and actions of the Prophet Muhammad. Everything in Islamic law and everything claiming to be Islamic has to be based on these two sources. In addition, there are subsidiary sources, such as analogical reasoning from these two sources, the principle of public good, and customary laws that do not contradict the spirit of the Qur'an and Hadith, and finally the laws of earlier revealed religions, which constitute part of Islamic law (*Shari'a*), provided there is nothing in *Shari'a* that contradicts them.[6]

4. 30:22.

5. 11:118–9.

6. Although this last source is listed in all books of Islamic jurisprudence as one source of *Shari'a*, it does not seem to receive any attention from non-Muslim scholars.

Throughout history, the test that makes any ruling binding on Muslims is that it has to be based on authentic sources in the Qur'an and Hadith, and indisputably mean what it is claimed to mean. If a ruling does not fulfil either of these criteria, a Muslim is under no obligation to accept it and can approach a different legal scholar for an alternative ruling. There is no one mufti or religious leader as, for example, in the Catholic Church. In the classical period, Islamic jurists and schools of law gave rulings on all varieties of matters including the politics of peace and war. In modern *Shar'ia* legislation, legislators select or reject and introduce their own rulings inasmuch as they have a basis in the Qur'an and Hadith and the objectives of the *Sharia* as a whole. Some writers on Islam (from both within and outside the Muslim world) are given to repeating rulings that may have been given thirteen centuries ago in a specific historical setting and presenting them as representing the "Islamic view" on something or another, or they may take the practice of some Muslims at one time and place as representing Islam. However, the vast majority of Muslims believe that authoritative stance on anything Islamic is flexible within the limits that it must indisputably be based on the Qur'an and Hadith.

Partly because of this, the Qur'an and Hadith are very much alive and operative in Islamic society to this day. Great numbers of people learn the entire Qur'an by heart and numerous Hadiths as part of their religious education, in addition to which in the Middle East, for example, they hear them many times a day in radio and television and in the mosques. All of this shapes the consciousness of Muslims.

Commonality and Mutual Respect

One solid basis for the politics of peace is to emphasise commonality and mutual respect among people. The Qur'an affirms that all religions before and including that of Muhammad are from one origin. God addresses all prophets saying: "This community of yours is one community and I am your Lord: therefore worship Me."7

A person cannot be a Muslim if he does not believe in all the messages and prophets, a group that includes the prophets of the Bible and

7. 21:92.

Torah.[8] In the Qur'an, it is the unalterable plan of God that there will always be different religions. Muhammad is told:

> If your Lord had pleased, he would have made all people a single community, but they continue to have their differences . . . for He created them to be this way.[9]

> Had your Lord willed, all the people on earth would have believed, so can you [Prophet] compel people to believe?[10]

This is a solid basis for the politics of peace.

One element of the avoidance of violence is abstention from the abuse of other people's gods or religion, even if they are idols (6:108). Thus, the Qur'an instructs the Muslims: "'Do not debate with the People of the Book (that is Christians and Jews) except in the best way' and say 'We believe in what is revealed to us and what was revealed to you and our God and yours is One. To Him we submit'"[11] This statement emphasises the common ground between the religions. God speaks in the Qur'an, saying:

> We revealed the Torah with guidance and light, and the prophets, who had submitted to God, [and] the rabbis and the scholars all judged according to it for the Jews. . . .
> We sent Jesus, son of Mary, in their footsteps, to confirm the Torah that had been sent before him: We gave him the Gospel with guidance, light, and confirmation of the Torah already revealed. . . . So let the followers of the Gospel judge according to what God has sent down in it.[12]

Indeed, the Qur'an instructs Muhammad to say: "People of the Book, you have no true basis (for your religion) unless you uphold the Torah, the Gospel and that which has been sent down to you from your Lord,"[13] and addresses Jews, Christians and Muslims: "We have assigned a law and a path to each of you. If God had so willed He would have made

---

8. The Qur'an refers to twenty-five prophets, including Noah, Abraham, Moses and Jesus Christ. Moses is mentioned in the Qur'an 136 times, Jesus and Mary seventy times, all greatly honoured by all Muslims.

9. 11:118–19.

10. 10:99.

11. 29:46.

12. 5:44–47.

13. 5:69.

you one community but he wanted to test you through that which he had given you. So race to do good: you will all return to God and He will make clear to you the matter you differed about."[14]

This is the best model, given in the Qur'an, for relations between the people of these three religions, and a sound basis for the politics of peace.

The Prophet's Example

The Prophet's character is set up in the Qur'an as a model for believers.[15] His whole character and teaching is an example of the avoidance of violence. In various hadiths he is reported as stressing a peaceful philosophy,[16] and whenever the Prophet was asked to choose between two options, he would opt for the more lenient (as, for example, in his reported sayings, "Make things easy and not difficult. Give good news and not bad,"[17] and "May God give mercy to the person who is easy-going and magnanimous when he sells, when he buys and when he demands his rights,"[18] both situations that could develop into conflict and violence without such an attitude). He also said, "The strong man is not the one who wrestles his opponent to the ground but who controls himself in the presence of anger,"[19] and counselled his community in how to maintain good relations: "Shake hands and rancour will disappear. Give presents to each other and love each other and enmity will disappear."[20]

---

14. 5:48.

15. Qur'an 33:21. Even before his mission began, whilst still in Mecca, he averted a conflict between tribes each competing to have the honour of raising the sacred Black Stone and setting it in its place in the newly rebuilt wall of the Ka'ba. He happened to arrive at the peak of their dispute and provided a famous solution: he spread his cloak, placed the stone on it and asked each tribe to take hold of one part of the cloak and lift the stone. He then took the stone and set it in place himself.

16. "Gentleness (rifq) adorns everything and lack of gentleness spoils it." "God is gentle and loves gentleness in all situations" (Bukhari: Istitaba 4); "Whoever is deprived of gentleness is deprived of goodness" (Ibn Majah: Adab 6) and many other hadiths to this effect.

17. Bukhari: 'ilm 11 and Adab 80.

18. Bukhari: Buyu' 16.

19. Bukhari: Adab 102.

20. Malik: al-Muwatta.

In a similar spirit, the Qur'an says, "Repel what is bad with what is better, and behold, he who is your enemy may become like a close friend."[21] These concepts can, obviously, be applied both on the level of both individuals and states.

The Prophet's mission started with his call for the worship of the one God and for equality between all people, specifically the protection of the rights of women and orphan children. His way of calling people was governed by the Qur'anic instruction: "Call people to the way of your Lord with wisdom and good advice. Debate with them in the most courteous way."[22]

Yet neither the theological nor the social aspects of his teachings were accepted by the pagan society in Mecca, which was based on a sharp hierarchy of tribes, so the new religion was met with fierce opposition and persecution of those who accepted it. In the fifth year of his mission, finding that persecution had gone so far, and in keeping with his character of avoiding conflict, he suggested to his followers, especially those who had no tribal protection, to flee with their new faith and seek protection under the Christian king of Abyssinia (Ethiopia), of whom Muhammad said, "He is a just king under whom no one will be unjustly treated.' These Muslims emigrated and stayed in Abyssinia for some years, and were only able to return when the Prophet himself and the remaining Muslims in Mecca were forced, in turn, to flee their home town and migrate to Medina, 300 km to the north, for protection.

When the Muslim community in Mecca was finally forced to leave, the Prophet received an invitation from some of the residents of the nearby oasis Medina (then called Yathrib) who knew of his reputation as a peacemaker, and wanted him to act as an arbitrator between the feuding tribes of Yathrib. On his arrival in Medina, many people competed to have the honour of welcoming him into their homes, but he decided to let his camel choose a place to stop. Nobody could object to such a decision and so dissatisfaction was avoided. This entire episode demonstrates the Islamic avoidance of conflict, both on a social level (in terms of the Muslims leaving Mecca to a place where they could freely practise their religion) and on the personal level of the Prophet's actions upon his entry into Medina. This characteristic of avoiding conflict was

21. 41:34.
22. 16:125.

manifested in a number of significant events in the Prophet's life, discussed briefly below.

The Constitution of Medina

After building ties of brotherhood between the Muslim residents and the immigrant Muslims from Mecca, and in keeping with his characteristic aim of getting people to live peacefully together, the Prophet drew up what became known as the Constitution of Medina, which stands even now as a shining example of civil society and citizenship. According to the constitution, everyone (Muslims, Jews, and all other non-Muslim residents of Medina) is recognized within their own identity and their own religion and all have the same rights and duties to co-operate in the defense of their city. That this was the first political and social act the Prophet undertook in Medina underlines the fact that the politics of peace is the foundation on which an Islamic state should be built. In keeping with the Qur'an's teachings he saw that only by recognizing people's identities and securing their rights can there be a durable and just peace. [23]

The Resolution of Conflict at Hudaybia

In Medina, six years after being deprived of seeing his beloved city, Mecca, the Prophet had a dream about taking a pilgrimage there (an ancient and time-honoured tradition). Accordingly, the Muslims, virtually unarmed, went towards Mecca in their pilgrim garb, with their sacrificial animals. The Meccans sent troops to provoke them but the Muslims stood their ground. Eventually the Meccans, aware that they would be criticized throughout Arabia for preventing people from reaching the sanctuary for pilgrimage, but not wanting to be seen as having been coerced into allowing Muslims to enter Mecca, realized they had to make an agreement with Muhammad. They proposed to him that he return to Medina on this occasion, and come back with the Muslims the following year to do the pilgrimage. In addition, they stipulated that if any of

23. The Meccans and their allies in Arabia did not accept the new situation, and came to wage war on the new state and whip up sedition in it. This culminated in the fifth year in the Battle of the Confederated Tribes that sought to finish off the new Islamic state in Medina once and for all. Eventually the invading tribes went back in disarray after the Muslims dug a ditch around the city to prevent them taking it (the Qur'an refers to this in 33:9–27).

Muhammad's followers left him to join the Meccan side, they would not send him back to Muhammad, whereas if any of the Meccans left Mecca and attempted to join Muhammad, he had to send them back to Mecca. In order to avoid violence and save people's lives, the Prophet accepted these terms.[24] At first his followers were reluctant to obey him and offer their sacrifices on the spot to end their attempt to do the pilgrimage. The Prophet was concerned about and complained to his wife, who advised him make his own sacrifice (as is required when the pilgrims are prevented from reaching Mecca) and that they would follow him, and this proved to be the case. This excursion led to the Treaty of Hudaybia, which was the basis for a ten-year truce between the Muslims and the people of Mecca.

There is a whole chapter of the Qur'an devoted to this event, the title of which is *al-Fat-h*, "the victory." It considers this avoidance of war as a victory and reminds the Muslims that God sent down His *sakina* (tranquillity) on the hearts of the believers, making them calm in the face of provocation on the part of the unbelievers. This is the essence of pacifism and non-violence, in which a positive force of spiritual peace, faith, and moral resolve have the power to counteract and overcome fear, emotional turmoil, and hostility.

The Conquest of Mecca

Two years later, however, the Meccans broke their treaty and killed Muslims kneeling in prayer at the Ka'ba in the Meccan sanctuary. The Prophet and the Muslims marched to Mecca, where they encamped within sight of the city. The leader of the Meccans, Abu Sufyan, came to the camp to negotiate with the Prophet, as a result of which Abu Sufyan himself accepted Islam and the Prophet entered Mecca without any fighting, promising that no one who stayed in their houses or in the Sanctuary would be hurt. Many families who had been split by the years of conflict were reunited and, at this supreme moment of triumph, the Prophet was magnanimous to the people who had, until now,

---

24. Just after this had been decided, a Muslim came from Mecca, complaining of persecution, but the Prophet said to him "I can not go back on a promise. You have to return and bear patiently and God will help you." The Prophet's companions protested to him, "Are we not in the right; are they not in the wrong? Why then do we accept such a humiliation?" but in his desire for peace, the Prophet could see that a delay in achieving the pilgrimage was a small price to pay to avoid confrontation.

persecuted the Muslims, putting the past behind them and starting a new era of peace.

The Prophet's Politics of Peace

Politics can be defined as "the art or science of government."[25] Another neat and more comprehensive definition is the following: "Politics is the process and method of making decisions for groups. Although it is generally applied to governments, politics is also observed in all human group interactions including corporate, academic, and religious."[26]

The Prophet Muhammad's politics of peace in reaching decisions with and for his community is described in the Qur'an as follows:

> By an act of mercy from God, you [Prophet] were gentle in your dealings with them—had you been harsh, or hard-hearted, they would have dispersed and left you—so pardon them and ask forgiveness for them. Consult with them about matters, then, when you have decided on a course of action, put your trust in God: God loves those who put their trust in Him. (Qur'an 3:159)

Islam attaches great importance to people being together in a group with a leader. Praying together, led by an *imām,* increases the reward for each individual twenty-seven times. The Prophet had a distinct desire for good management and said: "If there are three of you on a journey, let them appoint one of them as *amīr* (the one in charge)," and when he sent a group of people away for any purpose he would see that they had an *amīr.* Similarly, he advised that the pace of a travelling company should be set to suit the weakest among them, and the *imām* in prayer should set his pace to suit the old and the mothers who need to attend to their babies. He said, "The *sayyid* (chief) of a group of people is their servant,"[27] and "The best of your leaders are those you love and wish well, and who love you and wish you well, and the worst of your leaders are those whom you detest and curse, and who detest and curse you."

---

25. Merriam-Webster online dictionary.   http://www.merriam-webster.com/dictionary/Politics. See also *Concise Oxford Dictionary* (London: Oxford University Press, 1976).

26. The *Wikipedia* definition: en.wikipedia.org/wiki/Politics.

27. Al-'Ajilūni, I., *Kashf al—khafā',*1 (Cairo n.d.) p.562.

Cultivating Peace

The Qur'anic Stance on Conflict-Resolution?

It is clear from the Qur'an and Hadith that the whole character of Islamic teaching tends towards the avoidance of violence and conflict in all areas of life. The Qur'an makes working to bring about reconciliation between people a highly meritorious act.[28] Thus, in married life, the relatives of a couple, and society around them, are instructed, when they fear that a couple may break up, to appoint one arbiter from his family and one from hers to try to bring about reconciliation. God promises that if they have such an attitude, He will help them towards it.[29] In Islamic society, relatives and friends feel obliged by such teachings to try to contribute in a way that might be considered unacceptable interference in other cultures. It is a common practice in Islamic society, if one hears a quarrel in a neighbour's house to go in and try to help resolve the problem, or to help break up a fight and resolve any quarrel in the street. Likewise, if two cars bump into each other in a Cairo street, people will crowd around, estimate the damage, and ask the offending party to pay on the spot. If two parties fight, the Qur'an orders the Muslim community to

> ... attempt to reconcile them; if one of them is (clearly) oppressing the other, fight the oppressors until they submit to God's command, then make a just and even-handed reconciliation between the two of them. God loves those who are even-handed.[30]

The Prophet said, "Help your brother be he just or unjust." He was asked, "How can you help an unjust person?" He replied, "Curb his injustice: that is helping him." Thus the Islamic system protects peace.

An essential teaching of the Qur'an, which is relevant here, is *al-amr bi-l-ma'ruf wa-l-nahy 'an al-munkar* (commanding what is good and forbidding what is wrong), which is an obligation on every individual and the community at large. Indeed, the Qur'an considers this, in addition to believing in God, the feature distinguishing the Islamic

28. 4:114.
29. 4:35.
30. 49:9.

community, and adhering to it qualifies the community as "the best of communities."[31]

Part of the politics of peace in any society is to educate society in the benefits of peace and the blessing in avoiding conflicts. This is what the Qur'an teaches: "You who believe, remember God's blessing on you when a certain people were about to raise their hands against you and He restrained them. Be mindful of God: let the believers put their trust in Him."[32] Sowing enmity and hatred amongst people is the work of Satan: "Satan wishes to sow enmity and hatred between you with intoxicants and gambling."[33] Division into warring factions is viewed as a punishment with which God sometimes threatens disobedient people: "He is able to divide you into discordant factions and make you taste the might of each other."[34]

War is hateful,[35] and the changing of fear into a sense of safety is one of the rewards for those who believe and do good deeds.[36] That God has given them the sanctuary of Mecca is a blessing for which its people should be thankful.[37] Paradise is the Land of Peace—*Dar al-Salam*.[38]

Protecting Peace

Sometimes, in protecting this precious and blessed peace, active restraint of those who threaten that peace becomes unavoidable. In the Qur'an, the general stance is that war is prohibited: fighting is permissible only in defense of oneself and the oppressed, and the right to self-defense is given as permission in the Qur'an as follows:[39]

> Those who have been attacked are permitted to take up arms because they have been wronged—God has the power to help them—those who have been driven unjustly from their homes only for saying "Our Lord is God." If God did not repel some

31. 3:110.
32. 5:11.
33. 5:91.
34. 6:65.
35. 2:216.
36. 24:55.
37. 29:67.
38. 5:127.
39. 22:39.

people by means of others, many monasteries, churches, synagogues and mosques, where God's name is much invoked, would have been destroyed. God is sure to help those who help His cause—God is strong and mighty—those who, when we establish them in the land, keep up the prayer, pay the prescribed alms, command what is right and forbid what is wrong: God controls the outcome of all events.

What is noticeable here is that this passage does not just give Muslims permission to defend their mosques but includes all houses of worship in which God's name is much mentioned. The defending army is reminded that, after it succeeds in repelling the attack, God helps only those who, when given victory, will maintain the prayer and pay the prescribed alms, command what is good, and forbid what is wrong. Thus, even when given permission to defend themselves in the Qur'an, Muslims are at the same time instructed on the conduct and politics of peace. At this point, it is necessary to briefly address the concept of *jihad*, a gravely misunderstood term in Islam that is derived from a reciprocal verbal form in Arabic, and means "to exert effort to counteract and repel another effort," "to struggle against something," thus falling within the framework of the permissibility of war only as self-defense. It is unfortunate that this concept is nowadays misunderstood and misinterpreted by many, both non-Muslims and Muslims.

Self defense and protection of the peace is not just a right in Islam but a religious obligation. The Qur'an urges the believers in strong terms to defend themselves, and the Prophet himself said, "Whoever is killed in defense of his life is a martyr; whoever is killed in defense of his property is a martyr." Those who take such strong urging in the Qur'an and Hadith at face value to conclude that Islam is violent take the statements completely out of this context. Let us remember that at the time of the revelation of the Qur'an there was no conscripted army, and it could only persuade people to come out to battle, individuals who would be likely to get killed and leave dependents behind. If such people were ready to lay down their lives to defend themselves or to protect their religion and their community, it is no wonder that if they were killed they would receive great rewards in the hereafter, just like anyone else who does any good deeds: they are promised Paradise. In the Qur'an, faith is always coupled with doing good deeds. It is quite clear from the Qur'an that faith alone is not a way to salvation in Islam, and that it is faith together with good deeds that warrants the promise of great rewards in Paradise.

Restrictions on War: Discrimination and Proportionality

Even in the clearest and most decisive instruction about fighting in Islam, in 2:190–5, we see the maintenance of peace is still kept in mind. The verses begin with: "Fight in the way of God those who fight against you, but do not transgress. God does not love the transgressor."[40] "Those who fight against you" means actual fighters—civilians are protected. Accordingly, the Prophet and his successors, when they sent out an army, gave clear instructions not to attack civilians—women, old people, religious people engaged in their worship—nor destroy crops or animals. Discrimination and proportionality should be strictly observed. Only combatants are to be fought, and no more harm should be caused to them than they have themselves caused (2:194). Thus, wars and weapons of destruction that destroy civilians and their towns are ruled out by the Qur'an and the word and deed of the Prophet, these being the only binding authority in Islamic law. Statements in the Qur'an that deal with this are always couched in restraining language, with much repetition of warnings, such as "do not transgress," "God does not love the transgressors," and "He loves those who are conscious of Him."[41]

In fact, the relevant verses 2:190–5 are instructions given to people who, from the beginning, should have the intention of acting "in the way of God." Linguistically we notice that the verses always restrict actions in a legalistic way, which appeals strongly to the conscience. In six verses (190–5) we find four uses of the prohibition "do not," six uses of the restrictive "until," "if" and "who attack you" (all occur twice), as well as such cautions as "in the way of God," "be conscious of God," "God does not like aggressors," "God is with those who are conscious of Him," "with those who do good deeds" and "God is Forgiving, Merciful." It should be noted that the Qur'an, in treating the theme of war as with

40. 2:190.

41. Transgression has been interpreted by Qur'anic exegetes as meaning "initiation of fighting, fighting those with whom a treaty has been concluded, surprising the enemy without first inviting them to make peace, destroying crops or killing those who should be protected" (see al-Baydawi's commentary on 2:190).

many other themes, regularly gives the reasons and justifications for any action it demands. Such strict Qur'anic instructions on war are sometimes misrepresented. For example verse 2:191 begins: "Slay them where you find them and expel them from where they expelled you; persecution *(fitna)* is worse than killing."

The phrase "slay them wherever you find them," has often been misunderstood, as for example, in a recently published article by James Busuttil on war in Islam that takes this phrase as a title.[42] In this article the word "them" is removed from its context, where it refers back to "those who attack you" in the preceding verse. The phrase "wherever you find them" is similarly misunderstood: when examined in context, it becomes clear that the Muslims were anxious that if their enemies attacked them in Mecca and they retaliated, they would be breaking the law as Mecca had traditionally been regarded as a sanctuary. Thus the Qur'an here simply assured the Muslims that the persecution that had been committed by the unbelievers against them, for believing in God, was more sinful than the Muslims killing those who attack them, whether inside or outside Mecca.

Vigilance and the Desire for Peace

In order that Muslims may be able to defend themselves they are instructed in the Qur'an to make preparation so as to to deter those who would not be otherwise deterred. In chapter 8 the Qur'an refers to a group who broke their treaty every time the Muslims made treaties with them. The Muslim community is instructed:

> Prepare whatever forces you [believers] can muster, including warhorses, to frighten off God's enemies and yours, and warn others unknown to you but known to God. Whatever you give in God's cause will be repaid to you in full, and you will not be wronged. 61 But if they incline towards peace, you [Prophet] must also incline towards it, and put your trust in God: He is the

42. Busuttil, 127. The rendering he uses runs: "Idolatry is worse than carnage." This corrupts the meaning. It is clear from the preceding words, "those who have turned you out" that *fitna* means persecution. This meaning is borne out by the identical verb (turning out / expelling) preceding the only other verse (2:217) where the expression, "*fitna*' is worse than killing" appears. Here the statement is clearly explained: "Fighting in [the prohibited month] is a grave (offence) but graver is it in the sight of God to prevent access to the path of God, to deny Him, to prevent access to the Sacred Mosque and drive out its people."

> All Hearing, the All Knowing. 62 If they intend to deceive you,
> God is enough for you: it was He who strengthened you with
> His help, God is enough for you. . . . [43]

So, the Qur'an urges Muslims to be vigilant in case they are attacked but to take any chance for peace even if there is concern this might be a deceptive manoeuvre on the part of the enemy. This desire for peace is paramount. Likewise, hostilities are normally ended with treaties, such as that of Hudaybiya in the sixth year of *Hijra* and that made by Umar (d.16/637) with the people of Jerusalem in 635 CE.[44] Faithfulness to a treaty is a most serious obligation that the Qur'an and *hadith* incessantly emphasise:

> Believers, fulfil your agreements[45]

> Keep the agreements of God when you have made them and
> do not break your oaths after you have made them with God as
> your bond . . .
>   Covenants should not be broken because one community
> feels stronger than another[46]

Breaking treaties is described by the Qur'an as placing the culprit into a state lower than that of animals (8:55). The obligation to honor treaties takes priority, even over the obligation to defend an oppressed Muslim minority if they happen to live in a country with which Muslims have a treaty (8:72).

Prisoners of War

Magnanimity in treating prisoners of war reconciles people and is conducive to peace. There is nothing in the Qur'an or *hadith* to prevent the Muslims following the present international humanitarian conventions on war or prisoners of war. There is nothing in the Qur'an to say that prisoners of war must be held captive, but as this was the practice of the time, the Qur'an deals with the subject. There are only two cases in which it mentions their treatment:

43. 8:60–3.
44. See Tabari *Tarikh,* 1, 2405.
45. 5:1.
46. 8:91–92.

O Prophet! Tell the captives you have, "If Allah knows goodness in your heart He will give you better rewards than have been taken from you and forgive you. He is forgiving, merciful." And if they intend to be treacherous to you, they have been treacherous to Allah in the past and He has put them into your hands.[47]

When you have fully overcome the enemy in the battle, then hold your captives firmly, but thereafter set them free either by an act of grace or against ransom.[48]

As we can see, grace is suggested first, before ransom. While still in captivity, they are, according to the Qur'an, to be treated in a most humane way.[49] Safety from fear on the Day of Judgement is guaranteed for those "... who feed the wretched, the orphan and the captive, though they love it themselves, saying, 'We feed you for the sake of God alone: we seek neither recompense nor thanks from you.'"[50]

The Resumption of Peaceful Relations

We have already seen in 22:41 that God promises to help those who, when He has established them in a land after war, "establish worship and pay the poor-due and enjoin what is good and forbid what is wrong."

In 2:192, the Qur'an states: "If they stop, then God is most forgiving, merciful." And, as is often repeated in sermons in mosques and elsewhere, this is how the Prophet behaved when Mecca surrendered to him, after persecuting the Muslims and fighting them for over twenty years. He said to them, "What do you think I will do with you?" They replied, "You are a generous brother and the son of our generous brother," so he said to them, "Go free."

Generosity is recommended to Muslims in more general terms in terms of their dealings with non-Muslims: "God does not forbid you from being generous and equitable to those who have neither made war on you on account of your religion nor driven you from your homes. God loves those who are equitable."[51]

47. 8:70–71.

48. 47:4.

49. 9:60; 2:177.

50. 76:8–9.

51. This verse refers to the idolaters of Mecca who did not fight the Muslims.

International Co-operation

The Qur'an urges Muslims to co-operate with others, Muslims and non-Muslims, in what is good and right. "Co-operate in what is good and pious and do not co-operate in what is sinful and aggression."[52]

It is also reported in the Hadith that the Prophet Muhammad remembered an alliance he witnessed that was contracted between the chiefs of Mecca before his call to prophethood to protect the poor and weak against oppression and said: "I have witnessed in the house of Ibn Jud'an an alliance which I would not exchange for the best of red camels, and if it were to be called for now that Islam is here, I would respond readily."[53]

One of the most important aspects of the politics of peace in Islam is the protection, regulation, and encouragement Islam gives to trade. It should be pointed out that trade at the time was with non-Muslims, Christians in the north and Hindus from the south and east. This is reflected in the Prophet's statements to the Muslim community that "Nine tenths of your livelihood comes from trade" and "An honest merchant will take his position on the Day of Judgement amongst the messengers, those who bear witness to the Truth and the righteous," of which the Qur'an says, "What excellent Companions these are."[54] Instructions given in the Qur'an and the Prophet's teaching about the politics of peace and the protection of peace are thorough and clear. Whether all Muslims can always live by the standards set in the Qur'an and the Hadith for the politics of peace is a different matter, and is an issue that confronts all religions, not only Islam.

Conclusion

In his farewell speech to the Muslim community during the Pilgrimage to Mecca, the Prophet started by saying: "People, listen to me, so that I can explain matters to you. I may not meet you again after this year. Your God is One and your father is One: you are all of Adam." Muslims repeat daily the praise of God "The Lord of all"—everything and everyone are under his caring lordship. He made them into nations and

---

52. 5:2.

53. Red camels were proverbial in Arabia for the best one can have.

54. Tirmidhi.

tribes so that they may get to know one another than turn away from one another. The diversity of their tongues and colors are a sign of His power and grace, just as the diversity of religion is part of the unalterable divine scheme.

The Qur'an sees itself as part of a long succession of revelations. It does not set out to wipe out other religions or their followers, indeed it instructs them to adhere to their revelations. Thus it accepts other religions and lives with them. Since the beginning of Islam and for the last fourteen centuries, Jews, Christians and others have lived within Muslim societies and made a valuable contribution to Islamic civilization at all levels.

The objective of all religions according to the Qur'an is to uphold justice for everybody, without regard to enmity or favor to oneself, relatives, rich, or poor.[55] This political philosophy and these teachings help to uphold peace. The Qur'an instructs people to co-operate in what is good and right, to trade profitably with each other and race to do what is good. Jews, Christians and Muslims in particular should heed God's instructions to "Vie with one another in good works."[56] In fact, the Prophet instructed people to spend their time and energy doing what is good and productive and useful for everybody.[57] So important is this throughout one's life that the Prophet said: "If the Hour of Doom comes when one of you has a seedling it his hand, and he is bending to plant it, if he can do so before being overtaken by the event, let him do so."

Even in the face of the knowledge that when the Hour comes, the existing order in this world will come to an end, it is thus incumbent upon all those of faith to be productive and try to make the world better. As the Prophet of Islam, also declared: "The best of people are those who are most useful to people."

55. Qur'an 57:25; 4:135; 5:8.

56. 5:48.

57. "Each person must perform a charity for every joint in their body, every day the sun comes up: to act justly between two people is a charity; to help a man with his mount, lifting him on to it, or hoisting up his belongings on to it is a charity; a good word is a charity; every step you take to prayer is a charity; and removing a harmful thing from the road is a charity" (Bukhari *Sahih*). Also, "If any believer plants or cultivates a crop, from which a bird, an animal or a human being eats, it will all be counted as a charity he has given." Bukhari *Sahih*.

PART THREE

Religions and the Gendering of Violence

6

Gender, Religion, and War

Mary Condren

The problem is that when the father refuses to allow the mother her power of giving birth and seeks to be the sole creator, then according to our culture he superimposes upon our ancient world of flesh and blood a universe of language and symbols that has no roots in the flesh and drills a hole through the female womb and through earth in order to mark out the boundaries of the sacred space in many patriarchal traditions. It defines a meeting place for men that is based upon an immolation. Women will in the end be allowed to enter that space, provided that they do so as non-participants.

The fertility of the earth is sacrificed in order to establish the cultural domain of the father's language (which is called, incorrectly, the mother tongue). But this is never spoken of. Just as the scar of the navel is forgotten, so, correspondingly, a hole appears in the texture of the language.

. . . If we are not to become accomplices in the murder of the mother we also need to assert that there is a genealogy of women.[1]

OVER THE PAST THIRTY YEARS, THEORISTS HAVE ANALYZED THE DISTURB-ing relationship between gender and warfare. In the early days, some espoused theories based on male aggression and female peacefulness. However, several scholars quickly exposed the simplicities in such a

---

1. Irigaray, *Sexes et Parentés*, 16.

position, and challenged this correlation as academically sloppy and politically unhelpful.

Despite this, research shows that women and children now constitute the primary victims of war, that warfare is replete with images of masculine aggression, that war propaganda is eroticized and gendered, and that post-war situations reinforce patriarchal hegemony. But the exact way in which this works needs to be interrogated.[2]

In recent times, the role of right-wing and fundamentalist religions has underpinned various wars, conventional and terrorist. Most religions protest that the faith stances of their founders and all their sacred texts favor peace and condemn war. Nevertheless, often under the auspices of that same religion, wars are conducted to impose *democracy* or *Western values*, to rescue from perdition, or to bring various brands of *salvation* on particular peoples who, incidentally, quickly become *enemies* when the imperatives of war so dictate.

Even in technologically advanced societies, when religious fundamentalism strikes, religious texts, practices, and symbols often enable previously healthy gender relations to quickly collapse with devastating consequences for women who can no longer practice their professions, or play a role in the public workforce. Strict gender delineations through veiling, homophobia, propaganda, and other means become the norm (female suicide bombers notwithstanding; they demand a separate analysis).[3]

Guilt plays a major role in these dynamics. Adherents to various forms of religious fundamentalism are often obsessed with guilt, either because of past lives or because of a savior figure who *died for them* to save them from sin. This figure often apparently inspires such adherents to extreme political actions in emulation of the founding sacrifice, or through indebtedness for its effects. Such dynamics are gendered, inter-religious, and ecumenical, but have seldom been theorized.

In the twenty-first century, and despite great potential for alternative interpretations, and prophetic calls for *mercy* not *sacrifice*, the Abrahamic faiths, controlled by hegemonic males, underpin what

2. Brownmiller, *Against Our Will*; Barstow, *War's Dirty Secret*; Elshtain, *Women and War*; Hartstock, "The Barracks Community in Western Thought: A Prologemonena to a Feminist Critique of War and Politics"; and idem, *Money, Sex and Power*; Rose, *Why War?*

3. Condren, "War, Religion, Gender, and Psyche: An Irish Perspective."

Julia Kristeva has termed the *sacrificial social contract.* This *contract* generates combative cultural systems in which both women and men are sacrificed: men to war and women to the warriors.[4]

In this article, I will focus primarily on how some unconscious gender issues, largely neglected in scholarship, are played out in myth, religion, and war strategies. My focus will be on female and maternal issues. Although interrelated, a distinct focus on relationships between fathers and men is beyond the scope of the present work.[5]

I am bracketing (if this is ever possible) ontological, theological, and dogmatic issues in order to treat religion as a complex cultural, social, and psychic phenomenon that shapes and maintains social and gendered relations. I will argue that just as Christian sacrifice has historically been a performative act of gendering legitimation, so too contemporary warfare—conventional, nuclear, and terrorist—is the major performative and legitimation rite of *Western hegemonic masculinity*, culturally elaborated through various religious mechanisms to form the dominant Western social mythologies.

Since various forms of religion serve either to *inflame* or *contain* social imperatives toward war, my position is that all representational and social practices must be better theorized for their gendered underpinnings to promote those human communities and social orders whose primary commitments are directed toward finding peaceful solutions to the intractable dilemmas of civilization. My long-term aim is, by analyzing the unconscious elements of certain social myths that often take religious form, to bring to consciousness, undermine, and render ineffective the kinds of cultural propaganda or *sacred canopies* upon which warrior imperatives feed, and to support those political and religious practices and systems of representation that do the opposite.[6]

Warfare is an extensive phenomenon and, since Westerners enjoy no monopoly on war making, we cannot assume that Western variables contributing to war are universally applicable. We should, therefore, suspend judgment as to whether the Western recourse to war making as distinct from peacemaking (in stories, myths, propaganda) is the product of socialization, economics, access to natural resources, child-rear-

---

4. Kristeva, *Powers of Horror.*

5. Miller, *Dreams of the Burning Child*; Stein, "Fundamentalism, Father and Son and Vertical Desire."

6. Berger, *The Sacred Canopy.*

ing practices, or even theologically legitimated ontologies. At the same time, we can regard many observations of the major Western cultural theorists as emanating from *educated native informants*, reporting, as it were, on their experiences from the inside.

Current Debates

Two recent major works deal with war and, separately, implicate gender and religion. Joshua Goldstein's work, *War and Gender*, argues that *gender shapes war, and war shapes gender.* However, using extensive qualitative and quantitative analyses, he cannot elaborate on how this happens.[7]

Taking a cultural-anthropological approach, Carolyn Marvin and David Ingle in *Blood Sacrifice and the Nation* argue that the totem secret of Western societies is that we periodically send members of our own society out to die on our behalf. Sacrifice now takes place on the battle-field rather than on the altar. They assume that sacrificial victims are male, and that fighting soldiers (or their metaphoric substitutes, such as the flag) are their contemporary representatives. Marvin and Ingle do not interrogate gender relations, and their definition of *sacrifice* encompasses both religious and secular forms.[8] Neither Goldstein nor Marvin and Ingle interrogate the stories or the specific religious symbols and practices that form Western cultural values.

Cultural processes are not easily or necessarily amenable to quantitative or qualitative analytic methodologies. Similarly, whereas theologians usually focus on beliefs and tradition, these foci can ignore the role of representation, miss the unconscious social substratum, and fail to analyze the role of bodily and other practices, especially that of ritual. The challenge, therefore, is to find a way of interrogating the relationship between religious and political beliefs, rituals, and symbols; gender relations; and the combative mentalities that give rise to war. A theoretical minefield, the full complexities cannot be taken up here.

Cultures do not *think* consciously or otherwise, but collective actions have a language of their own. Psychoanalysts who participated in various wars and dealt with their aftermaths have observed that whole cultures sometimes act as *bodies, collective personalities,* or *love objects*

---

7. Goldstein, *War and Gender.* 6.
8. Marvin and Ingle, *Blood Sacrifice and the Nation.*

displaying human psychiatric symptoms. Likewise, whereas individuals might have reached certain states of psychic wholeness, at times of war, under the influence of group dynamics, major regression takes place.

In addition, religious actions (especially rituals) usually take place in groups, often under the auspices of collective stories of origin that serve to mediate or foster unhealthy psychic fantasies on the parts of participants. Rituals and systems of representation often depend for their efficacy on pre-conscious or *taken-for-granted* sets of social relations and symbolic systems. Interrogating such unconscious, gendered, and ethnocentric assumptions may enable us to understand the compelling power and violent nature of some of the central stories and other dynamics used in Western societies to rationalize and ritually reinforce the gendered social contract. In this sense, the relevant data will be derived not from *informers* but *performers*.

The most important stories, cultural strategies and motifs (although contested theologically or scientifically) have endured over time, often surviving the demise of religion and reappearing in myths of state and imagined communities.[9] Furthermore, there may be other stories that are equally available and potent but have yet to enter paradigms for social theory. Quite possibly this failure derives from the unconscious and gendered assumptions social theorists, psychoanalysts in particular, have themselves brought to their methodologies. These now need to be theorized.

Cultural Totems

Like Marvin and Ingle, Sigmund Freud and some early anthropologists, as well as some contemporary theorists such as René Girard, have argued that underlying the social contract is a totem figure whose death forms the system of representation (religious or secular) of a society. Societies differ only on the identity of the victim. Other anthropologists argue that the totem is by no means universal and, as in animistic societies, divinity is everywhere.[10] But, for the moment, let us assume that Freud et al. are *describing* Western social forms.

Freud argued in *Totem and Taboo* (1918) and re-iterated in *Moses and Monotheism* (1939) that societies are held together by post-sacri-

9. Anderson, *Imagined Communities.*
10. Sanday, *Female Power and Male Dominance.*

ficial taboos. In Freud's scheme, the specific taboos were instantiated following the murder of the primal father by the sons in order to gain sexual access to the mother. Freud's social analysis built on his Oedipal theories—*children want to sleep with their mothers and kill their fathers because they are the obstacle.* Freud placed the father at the center of psychic development. Having killed the father, the mythical band of brothers established the totem (the father) to remind them of *what not to do* in the future. These prohibitions formed the basis of the social contract and were reflected in classical and other myths. Freud's *sacrificial social contract* (as well as some current theories on the relationship between war and sacrifice) placed fathers and sons at center stage, a point to which we will return.

Underlying Freud's work and made explicit in the work of Girard is the notion that envy and its lethal consequences required extensive social prohibitions to keep it in check.[11] Relying on selective myths, Freud assumed that the totem figure was the father. Relying on literature, Girard considered that Freud was mistaken; that he inappropriately projected paternal death wishes onto infants; that the identity of the original victim was irrelevant; and that mimetic conflict was primary and resolved only at the expense of a victim. According to Girard, such victimage mechanisms resulted in sacrificial practices and sacrificial substitutions.

Neither Freud nor Girard was gender sensitive and here is not the place to reiterate the various gendered critiques of their work. However, the work of one of Freud's early successors, Melanie Klein, brings the relationship between gender and envy firmly into the equation.

Klein and Eumenides

When Klein made her (one and only attempt) to deal with myth, she turned to Aeschylus' *Eumenides* rather than *Oedipus.*[12] *Eumenides* forms part of the trilogy, *The Oresteia,* and here, as we will see, a very different sacrifice takes place.

Athens was riven by constant wars between competing social groupings as they played out seemingly interminable cycles of revenge under the age-old injunction: *An eye for an eye, a tooth for a tooth.* These

11. Girard, *Violence and the Sacred;* and idem *The Scapegoat.*
12. Klein, "Some Reflections on the *Oresteia.*"

civil wars were also hindering Greek imperial ambitions, and loyalty to natural bloodlines was being challenged by the competing claims of the state. Identity politics had lethal consequences, which the great philosophers and playwrights sought to tease out. Aeschylus' Oresteian trilogy was one such attempt.

Orestes was being tried for the murder of his mother, Clytemnestra. The old maternal goddesses of the kin, the Furies, sought his execution on the grounds of the most heinous ancient crime—matricide.[13] But the death of Orestes would have been the end of the Atreus line, making his survival important for maintaining the paternal ruling genealogy. The jury, the Greek Chorus, was tied. Significantly, a new, young, brash, and brazen goddess, Athena, arrives on the scene to adjudicate between the competing claims of blood and state.

Her qualifications?

> *No mother gave me birth, I came full blooded from the head of Zeus.*[14]

She decides in favor of Orestes, and she and her brother, Apollo, throw in, to boot, some revisionist biological lessons about mothers being merely *nurturers for the male seed.*[15]

Her social policy?

> *Let our wars*
> *Rage on abroad, with all their force, to satisfy*
> *Our powerful lust for fame. But as for the bird*
> *that fights at home—my curse on civil war*[16]

In other words, the problem of violence was not so much solved as merely projected outwards away from civil society. But just as important perhaps (and maybe even as a consequence), Athena reverses the natural order and effectively embodies some gendered sacrificial assumptions. Athena, the motherless daughter (a.k.a. *Virgin*), now rules above the earth.

---

13. The death of Orestes would have been the end of the Atreus line, making his survival even more important for maintaining the paternalistic system of determining who rules.

14. Aeschylus, *Oresteia: Eumenides*, line 751.

15. Ibid., lines 665–70, 750.

16. Ibid., 867–875.

At the end of the *Eumenides,* the old maternal goddesses of the kin, the Furies, whose duty it was to avenge kin murders, are led off stage. Their name changes to the "The Kindly Ones," but, nevertheless, they foment under the earth becoming the unconscious of the Western social order. Athena acknowledges the need to propitiate and pay homage to them, but those injunctions were quickly forgotten in logocentric economies.

These two narratives, *Oedipus* and *Eumenides* provide two seemingly alternative psychoanalytic accounts of the social order. In the first, according to Freud, taboos against the murder of the father found the social contract. In the second, (although not strictly a Kleinian interpretation—Klein left this essay unfinished), the institutions of the state supersede those of blood and kinship; the claims of paternity supersede those of maternity; and the claims of the father's head (Zeus) supersede those of the mother's womb. In *The Oresteia*, significant progress is made in superseding women altogether. Not just a stage play (as we know them today), the last part of the trilogy was regularly staged to reiterate in ritual form the terms of the Greek founding social contract.[17]

Myths and rituals exist in dialectical relationship to their environments. In *Totem and Taboo* and *Moses and Monotheism*, Freud focuses almost entirely on relationships between males and correlates the Oedipus myth with Jewish tribal society. The original impetus (the return to the Mother) is dropped from the analysis. *The Oresteia* relates to the foundation of the early Greek city-states: gender relationships come to the fore. However, when we move into the question of empire, quite a different mythological account of the social order begins to emerge.

Christianity

Theologians and philosophers traditionally interrogate Christianity for its *truth claims.* Few theorists interrogate the Christian story or system of representation for its unconscious origins, or political effects; even fewer theorists interrogate the gendered substratum.[18] The academic risks are enormous, especially for a theologian. However, at this time in history, when the future of the earth is in jeopardy from conventional

17. Ibid.

18. Jones, *Psycho-Myth, Psycho-History*; Kristeva, *Powers of Horror*; Irigaray, *Sexes et Parentés*.

and terrorist forms of warfare, the failure to interrogate the stories that derive from and shape Western consciousness (and arguably similar stories to be found in some of the other major religions) could be unconscionable.[19]

There is little need to recount the Christian story here. Suffice to say that the dominant (if reductionist) interpretation involves the sacrifice of the Son to the honor of God the Father, in order to atone for *original sin*. In traditional theology, this original sin is variously defined, but primarily, in relation to the *fall* that took place in the biblical Garden of Eden. Many cultures have *fall* stories that variously implicate animals, gods, or goddesses as having caused the *fall* from immortality to mortality. In the biblical version (more formative for Christianity than for Judaism), human mortality and death follow the sin of Eve, and derivatively, through disordered sensual passion at the time of procreation, to everyone else (Augustine).

Unlike the *Oedipus* story, where the sons kill the father to gain access to the mother, here (summarized in the classical interpretation of St. Anselm in the twelfth century) because of the *fall*, the honor of the Father, so badly insulted by *original sin*, could not be appeased by anything less than the sacrifice of his Son.[20] The death of the Son for the honor of the Father sets in train an order of representation, followed by misogynist propaganda, that questions the goodness of the natural order, and radically undermines the position of women.

Freud's early band of brothers wanted access to the mother, and killed the father. Klein's Orestes kills his mother, ostensibly in a crime of retribution. Orestes establishes the supremacy of social over biological ties, but Athena remained the (childless) Goddess of wisdom. Christianity went much further. Only the redeeming sacrifice of God's only Son (rather than Freud's father, or Klein's mother figures) comes clearly to the fore. Furthermore, the child is effectively killed by or for the parents, rather than the other way around.

Already (in relation to women) Freud's myth is beginning to look tame. God the Father bypassed women's wombs altogether, allowing Christianity to claim universal applicability. In the Christian story, women and mothers (except as virgins) are now radically super-

19. Ricoeur, *Freud and Philosophy* and "The Critique of Religion."
20. Anselm, "Cur Deus Homo."

seded. Furthermore, gender issues and explicitly sexual themes remain unconscious.

However, bypassing women's wombs only presaged a much greater development: patriarchal control of the origins of life. In traditional theology we are told that Jesus's death brought *new* life into the world, accomplishing the work of salvation. An early Christian seemingly innocuous epithet—*the blood of the martyrs is the seed of the church*— would have widespread implications in Western Christian history, and widespread gendered implications. The only *true life* comes through sacrificial death, a theme that would resonate throughout the succeeding twenty centuries. Athena had only emerged from the head of Zeus, but now sacrificial death superseded the natural birthing of women. This enormous mythical reversal has been left largely unchallenged.

Throughout Christian history, the question of sacrifice comes to center stage. The various Crusades and World Wars, as well as contemporary wars fought under the aegis of fundamentalist Christianity, have consistently drawn on such sacrificial discourses to legitimate their enterprises. After the break-up of the Roman Empire, sacrifice continued to be a major issue, and lay at the heart of Reformation disputes in Europe. The lines between ecclesiastical and military authority had become increasingly obscured. Questions of authority and legitimation of authority lay at the heart of the struggle. Who can sacrifice? Who authorizes them to do so? Has the sacrifice of Jesus taken place forever? Does it need to be re-iterated?

The Reformations did not dispute Christianity's sacrificial origins: they merely questioned whether the sacrifice was *once and for all* or needed to be re-iterated (as in Catholicism). Wresting control of sacrifice from Rome, therefore, was as much a political as a theological achievement. In European state mythologies, new life is brought into the world through sacrificial death and contemporary soldiers for Christ are simply in continuity with the original sacrifice. Even where Christianity was no longer the dominant cultural narrative, in contemporary warrior discourses (religious or secular), only the repeated sacrifices of men in violent death serves to regenerate the new social order. In addition, the Reformations further effected the relegation of women: statues were removed from churches; women were removed from convents (a sanctuary for many from oppressive patriarchal relations) and returned to the home.

Interpreting Jesus's death as a sacrifice (rather than as murder), accomplished several things. First, it effected healing from the *original sin* of the *first parents*. Second, it established God the Father as the only true social parent for lineage and political purposes. Third, it placed sacrifice at center stage as the mechanism that overcame our ignominious origins, superseded the lowly wombs of women, and re-opened the possibilities of immortality, or eternal life. Through the fatherhood of God, and through the sacrificial rites that follow on, men give birth (in sacrifice and war) not to mere children, but to lineages, nations, and ultimately, to immortality. Indeed, in many mythologies, one's fittingness to rule is established by the willingness to sacrifice the first-born son. Furthermore, the Christian version of that sacrifice (like *The Oresteia*) is regularly re-iterated through Western history in the various ritual celebrations that constitute the Christian liturgies.

These three stories, *Oedipus*, *The Oresteia*, and Christian, describe in stark terms the gradual appropriation of generative power from women to men, and the establishment of patriarchal lineages. Furthermore, they were highly successful in that the Western patriarchal social order has been considered by philosophers such as Hegel to be inevitable, normative, and even superior to all others.[21]

Only when the underlying assumptions and their warrior equivalents threaten the future of civilization as we know it are serious doubts raised, not only about the form such myths take in the religious realm, but more dangerously, as they appear in the mythologies of the state.[22] As Roger Money-Kyrle formulated the issue:

> the state they painted had all the qualities of a most jealous God. It demanded an absolute obedience, the total surrender of the individual will, and promised the rediscovery of perfect freedom by means of an identification with itself. The unconscious response to this leviathan is hate and fear, not love. Yet just because, as a projection of the most strict and sadistic type of super-ego, it was so feared and hated unconsciously, it had to be idealized into something deserving the most passionate, and masochistic love. And the work of transvaluation of spontane-

21. Avineri, *Hegel's Theory of the Modern State.*
22. Cassirer, *The Myth of the State.*

ous values was done with such consummate skill that those who did it deceived not only themselves but half the world as well.[23]

Who is the Totem?

The early anthropologists, then Freud, and now Marvin and Ingle assume that the sacrificial victim, and later totem, is male. By totem, they mean the representation (or its displacements) that reminds its culture of the terms of the social contract. That is to say, (in Freud's terms), *don't kill your father to gain access to the mother*. In Freud's version, the initial impetus (the brother's attempts to gain access—assumed sexual—to the mother) is lost.

At the outset, we mentioned the existence of a savior figure on whose behalf contemporary warrior fundamentalists continue to fight. Western history correlates this figure with Jesus Christ. In other words, in anthropological terms, at a conscious level, Christ becomes the totem figure governing Western history. But are things so simple?

In the *Eumenides,* the Christian story, and in contemporary warfare, women's generative functions have been superseded; women's genealogies (understood both as lineage and power) have been collapsed and serve the state. Therefore, even if the ostensible victim is male, behind the conscious sacrificial discourses another sacrifice has already taken place: that of the maternal body. As Luce Irigaray argues:

> When Freud, notably in *Totem and Taboo,* describes and theorizes about the murder of the father as the founding act for the primal horde, he is forgetting an even more ancient murder, that of the woman-mother, which was necessary to the foundation of a specific order in the city.[24]

In later centuries, ecclesiastical authorities would interrogate the issue of Mary's virginity in tones decidedly anti-sexual. *Alone of all her sex*, Mary had *conceived without* sin and given birth without losing her virginity.[25] However, originally the insistence on Mary's virginity was a political rather than a moral statement. Judaism was a matrilineal religion and, had Jesus been born (normally, as it were) of a Jewish

---

23. Money-Kyrle, *Psychoanalysis and Politics*, 160.

24. Irigaray, *Sexes et Parentés*, 11.

25. Warner, *Alone of All Her Sex.*

woman, his significance would have been confined to Judaism. Since Jesus was born of a virgin, God the Father became Jesus's social (rather than biological) parent, bypassing ethnic or tribal lineages and enabling the Christian religion to become universal, under God the Father's auspices.

The early Christian baptismal formula, *In Christ there is neither Jew nor Greek, slave nor free, male nor female,* offered a radical solution to the social and political inequalities then pertaining throughout the Roman Empire. Dispossessed or disenfranchised slaves, women, and countless others flocked to the early church, which offered them a new identity under the auspices of God the Father. However, as Christianity became the dominant religion at the fall of Rome, many forms of oppression were re-instated. No longer limited by tribal or ethnic boundaries, a new universal ambition could now be set in train, and sacrificial discourse played a major part.

Historically, many other interpretations of the Christian story have been offered and made possible. However, in Western history, sacrificial Christianity has been the dominant theology legitimizing both religious and political regimes and permeating sexual politics. The mythical solution of virginity, while temporarily surmounting the competing claims of tribes, ethnicities, and city-states to establish universal fatherhood, developed a life of its own to become (until the age of contraception) an anti-sexual vehicle controlling female sexuality in the interest of property rights and primogeniture.[26]

In other words, the primary totem underlying the sacrificial social order is female and this is reflected in the major rituals of state and church. In ancient Greece, women still had a role to play in the myths and rituals of state, albeit mostly as mourners.[27] But in those societies where sacrificial rites *perform* lineage establishment and maintenance (Apostolic succession), women are not allowed to sacrifice, their genealogies are superseded, and they are excluded from the productive effects of sacrifice as sacrificial beneficiaries.[28]

In Christian ecclesiology, we are usually told the story this way: *Women can't be priests because women menstruate, have children.* Women

---

26. Condren, *The Serpent and the Goddess.*
27. Huston, "Tales of War and Tears of Women."
28. Jay, *Throughout Your Generations Forever.*

are unfit to sacrifice because women are unclean. But if we use performative rather than sacrificial logic, we might formulate the problem differently and say something like this: *Sacrificial rites create the conditions under which menstruation, or childbirth becomes unclean, or where hegemonic masculinity is instantiated.*

In a recent version of this theme (the Vatican's 1976 "Declaration on the Question of Admission of Women to the Ministerial Priesthood"), we were told that women can't be priests because there would not be this *natural resemblance* between *Christ and his Minister.*

> The Christian priesthood is therefore of a sacramental nature: the priest is a sign, the supernatural effectiveness of which comes from the ordination received, but a sign that must be perceptible (18) and which the faithful must be able to recognize with ease. The whole sacramental economy is in fact based upon natural signs, on symbols imprinted upon the human psychology: "Sacramental signs," says Saint Thomas, "represent what they signify by natural resemblance."(19) The same natural resemblance is required for persons as for things: when Christ's role in the Eucharist is to be expressed sacramentally, there would not be this "natural resemblance" which must exist between Christ and his minister if the role of Christ were not taken by a man: in such a case it would be difficult to see in the minister the image of Christ. For Christ himself was and remains a man.[29]

Supported by Thomas Aquinas, this is probably the clearest formulation in Western history as to how the Christian Eucharist, understood as sacrifice, became, not a banquet table instantiating relations of justice (as in the early church), but a performative rite of hegemonic masculinity, and the dominant political legitimating narrative.

Furthermore, whereas social theory statements from the Vatican are rarely accorded much credence, social scientists themselves provided more concrete enforcement of the underlying dynamics when they took the supremacists stories of the successful sacrifiers (especially *Oedipus* and Christian), and applied them uncritically to social and psychic development.

Generations of Western social philosophers—Hegel, Marx, Engels, Freud, and Durkheim—assume that patriarchal social organization (and

29. Vatican Document "Declaration on the Question of Admission of Women to the Ministerial Priesthood."

patriarchal religion) is normative, universal, inevitable, and achieved by various types of sacrifice: psychic, linguistic, or economic. They differ only on the source of that inevitability: inferior anatomy, private property, and psychic undifferentiation. They legitimized their narratives, rather than interrogating them for signs of struggle. In other words, these theorists *took for granted what needed to be explained,* further contributing to the effective sacrifice of women in the social order.

Adding insult to injury, theorists such as Marx then assume that the patriarchally constructed sacred (a form of alienation in itself) is mystifying, and needs to be superseded by advanced forms of rationalism. Ironically, he missed the role that such instrumental rationality played in the development of capitalism.

But why did such stories enjoy such commissive force? To what psychic realities did they speak? What political realities did they legitimate? These are questions that can only be touched on here. Two questions, however, are crucial. If Freud assumed that the original brothers merely wanted sexual access to the mother, why did so many other features of the dominant Western narrative (the Garden of Paradise) not receive much analytic or political attention, apart from that of theologians anxious to reinforce gendered inequalities and propaganda within the dominant Western tradition? Why spend so much time disputing Freud's Oedipus interpretation while ignoring the opposite reality: fathers sending sons out to die for the sake of their honor? To help understand this we will return to Melanie Klein.

Melanie Klein: Gender and War

> The most terrifying qualities of the object idealized tended to be split off from it and to appear elsewhere. The God of medieval Christianity was a mixed object, a compound of the most selfless love and the most cruel sadism that could be conceived. But while the terror he inspired increased the need to worship him, his sadism which was the source of the terror, tended to be split off and attributed to another figure—the Devil.[30]

Whereas Freud focused on the trauma behind the Oedipus complex, Klein argued that psychic trauma takes place earlier, primarily in relation to our first object. Even before we emerge from the womb, we

30. Money Kyrle, *Psychoanalysis and Politics,* 161.

begin to be formed by the security and holding we experience in what is literally (if unconsciously) a garden of paradise. Rudely cast out at birth into independence (a precursor of death), we long to return to the security of womb holding. However, we usually displace that longing onto our mother's breast (or breast substitute). Mediating our relationship to the breast, according to Klein, constitutes our first major psychic struggle and issues in two positions, both related to the mother as the source of feeding (and implicitly, vital goodness).

Infants attempt to control the mother in what Klein calls "omnipotent moves." Failing this, we split the real mother into two: the *good mother* and the *bad mother.* The *good mother* is she who gives plenitude (breast or bottle) and restores us to original unity. The *bad mother* is she who withholds and deprives us of the garden-of-paradise security that we experienced in the womb. She exposes us to independence, an ambivalent move if ever there was one.

As infants, we cannot hold onto the strength of the emotions we feel and we project the *Inner Terrifier* out of ourselves, usually into the mother. Known as *projective identification,* in this process we now fear that the terror we projected outwards will return. The infant expects *an eye for an eye, a tooth for a tooth,* and only maternal *containment* prevents psychic fragmentation.

Klein identified two of the major psychic positions we take up in the developmental process. The first derives from the splitting process and is called the *paranoid/schizoid position.* When Athena said, "let our wars rage on abroad to satisfy our powerful lust for fame," she encapsulated the problem beautifully. Athena was ensuring the psychic health of the Athenians—at the expense of its enemies.

Klein called the second position, the *depressive position,* achieved only after a period of *mourning for the lost object* (the womb or breast displacement). Here we begin to grow up, reconcile ourselves to primal object loss and to the fact that the *bad mother* who withholds the breast is also the *good mother* who sustains us. In other words, we embrace the complexity (and tragedy) of the human condition, and the knowledge that we can never return to her *garden of paradise* (at least on this side of the grave). We attain a certain psychic stability, but never for long. *Omnipotent fantasies* and hopes remain with us.

Religion, Envy, and the Death Drives

The Garden of Paradise story has other dimensions. The first concerns our rude ejection into independence—a traumatic event with ongoing consequences, called *death drives*. In Freud's *Beyond the Pleasure Principle*, he argued that infants engage in repetitive compulsive behaviors, often in the form of games, risking dissolution (primarily separation from the mother) for the sake of mastery.[31] Freud called these alternations *death drives* in that they oscillate between *Eros* and *Thanatos*. Psychoanalysts and psychologists differ between themselves as to whether these oscillations are biological, instinctual, conscious, or energetic.[32] These debates need not concern us here.

The second dimension concerns the question of envy. In the Garden of Paradise story we know that a massive act of reversal took place: Eve was created from Adam's rib. Here we see what theorist Teresa Brennan calls *a foundational fantasy* in which envy of the female body plays a crucial role.[33]

According to Klein, whereas jealousy is triangular, envy occurs when we fantasize that someone else has or has achieved something that we can secure only through their annihilation.[34] Primary envy (in the technical rather than moral sense) is not initially directed toward the father's penis, but toward the mother's breast—the source of all goodness, nourishment, life, primal holding, and the origins of every human life. In other words, our attempts at mastery take place primarily in relation to the body of a woman and her life-giving powers.

In Freud's *Totem and Taboo,* and *Oedipus*, envy plays a major role but then appears to be magically resolved through totemic institutions and fraternally based social structures. In Klein's version, however, the phenomenon of envy remains a significant feature. For Klein, underlying the death drives are painful quests for certainty, psychic holding, and identity—a longing to return to the safety of the womb/origins. Furthermore, the original source (the mother's body) is primary. Klein,

31. Freud, *Beyond the Pleasure Principle.*

32. More recently, however, some psychoanalytic theorists have identified the roots of aggression as relating not so much to drive energy, but to the inability to overcome *insurmountable obstacle(s)*, especially in relation to what they describe as *omnipotent figures*. Rizzuto et al., *The Dynamics of Human Aggression*, 31–36.

33. Brennan, *Exhausting Modernity*, 189.

34. Klein, "Envy and Gratitude."

therefore, argued that the struggle occurs, not between life and death, *Eros* and *Thanatos* as in Freud, but between love and hate, envy and gratitude.

Both women and men experience envy toward the mother's body, but the possibilities of resolution for women are different from those of men, not only for biological reasons, but also because of relational strategies. Religion and mythology and, in particular, the patriarchal monopolization of divinity, now play a crucial role. Men may not give birth biologically, but in *acts of omnipotence*, their sacrifices on the altar and the battlefield supersede women's birthing, thereby triumphing over envy by removing its primary cause, a strategy that occurs in war as much as in religion.

Many social theorists ignore the foundational nature of religious imagery and symbolism as the social contract, but have little difficulty using secular language (parasitic on the religious) as sacrifice moves from the altar to the battlefield. In wartime, warriors strive to give birth to what become new *Motherlands*, or at the very least, to renew or regenerate the existing one, preferably fertilized by the blood spilled in war. Political forces are unleashed. The regression that takes place in the public rites of sacrifice/war effectively wrests fertility from the maternal realm, appropriates it to legitimize male religious and political authority, and performs massive acts of reversal. When such dynamic forces are underpinned by religion, and when such forces are secured by a political world dominated by hegemonic male morphologies, the consequences are lethal.

In a unique move toward what Klein calls "omnipotence," warriors even give birth to their own mothers. As one theorist wrote of the conflict in Argentina:

> What made the Patria acceptable, perhaps even necessary, within this discourse was that she was not credited with giving birth to her children—on the contrary, the glorious military men gave birth to her. The Patria was empowered by her heroic sons[35]

In this sense, the rhetoric of birth and death that permeates warfare (and sacrifice) represents what could be considered a socially pathological attempt to gain omnipotence or control over one's ignominious origins, often represented as female.

35. Taylor, "Spectacular Bodies," 21.

Psychic Mourning

For both Freud and Klein, mourning was a normal feature of the human condition. In different ways they argued that we often continue to *mourn* the loss of psychic unity and try desperately to regain it. In various mythologies, the theme of returning to the mother recurs over and over again. Even the gates at the Garden of Paradise were closed against that possibility.

Religious images and discourses offer both beneficent and maleficent forms of *mourning*. For instance, every night in monasteries throughout the world, the last hymn, *Salve Regina,* is sung with such themes as *the banished children of Eve, and after this our exile.*[36] However, religion and war are closely connected in that religion (and political ideologies) also provide ready made sets of symbols and discourses to fuel the *paranoid elaboration of mourning.*[37] As Fornari argues:

> Anti-Semitism offers Christians a way to avoid mourning and the sense of guilt for the death—loss of the love object by projecting into the Jews the cause of the death and betrayal of Christ.[38]

In Freud's early work on war, focusing on what he called the *severity of the Superego,* he understood war to be a lifting of instinctual repressions. Individuals had to take a *holiday* from civilization, or their superegos. However, more recent psychoanalytic work, building on Freud's later reflection, considered war to be a form of the *paranoid elaboration of mourning.*[39]

By the *paranoid elaboration of mourning,* Freud meant that our ambivalent attitude to death (grief for the dead, but also fear of their continued existence in the form of ghosts) derives from an inner ambivalence that remains with us, even toward our most loved ones. Under normal circumstances, we cope with this ambivalence by *externalizing* our fears outwards onto others in the human, mythological, or religious world. Franco Fornari synthesizes Freud and Klein's approach to war:

36. Condren, 1997.
37. Fornari, *The Psychoanalysis of War,* xxii.
38. Ibid., xxv.
39. Ibid., xiv.

The exportation of the problems of the inner world into the outer world, which is an essential part of the mechanisms of paranoid schizoid elaboration of mourning, may be considered the presupposition which renders it easy for certain political operators to present war as a dramatic but definitely desirable event because it allows the externalization of both the fear of being killed by what we love and the fear of killing what we love.[40]

Fornari continues, stating that:

If it were not for war, society would be apt to leave men defenseless before the emergence of the Terrifier as a purely internal foe.[41]

For Freud, that *Inner Terrifier* was primarily the primeval father. But Klein's identification of the *Inner Terrifier* with the pre-Oedipal mother brings us closer to the role played by religion and gender fantasies in war.

Behind such warring strategies, therefore, often lie painful quests to regain psychic unity or to overcome fragmentation. Regaining such unity at a personal level can happen, sometimes through genuine love. However, given certain group dynamics, the same attempts can often issue in violent acts of desperation. Wars are made more desperate since they take place not because we hate the enemy, but because we wish to protect the collective love object, a fantasy that also disguises and absolves whatever atrocities we commit in its name.

Klein and the Collective Love Object

The war then provides a set of surrogate progenitors, a maternal womb, and a patriarch operating through industrial processes that *hammer, cast and temper* an entire generation.[42]

Religion and war engage in other forms of lethal marriage. Klein did not attempt any full-blown social psychology, but systemic group analysts (building on Klein) argue that groups often act collectively much like *bodies*. Collective group dynamics simulate a form of womb holding, and relatively healthy individuals, once put in groups, often radically *regress*. Warfare and sacrifice foster group dynamics of social

40. Ibid., xxvi.

41. Ibid., xvi.

42. Leed, *No Man's Land*, 153.

wombs where regression often takes place to infantile states. The group becomes the *symbolic mother/womb* whose security (through torturous psychic processes) is threatened. All the painful dynamics that usually characterize individuation and identity are played out, together with the potential for splitting, projection, and introjection.[43]

As stated above, the play *Eumenides* was regularly staged in ancient Greece to reiterate the terms of the founding social contract. In Western Christianity, the mass fulfilled a similar function. However, in today's world, the theatre of representation has shifted and the battlefield, its multiple paraphernalia and rituals, forms the sacred theatre. Military generals are the priests, and Christian officiaries mere handmaids, in the birthing pangs of whole nations.

Psychic struggles take on lethal and often infantile dimensions. *Omnipotent fantasies* can run riot, and the early pre-Oedipal struggles now take place on the world stage, complete with lethal weapons. Group thinking, collective love objects, *Motherlands*—all these serve to legitimate and make it possible for participants to abdicate responsibility for their actions and follow the commands of military leaders, usually backed up by religious authorities.

At the heart of any war, therefore, is a prized and often unattainable object for which there are multiple displacements or concrete substitutes: the flag, land, perfect genealogy, or ethnicity. Items such as the national flag symbolically represents the nation; they are the ostensible totem, and warfare represent a time when the totem is apparently, *up for grabs.* However, if, as has been argued here, underlying this totem is another totem—the omnipotent mother of fantasy—then we can also begin to understand the gendered themes and atrocities that take place in war. In other words, finally we can begin to bring Goldstein, and Marvin and Ingle's work together in relation to sacrifice.

Ordinary logic would suggest that soldiers are motivated by hatred for the enemy. But in Klein's framework, it is not *hate*, but *love* of one's *internal objects* that motivates soldiers to go to war. The *good mother* becomes the collective love object and takes the form of the *Motherland* (who now needs to be defended). In other words, and contrary to popular logic, warriors are driven, not by hate, but by love.[44]

43. Money-Kyrle, *Psychoanalysis and Politics*; Bion, *Experiences in Groups and Other Papers*; Fornari, *The Psychoanalysis of War*.

44. Fornari, *The Psychoanalysis of War*.

The preservation of this collective love object—the nation, country, state, church—impels soldiers to commit atrocities of which they might not otherwise be capable. The communal regression fostered at wartime often serves as a powerful aphrodisiac impelling soldiers to *die for their country,* as though to preserve a collective ideal that offers such libidinal satisfaction.[45]

Foremost in any war is the question of *just cause.* In the midst of warfare (or even before), politicians and propagandists struggle desperately to espouse the legitimacy of their *cause.* Perceived threats, shame, humiliation, grievances (however justified), the paranoid/schizoid dynamics, and *projective identification* both *cause* and *effect* warrior dynamics to roll into operation. For these reasons, Fornari writes that:

> In this manner we arrive at the incredible paradox that the most important security function is not to defend ourselves from an external enemy, but to "find a real enemy."[46]

Religious theorists and practitioners usually confine themselves to analyzing the conditions under which *just wars* might take place. But in this context such discussions are already too late. As Nietzsche wrote:

> Ye say it is the good cause that halloweth every war? I say unto you: it is the good war that halloweth every cause.[47]

Religion, therefore, can play a lethal role, not strictly because of religious beliefs, but because religious groups enable the suspension of previous healthy psychic states. In addition, and more recently, theorists such as Brennan have argued that group formation allows the *transmission of affects,* the intensity of which often supersedes rational consciousness. According to Brennan (re-inforcing Nietzsche), affects often find thoughts that suit them, rather than the other way around.[48]

Female Bodies and War

The maternal imagery of war often persuades participants that they are fighting *for* beleaguered women, but this is far from being the case.

---

45. Ibid.
46. Ibid., xvii.
47. Nietzsche, *Thus spoke Zarathustra*, 74.
48. Brennan, *The Transmission of Affect*, 7.

During warfare, women's bodies become the symbolic fields or totems over which identity—positive and negative—is formed. The Kleinian mother is profoundly ambivalent, and the Kleinian child profoundly schizophrenic. In wartime such splitting takes on pathological proportions and the *paranoid/schizoid* position starts to run riot. We develop various forms of splitting: the *goodies* and the *baddies*; the *saved* and the *unsaved;* the *elect* and the *non-elected.* But in terms of gender, the primary splitting takes place between *good mothers* and *bad mothers.* The *good mother* is to be idealized and preserved; the *bad mother* is to be desecrated and defiled, in whatever ways prove possible. One way or the other, the discourses of motherhood play an enormous part in making wars ever more lethal.

In the collective libido, the *good mother* becomes the *Motherland,* who plays a powerful role, signifying a primal libidinal unity, now threatened or lost. Recovering this primal unity develops logical structures that supersede any immediate self-interest. She can take the form of Brittania, Mother Ireland, or some other version of the *Motherland.* In Nazi Germany mythologies centered on romantic myths of *Fatherland/ Motherland.* Psycho-historian David Beisel argues that really the *Motherland* was at issue, but this was disguised for fear of the accusation of incest.[49]

However, *Motherland* rhetoric should not deceive us into thinking that real women are revered. As A. E. Housman put it so poetically:

> For the calling bugle hollows,
> High the screaming fife replies,
> Gay the files of scarlet follow:
> Woman bore me, I will rise.[50]

Bad Mothers

In contrast to this *good mother,* the *Other's Women* become the *bad mother,* a legitimate target of aggression. Rape and other sexual atrocities symbolically signify military triumph (penetration) over the *Other's Mother,* or his *Women.*

In the dynamics of hegemonic masculinity, soldiers who desert are cowardly or otherwise considered unfit to fight, and captured enemies

49. Beisel, "The Group Fantasy of German Nationalism, 1800–1815."

50. Housman, *A Shropshire Lad,* 47.

become *mere women* and are insulted with feminized epithets. As was the case with female martyrs in the early Christian church, women who join in the battle, *become like men*. In patriarchal culture, this is the highest accolade that can be paid to a woman.

Further implications could be drawn regarding rape and other forms of female desecration, the feminization of enemies, the brutality of soldiers' male initiation rites, the rites of purity in fundamentalism, and the gendered pornographic underpinning characteristic of Western warfare.

Guilt, Salvation, Redemption

> With *Melanie Klein*, the fantasy connected to the mother lies at the heart of human destiny. In our Judeo-Christian culture, this important revaluing of the mother should not be underestimated. The fertility of the Jewish mother was blessed by Jahwe but removed from the sacred space that harbors the meaning of speech. The Virgin Mother then became the empty core of the Holy Trinity. Two thousand years ago the Man of Sorrow, Christ, founded a new religion that lays claim to the father, without wishing to know what he shared in common with his mother. The Kleinian child, phobic and sadistic, is the inner double of this visible and crucified man, his painful inside that is consumed by the paranoid fantasy of an omnipotent mother. That fantasy is one of a killing mother who must be killed, of an incarnate representation of female paranoia in which we discovered the projected paranoid-schizophrenia of our primitive and feeble ego. The subject is nevertheless able to free himself from this mortifying depth, provided, that is, that he can work through it indefinitely until it becomes the only value we still have: the depth of thought.[51]

Such psychic processes as those of which Klein and Freud write may (or may not) be common to all infant human beings. However, in the Western world we have constructed identity politics in such a way that we only know who we are by projecting unwanted thoughts outside of ourselves, in particular, toward the M(O)ther who gave us birth. The Western *foundational fantasy* (brutally reinforced by various theologies) is that, rather than acknowledging that we *project* all our

---

51. Kristeva, *Melanie Klein*, 246–47.

unwanted thoughts, emotions, and affects into our mothers, she actually *is* responsible for *our* psychic and other discomforts.[52] As Brennan summarizes:

> Envy, anger, aggressive behaviour—these are the problems of the other. Overtolerance, overgenerosity—these are our problems.[53]

In religious rites, for instance, the M(O)ther, her body, and all her bodily fluids (menstrual blood, in particular) are *abject,* that is to say, repudiated as a condition of a particular kind of consciousness. In Brennan's terms:

> *there is no reason why one person's repression could not be another man or woman's burden, just as the aggression of the one can be the anxiety of another.*[54]

Through either saving or triumphing over the *good* or *bad mother,* individuals who were formerly abject, humiliated, despised, or otherwise psychically marginal, achieve *salvation,* or *redemption.* For these reasons the discourses of *salvation* and *redemption* permeate warrior discourses.[55]

In her infant analysis, Klein spoke of the dynamics of guilt and reparation that affected her very young clients and that far exceeded any possible act they might have committed in their young lives. In their struggles with the *good* and *bad mothers,* infants wavered between envy and gratitude. But their guilt, deriving from *envious attacks* on their mothers, was often overwhelming and underlay serious psychic conditions. She concluded that such guilt and reparative strategies arose from deeply unconscious dynamics, specifically their envy of the life-giving mother.

In Western societies, the male cultural totem bears a double layer of guilt. The first relates to the primordial mother of the unconscious whose life-giving powers are envied and feared. The second relates to the guilt at completing this double erasure of the mother—denial and erasure of lineages—from the social worlds of religion, politics, and

---

52. Brennan, *The Transmission of Affect,* 13.

53. Ibid., 13.

54. Ibid., 12.

55. Stromberg, *Redemption by War;* Linenthal, *Changing Images of the Warrior in America.*

representation. In contemporary warfare, especially in fundamentalist religions, guilt appears to play a major role driving individuals to desperate lengths, especially in war.

Kleinian analysts typically struggle to bring such envy and guilt to consciousness, thereby mitigating their effects over their clients' lives. What happens, however, when such sacrificial dynamics are culturally elaborated and played out on the world stage, legitimated by the major religions, and appropriated by devotees who can envisage no greater tribute to their gods than to blow themselves up in a crowded station, or bomb and threaten whole cultures into submission? Guilt goes so far underground as to become impervious to analysis.

If Freud identified guilt to be at the heart of the Oedipal complex, how much greater is the unconscious guilt now waiting to be harvested in the cause of the M(O)ther? Religion (and especially those forms of fundamentalism that *write* their insecurities onto the bodies of women—veiling, sequestering) plays a lethal role in relation to the unconscious M(O)ther under the ground, waiting to disturb the precariously achieved psychic contract.

In Western culture, above the earth (as it were), through various forms of cultural representation, the conscious male cultural totem has effectively appropriated the life-giving power of the mother: real life (the only one that matters) enters the world through sacrificial death. Under the earth, the unconscious female totem (Mother) lies seething. In the *Eumenides,* Athena recognized the need to propitiate the Furies,[56] to pay them honor and to recognize their role in the social contract, but her promises were soon forgotten in the phallic order, and women were largely excluded from education, lest they remember.

And so the myth is perpetuated; *Eve's sin* cast us all out of paradise and only the sacrificial blood of men will ever allow us back.

Religious Leadership

In Western culture, the erasure of women from systems of representation and the failure to acknowledge what Irigaray calls the *maternal*

---

56. Athena increasingly emphasizes the Furies' capacity for good, especially after the verdict absolving Orestes is delivered. Throughout the last pages of the play she assures they that they will be honored and keep a powerful place in Athenian society.

debt, far from minimizing the role of the psychic mother of fantasy, in fact elevates her to enormous, albeit unconscious, proportions.

Throughout all of this, real women are kept in their place, the unconscious mother is kept underground, and the cultural totem and his priests inherit primitive emotional dynamics, positive and negative, leading to various forms of toxic leadership.

In religious leadership today, the failure to interrogate the psychic underpinnings of cultural mythologies could be said to be morally culpable. However, leaders often have a vested (and libidinal) interest in failing to do so.

As Jessica Benjamin, drawing on Kleinian theory has pointed out:

> Unfortunately, the fear of dominance does not lead groups of people to avoid being dominated; on the contrary, it draws them towards a specific or chosen domination.[57]

As Roger Money-Kyrle, wrote of the participants in the World War II:

> The impulse to dominate grew in proportion to the impulse to submit, and both combined to mould the state into something that could be worshipped as a god and in whose apotheosis they could also feel their own.[58]

Guilt and fear are the major currencies of apocalyptic and fundamentalist religions and political strategists. Cutting, flagellation, starvation, abnegation, and other sado-masochistic practices become normative.

Religious and political leaders often perform the role of the *Chosen Dominators.* Feeding psychic fantasies, rather than witnessing with their lives, often forms their pastoral strategies. Highly armored males, immune to any psychic penetration, they become androgynous figures capable of receiving (and appropriating) the displaced projections of the mother.

Their adherents and followers (often the most despised and abject members of society—*poor white trash* or *colonized ethnicities*) rely on their various priests to absolve, punish, or otherwise recognize their agency. In certain circumstances, becoming a suicide bomber (under

---

57. Benjamin, *The Bonds of Love,* 82.
58. Money-Kyrle, *Psychoanalysis and Politics,* 114.

religious or secular auspices) becomes the ultimate omnipotent act: re-birth through death, the ultimate form of purification.

Psychic Individuation

The failure to theorize critically the garden-of-paradise motif speaks of an unconscious imperative to deny its significance especially in relation to the death drives, and especially the deep longing to return to stasis, or nirvana. Theologically, the return to the lost paradise is achieved only through violent acts of redemption, reparation, and sacrifice. Politically, the return to lost origins, pristine lands, or pure ethnicities takes similar forms.

This paradise is the source of infinite, unspoiled goodness—the perfect breast, unimpeded by the demands of psychic independence, or unreliable mothers. Such controlled *omnipotent fantasies* are allowed to run riot in the public world, unhindered by analyses that take their gendered underpinnings and consequences into account.

However, even wars must come to an end. In many initiation rites, definitive splitting from the world of mothers takes place as a condition of entry into hegemonic male political formations. Today, this is often facilitated by a final act, designated as sacrifice, that mimics male individuation, or is theorized as the Oedipus complex.

Contemporary acts designated as sacrifice *perform* a similar role and are, therefore, performative and hegemonic. Most Western philosophies and theologies, far from attempting to heal the split, celebrate the triumph of one over the other, often (like Hegel's distinction between the male and female reproductive organs) resorting to some fairly basic biological fundamentalisms to do so.[59]

Through cultural elaboration in the form of myths and rituals, therefore, Western representational strategies reinforce, rather than undermine, male infantile unconscious. As Irigaray argues, whereas

---

59. ". . . in the male, the uterus is reduced to a mere gland, so, on the other hand, the male testicle remains enclosed in the ovary in the female, does not emerge into opposition, does not develop on its own account into active brain; and the clitoris is inactive feeling in general. In the male, on the other hand, we have instead active feeling, the swelling heart, the effusion of blood into the *corpora cavernosa* and the meshes of the spongy tissues of the urethra; to this male effusion of blood correspond the female menses. In this way, the reception (*Empfangen*) by the uterus, as a simple retention, is, in the male, split into the productive brain and the external heart." Hegel, *Philosophy of Nature*, 413.

women and men both need to deal with the *death drives,* men symbolize their death drives *at women's expense.*[60] *Pandora opened the box. Eve made me do it.*

Meanwhile, since female psychic struggles or agentic forms of representation are seldom culturally elaborated, women are often left culturally bereft. In the Western representational economy, only virgins, martyrs, and a few mothers with large families who died in childbirth are admitted to sainthood: in other words, they are a-sexual, or died enforcing their biological and theologically enforced imperative to reproduce.

As Irigaray points out, in Western cultures there are few, if any, mother-daughter representations or images of agental females.[61] The overriding myth is that only the sacrificial deaths of men can regenerate the culture: the natural birthing of women or their cultural labor of nurturing and nourishing is never culturally elaborated and never publicly acknowledged. In other words, Western definitions of sacrifice so completely reverse the natural order that only a theory as outrageous as envy could possibly begin to explain what is going on.

Individual Health: Collective Madness

At the outset, I mentioned that the theorists used here would be regarded as *highly qualified native informants* reporting on the psychic fantasies of their respective cultures. In other words, while we can use their work to understand or elucidate cultural fantasies, we need to suspend judgment as to whether the developmental models they describe are a necessary or contingent (Western) feature of the human condition. The question of *causality* here is crucial and needs to be re-theorized in the light of psychoanalysis.[62]

Psychoanalytic *descriptions* quickly become *prescriptions*. Individuals are assumed to have attained psychic health when they attain whatever culture considers the psychic norm. Meanwhile, the entire collective gears up toward war (actively, ritually, symbolically). Moreover, because of the extent of most nation-state's GDP dependence on

60. Irigaray, *Sexes et Parentés.*

61. Ibid., 189.

62. Rose, *Why War?*, 98.

weapons manufacturing, the process is left unanalyzed and considered to be substantively *rational*.[63]

Traditionally, psychoanalysts focus primarily on infant projections, and complete their training through various forms of *infant observation*. Such micro focuses can yield valuable information about infant projections. However, as Brennan points out, whole cultures, through their various forms of representation and economic modalities can equally *project* cultural expectations into infants through the transmission of adult and cultural *affects*.[64]

Similarly, Peggy Reeves Sanday argues in *Divine Hunger* that cultural ontologies exert powerful influences over the meaning of ritual practices to communities and individuals, often superseding their immediate material interests.[65] Social researchers who dismiss such ontologies or myths as *meaningless* or epiphenomenal effectively discount a valuable analytic tool of discernment and miss out on valuable possibilities of cultural interventions.

We know that societies have very different ways of imaging, othering, and resolving potential oppositions including those of gender, and that systems of cultural representation also impact on how potential oppositions are mediated and finally resolved. But where power and libido congeal, where weaponry increases the potentialities of force, and where envy is so firmly directed toward the mother's body, the combination becomes a lethal cocktail. In Western society, this is precisely what has happened. At every turn, struggles for individuation, and recognition are played out between hegemonic males, or those struggling for hegemony in any particular culture (often supported by women, unconscious of their own substantive best interests).

Sacrificial warrior discourses and their accompanying theological themes—guilt, reparation, salvation, redemption—plug into the collective psyche almost like an electronic probe that renders its object immobile, incapable of resistance. Uncritical, unconscious, and hegemonic, such discourses function to legitimate war efforts at the same time as they *perform* a collective initiation rite for men, psychically

63. Wallace, "Reason, Society and Religion."

64. Brennan, *The Transmission of Affect*.

65. Sanday, *Divine Hunger*.

splitting from the omnipotent mother, and psychically entering worlds of fantasy where new forms of omnipotence hold sway.

Sacrificial rites and discourses split the world open reflecting and effecting political and psychic dualisms. The *Other* is defined derivatively in relation to the dominants, but the primary *Other* over against whom we achieve identity is female; men give birth through death; ends and means are reversed; the public world takes priority over the private and, by implication, the world of men over that of women. Male morphology defines *true sacrality,* superseding and discounting that of females. Even the earth on which we stand and that forms our being becomes instrumental, to be sacrificed whenever political expediency so dictates.

Far from deconstructing such imperatives, in the Western world the cultural stories—*Oedipus, Eumenides,* and versions of the Christian story—beloved by our earlier theorists, reinforce the abjection of women. Those religious traditions that exclude women from representation and officiation collude with, rather than deconstruct such psychic potential, providing various forms of toxic androgynous leadership, often sustainable, as has been revealed in recent decades, only through massive sexual hypocrisy.

Conclusions

In the Western world, phallic myths dominate the cultural landscape and seem to be almost impervious to critique, or alternative possibilities. Religious mythologies that offer instant routes to the moral high ground and superior identities provide powerful defense mechanisms against conditions whereby individuals might seek psychic wholeness. Sacrificial motifs enable *Internal Terrifiers* to be personified, externalized, and scapegoated. Splitting and projection fosters group coherence, but at the expense of victims both within (sinners) and without (heathen). Furthermore, religious group cultures often uniquely enable forms of *group thinking,* or religious group formations that feed (rather than challenge) unhealthy maternal psychic fantasies.

Even though the links between warrior and religious discourse are not theoretically inevitable, historically, and with few exceptions, patriarchal religious discourse of all kinds (especially silence) support the war efforts—conventional and terrorist—of their various constituencies. Political, international, ecumenical, and inter-religious, such discourse makes conflict ever more lethal, especially when communal religious energies, culpably unconscious at the best of times, are now focused uncritically to serve the war efforts.

Mythical reinforcement of phallic narratives leaves few options for males other than to meet the socially sanctioned imperative of culture. Given that both religions and state worship offer powerful defenses again psychic anxieties and trauma, such libidinally charged group dynamics will not easily be overcome. As Fornari has argued: while pacifists often show good will, their work has *never given rise to social institutions capable of performing the security functions (against deep-seated anxieties) served by war.*[66]

However, if religions are to aspire to the condition of ethics (focused on war rather than sex), religious leadership must begin to become conscious of the lethal power that often rests in their hands. Humanity simply cannot afford the current scenario: medieval mindsets and worldviews, combined with twenty-first-century weapons.[67]

As a species we simply cannot afford the only two alternatives seemingly on the table: *the permanent war machine (or permanent security state) or the regime of holy terror.*[68]

Where do we find hope?

Mercy not Sacrifice

Prophets of various religions usually have more in common with their interreligious counterparts than with the priestly castes of their own traditions. Such prophets cry out to their assembled peoples: *take the smell of those sacrifices out of my nostrils. Give sight to the blind, food to the hungry, and comfort the widow and orphan.* Espousing practices of mercy, they urge us not to split off those unwanted parts of ourselves onto others, but to develop inward compassion for ourselves, to be extended outwards in ever increasing circles. Yet, in religious circles, even where ecumenical dialogue takes place, it takes place largely among the priestly castes, fighting over the sacrificial spoils, rather than returning to the radical roots of their traditions.

66. Fornari, *The Psychoanalysis of War*, xxii.

67. Habermas, *Religion and Rationality.*

68. Petchesky, "Phantom Towers," 316.

If indeed *war is a womb,* and if, as other theorists imply, radical regression regenerates the social order then perhaps we need to return to another source to find social, political, and personal replenishment.[69] As Bracha Ettinger argued:

> In the Hebrew Bible one of the many names for God is *El Harahmim,* translated as "God full of Mercy" or compassion, and also as *misereri misericordiam, caritas, pietas, gratia* and so forth. These are indeed the figurative means of *Rahamim.* But the literal meaning, the signifier is: wombs, uteruses, Matrixes. The text literally signifies a "God full of wombs" or (in Latin) full of "matrixes."[70]

Such an approach demands that we theorize the *maternal debt* and that we challenge the valorization of some very common theological motifs. In Klein's work, psychic health comes about when infants (or clients) understand that the person who offers the breast is the same person who sometimes withholds it. The mother becomes, not a *part object* (which leads to various forms of perversion) but a *whole object—* in other words, a person in her own right. Gratitude towards the mother ensues, and human life (with all its complexity) is made possible. Envy and idealization, (worship and awe), is replaced by love, guilt, and reparation (gratitude and responsibility).

In right-wing apocalyptic fantasy, redemption through death has replaced the cyclical redemption of the natural earth. Specular value is currently afforded, not toward the natural earth in all its beauty, but toward rituals of death and sacrifice, in which death, the threat of death, or the performative rites of death instantiate truth—albeit allied sharply with victory.[71]

Whatever realities lie beyond this earth, for now, in contemporary feminist rituals we chant, *the earth is our mother, we will take care of her, she will take care of us.* The work of actively recuperating and instantiating a life-supporting and life-giving symbolic system for our time is also acutely prophetic.

---

69. Caillois, *Man and the Sacred.*
70. Ettinger, "Transgressing with-in-to the Feminine," 75.
71. Fornari, *The Psychoanalysis of War,* 24.

Prophetic strands (especially those espousing non-violence) are usually silenced or canonized (two sides of the one coin). However, as one such contemporary prophet once wrote:

> I had rather a hundred times spend my life's energies working to heal the injustice around me, and never once speak of God; of doing it for God, of clarifying my motives! Than spend life converting others to God, while I gave not a snap for the prisoners, slave camps, wars, starving peoples, the sins of the mighty. To what God would I be converting others, in such a demented case? In what God would I believe?[72]

72. Berrigan, *Uncommon Prayer*, 25.

7

The Gendering of Post-Holocaust Jewish Responses to War and Collective Violence

Melissa Raphael

JEWISH MEN IN THE DIASPORA HAVE BEEN BOTH CONSCRIPTED INTO the collective violence of war and revolution and also been the target of collective violence, especially that of persecution and genocide. This essay will begin by outlining how biblical and rabbinic law have sought to regulate acts of violence and war, noting the difference between the prescriptions in classical sources and their interpretation in contingent historical situations, as well as the complex interaction of the legal and cultural norms implicit in ideologies of gender. The essay will then go on to discuss how secular and religious male Jewish responses to the Holocaust illustrate how the gendering of Jewish responses to war and violence is ambivalent, plural, shifting, and multiply determined. This is of significance to scholars of religion, war, and gender because Ashkenazi (eastern, western, and central European Jewish) men's attitudes to violence unsettles the customary second-wave feminist assumption that patriarchal religion *either* supports, *or* less commonly, protests regimes of violence. Generalizing somewhat, the diaspora ethics and culture of Ashkenazi Judaism complicates the options; there is a spectrum of positions between the prophetic criticism of violence and complicity with violence, reminding the feminist student of religion that religious patriarchies do not take one single, universal, and consistently oppressive form. That a religion is male-dominated does not mean it always sanctions a macho or warlike stance, glorifies violence, or offers a clear and direct impetus for a community's defense against violence.

It can be argued that post-biblical Judaism's reluctance to glo rify war and its preference for scholarly and family life has produced a non-macho—even "feminized"—Jewish masculine ideal that, despite being essentially patriarchal, does not sanction a militaristic stance. Militaristic values and postures cannot be assumed even where a religion, in this case, Judaism, is clearly male-dominated and broadly ascribes femaleness a second order status in its spiritual and intellectual hierarchy. Until the Holocaust, Ashkenazi men constituted a community of outsiders whose valorization of scholarship as the highest attainment in life and whose vulnerability to collective violence is widely considered to have "feminized" them or, at least, unsettled the typically patriarchal bi-polar construction and distribution of gender attributes, tasks, and goals. Indeed, quite differently from the highly derogatory anti-Semitic "feminization" of the Jewish male, the phenomenon of what the Jewish scholar Daniel Boyarin calls the "sissy Jew" persists in ironical and knowing forms in some Anglophone diasporic intellectual circles to the present day.

However, the essay will conclude by observing how, since 1948, the historical, political, and cultural conditions obtaining in Israel have produced, among Israelis at least, a widespread rejection of the "sissy" Ashkenazic Jew in favor of a neo-biblical and secular Zionist masculine ideal derived from the Israelite military hero of the Hebrew Bible, so erasing the "humiliating" memory of the male Ashkenazic victim of the ghettos, pogroms, and death camps, and buttressing the military defense of the Jewish family and Jewish territory. The aggressive posture and rhetoric of the Israeli masculine ideal (whose cultural influence has been limited in the European and North-American diaspora) has newly sexist dimensions and has been sharply criticized by feminists and others critical of the militarization of Israeli culture.

Attitudes to War and Violence in the Jewish Tradition

Diderot once attributed the survival of the Jewish people to the fact that they were not liable for military service. This was not entirely true: Jews had helped to defend cities in the middle ages and, after their emancipation, Jews were to serve in the French revolutionary armies. In the nineteenth and early twentieth centuries Jewish men were also conscripted into the Tsar's army (as was my great grandfather, who contrived to complete his military service by playing the clarinet at the Bolshoi). Jewish men also served with distinction for Germany, Britain, and other countries during the World War I. Around 30,000 Palestinian Jews served in Jewish military brigades within the British army during the World War II, with an estimated 700 of them killed in active service.[1]

Although, as in other traditions, Jewish observance is founded upon its belief in the sanctity of life, Judaism is not an inherently or widely pacifistic religion. Although some modern Jews have espoused pacifism, Jewish participation in war is supported by religious law (*halakhah*). Jewish law elaborates a highly complex typology of legitimate wars, with careful attention to their proper conduct and environmental impact. Although *halakhah* requires careful interpretation before it can be applied to the conditions of modern warfare and defense against contemporary terrorist attacks on civilians, it is generally halakhically clear that Jews must, if only for their own safety, comply with the civil law wherever they live, including compliance with national conscription orders. And, as already indicated, Jewish soldiers have done more than merely comply with the civil authorities. In the United States, for example, not only Jewish men but also Jewish women have served as nurses, marines, and airwomen in wars over the last 150 years, from the American Civil War through World War II, to Vietnam and Operation Desert Storm. During Operation Desert Storm, for example, Lisa Stein, a practicing Jew, put in 1,800 hours of combat flight time despite the then rule that women could not fly combat missions; despite the fact that the Saudis opposed the presence of both Jews and women in the war zone; and despite the fact that women soldiers were generally under orders to cover their hair and wear a black gown over their battle dress.

Although a comprehensive or detailed survey of Jewish attitudes to war and its legal regulation is beyond the scope of this essay, it is important to note that the Hebrew Bible, which sets out some basic commandments concerning the prosecution of war that were later elaborated in rabbinic law, contains a variety of attitudes to war and violence that cannot be synthesized into a single position. Nonetheless, in some important respects, military conquest is the means by which biblical covenants are fulfilled. God's fidelity, providence, and blessing

---

1. See further, e.g., Beckman, *The Jewish Brigade*; Eshel, *Bravery in Battle*, 153–63.

are predicated on his loyalty to, and his command of, Israel's territorial cause. This is a God who, before Israel's "very eyes," "ventured to go and take for himself one nation from the midst of another by prodigious acts, by signs and portents, by war, by a mighty and an outstretched arm and awesome power (Deut 4:34)." The Bible narrates God's role in securing victory for the Israelites in a series of ferocious wars and there is no doubt that the Israelites, under God's command, committed genocidal acts of war and the sexual atrocities that are themselves the instruments of genocide. The book of Numbers, for example, condones the abduction and rape of women from other tribes during warfare (Num 31:17–18, 32–35), even though Deuteronomy and its rabbinic commentators seek to control and limit the suffering of female captives.[2]

Yet while the Hebrew Bible assumes that war will occur, it also displays a prophetic distaste and a cultic repugnance for war: Deut 27:5 proscribes the placing of iron tools or weapons on the altar as a profanization of the sacred, and Isaiah dreams of a messianic age when swords will be beaten into plowshares and spears into pruning hooks and "nation shall not take up sword against nation; they shall never again know war (Isa 2:3–4)." To accept that war is a tragic possibility of human life is not to glorify it. The rabbis, for example, commenting on Isa 2:3–4, thought it disgraceful to wear a sword as a personal ornament (Mishnah Shabat 63a). The refusal to glorify military valor and bloodshed is not merely rhetorical. Biblical law offers certain exemptions from war that protect young men and the material welfare of their offspring. Deut 20:5–8 excuses a man from service if he is newly married and has lived with his wife for less than a year. Likewise, he is exempt if he has built a new house and has lived there for less than a year or if he has planted a vineyard that he has not yet harvested. Interestingly, the Bible also exempts those men who are, quite simply, afraid.[3]

Modern Judaism has a pacifist strand that has been articulated and practiced by a number of well-known activists. The late Steven Schwarzschild believed pacifism to be "the best, the most authentic

2. Elman, "Deuteronomy 21:10–14," 1–18; Fein, "Genocide and Gender," 43–63.

3. In continuity with the biblical tradition, in Israel today there is some recognition that there may be religious objections to military service or that warfare may be incompatible with the daily observance of Jewish law. Ultra-Orthodox Jews are excused military service if they are full time seminary students and women are also exempt if service would interfere with their religious life.

interpretation of classical Judaism."[4] Schwarzschild, arguing from his knowledge of modern twentieth-century warfare, notes that Jewish law permits limited wars, though limited warfare was the *only* kind of war known to the talmudists. Schwarzschild notes that Jewish law legislates the limits of war: all women and children must be spared, as must water, springs, fruit trees, food, and household goods. The enemy must also be granted a safe line of withdrawal. Maimonides deemed war permissible only after an offer of peace had been made on the grounds that Deut 20:10 requires the offer of peace and forced labor to the inhabitants of an enemy city before any attack is made. Since these conditions are difficult, if not impossible, to obtain in the contemporary age where civilian and military targets are too often indistinguishable, Schwarzschild argues that contemporary Judaism should not permit any wars. Again, since the Hebrew Bible accepts that men who are afraid can be sent home, and since any man would be afraid of dying or being wounded in battle, Schwarzschild sees no reason why Judaism should call on any man to fight in any war.[5]

Jewish pacifism has also been notably represented in the twentieth century by Judah Magnes, Abraham Joshua Heschel, and Bella Abzug, whose espousal of pacifism was not, in her case, religiously motivated. Jewish pacifists have used the theological anthropology of humanity's creation in the divine image as that which makes "brothers of us all" and which grounds the commandment prohibiting murder. The Noahide code, a basic and general ethic held by Jews to be applicable to all humanity, states that "whoever sheds the blood of man, by man shall his blood be shed; for in his image did God make man (Gen 9:6)." It was in this spirit that Abraham Joshua Heschel spoke out against the Vietnam War, refusing to see the Vietnamese as anything but his brothers. For Heschel, God is a God of love and compassion encountered in shared suffering, shared responsibility: "God's presence unites us and God is present wherever man is afflicted and all of humanity is embroiled in every agony wherever it may be." There is no dichotomy of "here and there," "me and them." Heschel reminded American Jewry that Judaism

---

4. Wilcock, *Pacifism*, 191. Citing "Shalom" in *Holy Land* 7 (1987) without a page reference.

5. Wilcock, *Pacifism*, 190.

does not absolve any one from responsibility for their own acts and any individual may challenge those in authority who order a Jew to fight.[6]

A marked reluctance to engage in warfare, even if it stops short of pacifism, can be derived from rabbinic literature. As Yeshayahu Leibowitz points out, in classical Judaism, heroism (*gevurah*) is understood as the victory of the moral imperative or binding obligation over the satisfaction of "natural" urges such as those for economic success, sexual pleasure, or military triumph (Shulkhan Aruch 1.1; M. Avot 4.1). In other words, although *gevurah* is defined in masculine terms and from the perspective of masculine experience, characteristically masculinist forms of heroism are downgraded. While other nations link a heroic death with death in battle, Judaism understands a heroic death as the sacrifice of the self, not for land or power, but for the sake of one's values and, ultimately, in for the sake of the transcendental value that is the holy (*kadosh*). In the memorial prayer for the dead in the daily prayer book, or *siddur*, it is those who give their lives for the sanctification of God's name (*Kiddush Hashem*) who are described in the words of 2 Samuel 1:23 as "swifter than eagles, stronger than the lion." To go to one's death "like a sheep to the slaughter" is to be a true servant of the Lord (Isa 53:7).[7] Classical Judaism, and even the Hebrew Bible itself, regards military heroism as "the least worthy" form of heroism:

> Heroism in battle is no indication of a person's stature as a human being. If one is a hero in the military sense (an excellent soldier), it is no guarantee that he is a superior person, either in terms of wisdom and intelligence or in honesty and integrity. On the other hand, a person who has heroically withstood urges arising from envy, hatred, or lust is certainly one of the elite few.[8]

While the Hebrew Bible narrates numerous wars: the conquest of Canaan, David's conquest of Jerusalem some four hundred years later, or Jereboam's restoration of Israel's territories two hundred years after, none of these are commemorated by any festival or thanksgiving. These victories are more or less ignored in Israel's theological tradition. Only the post-canonical war and victory of the Maccabees is commemorated,

---

6. Heschel, "The Moral Outrage of Vietnam," 48–61.

7. Leibowitz, "Heroism," 364, 369.

8. Ibid., 365.

because this was waged on behalf of Torah or the law, not territory.[9] Merely "nationalist" war is without theological-historical significance. Consequently Leibowitz believes that contemporary Israel has betrayed this spiritualized response to collective violence and followed "the nations" in the militarization of Jewish death.

It is possible that Schwarzschild and Leibowitz place too heavy a reliance on textual evidence and theological propositions. Judaism's traditional reluctance to endorse militarism probably owes as much to historical contingency as it does to its spiritual ethic. Reductively, it could be argued that post-biblical, diasporic Judaism made a religio-ethical virtue of stateless Jewish men's incapacity to wage war. More positively, though, it should be remembered that Judaism as we know it only came into being in the period after the destruction of the Second Temple when biblical Judaism was transformed by the sages into a largely domesticated religion of prayer and worship, without the apparatus of nationhood and without the cultic violence of ritualized blood sacrifice. Deliberation on the prosecution of war became literally academic. As Sandra Lubarsky observes, after the failure of Jewish military strength and the destruction of the Second Temple, the rabbis "created a Judaism that could survive without political power" and an image of God whose power was deferred and whose present imitation was located not in victory but in prayer and the "service of the heart."[10]

The Gendering of Jewish Approaches to War

The "domesticatication" or even "feminization" of Judaism after the destruction of the Second Temple does not imply that actual Jewish women's moral positions had any authoritative influence on cultural or legal discourse on war. In Judaism, as in other of the world's religions, women are not the speaking subjects of their own thought and experience. We therefore know very little of Jewish women's thoughts and feelings about war and violence before the middle of the nineteenth century, and this silence was only widely broken in the latter part of the twentieth century when second-wave feminism, with its roots in the redemptive social critique of first-wave Jewish feminism, took root to varying degrees in most Jewish denominations.

9. Ibid., 367–68.
10. Lubarsky, "Reconstructing Divine Power," 310.

The Hebrew Bible, however, shows women to be actively involved in military campaigns, though more by a combination of intelligence, wits, and sexual allure than by physical prowess. Deborah—a decisive player in the defeat of the Canaanites (Judges 4–5)—is a military leader but does not go into battle. It was her brilliance as a military strategist, and Jael's cunning seduction and gruesome murder of their enemy Sisera, that these two women brought the Israelites victory and forty years of peace. Nonetheless, it is notable that, on a rabbinic reading at least, the Torah assumes that women's "natural" inclination is to reproduce not kill. In Judaism, only men are commanded to procreate, not women, because it is held that men's "natural" inclination is to go to war or otherwise engage in projects that augment their power, whereas women are "naturally" inclined to the nurture of life; it requires no commandment. In rabbinic literature there is one exception to female silence on the matter of killing (and most other matters). A story is told, by male rabbis, of Beruriah (the only woman teacher in the Talmud of the second century CE) whose husband, an eminent rabbi, was praying for the death of a highwayman who had attacked him. Beruriah is said to have chastised him and used a biblical text to remind him that it is the cessation of sin, not the death of the sinners, that will produce repentance and an end to suffering (BT Berakhot 10a).

Israel was one of the first, and remains one of the only, states to make military service compulsory for (Jewish) women as well as men. Yet, in the mid 1980s, research suggested that on top of the pregnant, illiterate, religious, and married women who were exempt from conscription, only about 50 percent of draftable women actually served in the armed forces. For many of those who have served, the egalitarian rhetoric and certain legal changes made under pressure from liberal Israeli feminist groups[11] have not fulfilled their promise. Military services remain male-dominated and most women act in auxiliary roles as drivers, clerks, teachers, nurses, and secretaries rather than taking front-line roles in combat.[12] On the other side of the spectrum, Jewish

11. In the mid-1990s a lawsuit successfully challenged the exclusion of women from the Israeli Air Force's training courses for military pilots.

12. Fuchs, "Images of Love and War in Contemporary Israeli Fiction: Toward a Feminist Revision," 192.

feminists have been active in the Israeli and other peace movements for several decades.[13]

But surveying what Jewish women do or do not believe about war and peace is not entirely to the point. One cannot understand the gendering of violence in relation to Judaism without recognition that the Jewish diasporic (Ashkenazi) construction of masculinity shares in some of the roles and attributes commonly ascribed in Western culture to virtuous women without, at the same time, in any way forfeiting actual men's hierarchical dominance as master of the household and God's primary interlocutor. There is a substantial literature on the "feminization" of the male Jew in both anti-Semitic and intra-Judaic discourse. While popular anti-Semitic discourse often "feminized" male Jews as a means of victimizing them and of symbolizing their political condition of statelessness, *intra*-Judaic cultural, ethical, and theological values have complicated the customary duality between aggressive masculinity and passive or pacific femininity.[14] Culturally, Jewish masculinity in the diaspora is not affirmed by violence, but by the power derived from ethical virtue and scholarship. Daniel Boyarin's study of Jewish masculinity warns against making gender-stereotypical assumptions about Jews and violence, since the construction of masculine ideals in Judaism are particular to its own history, culture, and theology. Rebutting a Western construction of gender that can be traced from Roman culture to Freud, Boyarin finds that in both ancient and modern religious texts the talmudic exemplar of the ideal male Jew is not defined by physical prowess. Ritualized scholarly combat (*pilpul*) in the interpretation of sacred texts, feats of halakhic memorization, knowledge, and erudite wit are an alternative source of power and prestige.[15]

Before the Holocaust and the establishment of the state of Israel in 1948, the male Jew could cut a figure of great pathos and dignity; he could be romanticized by non-Jews as the representative of an ancient and noble tradition. But more commonly the Jewish male bore the brunt of actual or potential violence stirred up by centuries of demonizing

13. See e.g., *Nashim: A Journal of Jewish Women's Studies and Gender Issues* 6 (2003). This issue, edited by Alice Shalvi, is devoted to "Women, War and Peace in Jewish and Middle Eastern Contexts" and contains contributions from feminist peace activists such as Erella Shadmi and Judith Peck Stern.

14. See e.g., Brod, *A Mensch Among Men*; Boyarin, "Justify My Love," 131–37.

15. Boyarin, *Unheroic Conduct*.

rhetoric of a Christian and later racist or nationalist character. The Jew as scapegoat is typified by the male figure of the *Lamedvovnik* of talmudic legend (BT Sanhedrin 97b; Sukhah 45b)—the just man who spares the heart of God by carrying the sin and pain of the world on his back as he journeys, unnoticed, through the *shtetls* of old Jewish Europe.[16] Rather differently, there was also the abjected figure of the Jewish tenant farmer who, in pre-Holocaust Poland, was sometimes brought before the squire or *poritz* and his drunken party to sing and dance to the traditional Jewish Sabbath hymn. Jeered at by the *goyim*, this Jew was also sometimes referred to contemptuously by his own kind as a bootlicking *Yid* or *mahyofis Yid* (a term later used in the mid-twentieth-century of self-effacing *galuti*, diaspora Jews by Zionists wishing to cast off the old Ashkenazic "victimized" identity).[17] If one accepts the patriarchal notion that masculinity is defined by power over the subject other, then it is arguable that Jewish men have been in some senses "emasculated" by centuries of persecution. As an often-beleaguered minority group consisting predominantly of scholars and traders in small townships, Jewish men were culturally and materially ill equipped to protect themselves and their families from murder and attack.[18]

Theologically too, as Howard Eilberg-Schwartz has pointed out, there are dimensions of the characterization of the quasi-marital relationship between God and Israel that feminize Jewish men and Jewish spirituality and weaken the customary association of masculinity and aggression.[19] It is possible that gender slippages within Jewish culture reflect gender slippage in Jewish theological conceptions of God, and vice versa. It is this sense that the Jewish God is not, in fact, a relentlessly

16. See Raphael, "The Face of God in Every Generation." See also Schwartz-Bart, *Last of the Just*. This is a literary evocation of the twentieth-century just man, Ernie Levy, whose active resistance to violence is precisely a chosen and self-sacrificial passive acquiescence to violence.

17. Friedman, "The Haredim and the Holocaust," 90. However, anti-Zionist Haredim construed the *mahyofis* Jew as a hero of sanctity, of "a people that dwells apart, not reckoned among the nations." So that even when dancing before the *poritz*, the Jew knew himself to be noble, exalted, proud and joyous in his otherness (Ibid., 101).

18. The vulnerability of both Jewish men and women to collective violence has not always led Jewish men to abstain from spousal abuse. Although it is strongly discouraged in the classical Jewish sources, spousal abuse is as prevalent in Jewish marriage as it is in the rest of Britain and the United States. See Spitzer, *When Love is not Enough*.

19. Eilberg-Schwartz, *God's Phallus*.

and exclusively masculine Father and Lord of Hosts that informs Judith Plaskow's notion of a transgendered God. Examining the classic tradition, feminist readings of tradition, and the work of Eilberg-Schwartz and Boyarin, she finds that gender essentialism is countered by the instabilities and contradictions of image and discourse generated by the Jewish model of God as the husband of Israel (that is, of Jewish men). The literature is reticent about the quasi-sexual relationship between God and Israel, not least because the implication of God's being effectively married to Jewish men has unacceptably homoerotic overtones. Yet Plaskow goes beyond Eilberg-Schwartz in arguing that the Jewish God is neither a bi-polar union of the male and the female, nor androgynous, but, rather, transgendered. Although the Hebrew Bible refers to God as a woman in labor and as a woman nursing her baby, God is also Israel's husband. The indeterminacy and ambiguity of the bond between God and Israel (comparable to the *Song of Songs* subversion of gender stereotypes and its evocation of the mutuality of love by blurring normal distinctions between the speaking subject and its object) suggests, to Plaskow, a transgendered model of God that can produce an actual and potential Jewish theology where gender is performative and playful. For "if gender is something we perform, the possibilities for divine performance are infinite."[20] Compulsory heterosexuality loses its divine ordination. Human masculinity need no longer mime or defer to divine omnipotence. Plaskow does not present her model of a transgendered God as a cure-all for violence and coercion in the tradition, but argues that it does allow all Jews to experience the more relational possibilities afforded by "fluid and shifting subject positions."[21] The relevance of Plaskow's argument to the present paper is that if the Jewish God were in some senses transgendered, this would undermine the widespread theistic patriarchal association of divine power with providential deliverance and his vindication with military victory. In Judaism, God can adopt roles and also cast them aside. God is the Lord of Hosts, but not always.

20. Plaskow, "The Sexuality of God," 9.
21. Ibid., 11.

Jewish Men's Responses to Collective Violence in the Twentieth Century

Any religious tradition's values, theology, textual interpretation, and cultural mores are tested by the *extremis* of war and catastrophe. The violent and ultimately murderous assault of the Holocaust was to become a defining moment in the late modern construction of Jewish masculinity. Yet as the preceding discussion suggests, to polarize masculine and feminine Jewish responses to violence may be misleading. I have recently argued that the values and imaginary of post-Holocaust theology in the second half of the twentieth century are broadly masculinist, but its masculine God is, nonetheless, a vanquished God. To be a Jewish man in the ghettos and camps was in almost all cases to be the paradigmatic *Other*; the defenseless victim.[22] The male Jewish theologians who reject or remain faithful to God speak in identification with Jewish victims who have been "feminized" by their helplessness before the forces of hyper-masculine Nazism.

Moreover, it is well known that gender roles can slip and reverse in times of war. When men are drafted or killed, women's status can alter rapidly from that of passive dependent to that of head of household and primary wage earner with a far more prominent role in the civilian community than might previously have been the case. Soldiers' emotional dependence on wives and mothers at home can increase, and the restoration of wounded men's health often depends on the training and skills of female nurses.[23] In the early stages of the Holocaust, Jewish women often had to take over the roles and attributes of the husbands, brothers, and fathers who had been stripped of their livelihoods, deported, or killed. Nechamah Tec's study of gender and the Holocaust has demonstrated that, as the subordinate partners in marriage, Jewish women were used to adjusting their behavior to those in power over them. In the early days of the Nazi occupation, when men were publicly humiliated with beatings and other tortures and robbed of their livelihoods, they tended to succumb to depression and "give up." Even though very few would be ultimately successful in their efforts to survive, many women, deprived of emotional and financial support from men, had

22. Raphael, *The Female Face of God in Auschwitz*.
23. Fuchs, "Images of Love and War," 191.

to use their flexibility and resourcefulness to organize the family into a unit that could at least continue to eat an increasingly meager diet.[24]

And not all Jewish men responded to the unfolding horror in the same way; religiously observant men were less inclined to pursue armed resistance than those with secular political commitments. The class and economic standing of men, as well as religion, politics, and gender, were also factors of experiential difference. In the ghettos and later in the camps, lower-class men were already acclimatized to varying degrees of deprivation and injustice. Elite men and male intellectuals for whom the shock and humiliation of genocidal persecution were more debilitating were also often singled out for the most degrading jobs.[25]

The gendered division of religious opportunity and labor in Orthodox Judaism produced further differences in the way religious men and women met violent attack and death. Religious (Hasidic) men often met violence with the non-violent resistance of ecstatic payer: Rabbi Elchanan Wasserman in the Kovno ghetto; Rabbi Yerucham Hanushtate in Treblinka or the Ostrovzer Rebbe; Rabbi Yehezkel Halevi Halstuk who, in 1943, garbed in his prayer shawl and kittel, faced the German guns in Zusmir with the words, "For some time now I have anticipated this *zekhut* (privilege) (of *Kiddush Hashem*). I am prepared."[26] Certainly, only such men were given the roles, costumes, and lines of a religiously performative death. The Jewish ideology of femininity as properly private and modest and whose glory, according to the halakhic maxim "is to be out of public view," was such that public religious utterance of the prophetic kind was culturally and religiously alien to women in the gendered division of religious labor. At chaotic sites of mass execution, ringing with screams, barking dogs, and gunfire, it was possible for Hasidic Jewish men to dance and sing, rejoicing in their opportunity to die for *Kiddush Hashem*, "completely ignoring" the Germans surrounding the graves who were preparing to shoot. Indeed, as Eliezer Berkovits comments: "At that moment (when the men jumped into the pit) they lived their lives as Jews with an intensity and meaningfulness

24. Tec, *Resilience and Courage*, 10, 26, 349.

25. Ibid., 51, 169. Similarly, poorer rural women of lower education and expectations of life from the harsher eastern-European climate adjusted better to the appalling conditions of the camps than middle and upper class women who were used to service, comfort, and courtesy.

26. Cited in Schindler, *Hasidic Responses to the Holocaust*, 61.

never before experienced."[27] If Berkovits is right, it is not immediately apparent how a Jewish woman at such a site of execution, perhaps holding a baby in her arms and with terrified children clinging to her legs, could have died that fully Jewish, and indeed fearless, masculine religious death in which there is not merely a non-violent protest against a moral atrocity, but also an obliviousness to human hatred in the ecstatic joy of transcendental love.[28]

Although contrasts between religious "passive" resistance and secular "active" resistance are invidious, there is little doubt that although secular Jews construed and engaged the Nazis' genocidal assault very differently, their non-religious responses were as profoundly gendered as that of religious Jews. As Tec has demonstrated, secular women partisans' resistance to Nazism was constrained by cultural prejudices against their participation in military planning and battle and it was secular custom rather than religious observance that kept women's contribution to resistance a generally domestic one of "household" duties and sexual favors.[29] While some women were, nonetheless, active in the Jewish ghetto underground, in forest partisan groups, and one, Gisi Fleishmann, was the courageous leader of the Slovakian Jewish community,[30] it is male ghetto fighters such as Mordecai Anielewicz who are celebrated for their determination to die a manly, that is free or autonomous, death.[31]

It has been male underground and partisan resistance in the Holocaust, rather than religious or spiritual resistance of the sort described by Berkovits and others, that has been celebrated in post-war Jewish culture, especially in Israel. Post-Holocaust Jewish masculinity has been, if not redeemed, then certified by male Jewish resistance during the Holocaust and in the establishment and security of the state of Israel. Here rabbinical military reluctance has been widely eschewed even by the Orthodox in favor of national survival. Traditional notions of Jewish moral difference from the "nations" have also been widely

---

27. Berkovits, *With God in Hell*, 75, 112.

28. Raphael, *The Female Face of God in Auschwitz*, 22–24.

29. Tec, *Resilience and Courage*, 347–349.

30. See Meed, *On Both Sides of the Wall*; Tec, "Women among the Forest Partisans," 223–64.

31. See Kurzman, *The Bravest Battle*, 98.

repudiated as an intolerable burden and a sentimental indulgence that the cause of national survival cannot afford.

Indeed, some feminist commentators have argued that the macho, secular Israeli military establishment has defined its rights of occupation and domination by "feminizing" male Ashkenzic victims of persecution, especially the immigrant survivors of Nazism. Outside Orthodoxy, the virility of the male Jew is now, above all, embodied in the Israeli soldier: a secular reincarnation of the Israelite warrior of the biblical period.[32] The sexual political consequences of this move have not been desirable for women or for men who do not or cannot live up to this ideal. The militarization of Jewish masculinity tends to cast women as mere refugees from the horror and chaos of war; grieving mothers; or sex objects whose function as female conscripts can be regarded by those who harass and assault them as that of relieving the psychological and physiological pressure of military service.[33] Women are also often resented as those who, by "sitting at home," are not quite "doing their bit" to combat the constant threat of national catastrophe. Yet any encroachment by women into the domain of Israeli military power and into the military elite (who have often gone on to take important roles in government) can also be resented as that of amateurs trivializing the serious project of national defense.[34]

This is not to say that the defense of Israeli citizens is an inherently patriarchal project. A Jewish state has as much right to defend its borders and population as any other state. The suggestion that a Jew betrays his or her heritage by fighting for land on which to build a home may be dependent on the outmoded caricature of the wandering Jew whose normative state is that of the essentially homeless, disembodied *Luftmensch.* It is the militaristic ethos of much Israeli politics (including that of many Torah-observant political groupings) that feminists and others have challenged, not so much the notion of Jewish state as such. It has not, however, been the purpose of this essay to judge the conduct of contemporary Israel's military leadership. Rather, this paper has suggested that Jewish constructions of masculinity, which are historically contingent as well as legally and theologically produced, do not

32. Lentin, *Israel and the Daughters of Shoah.*

33. Mazali, "'And What About the Girls?'" 44–47.

34. Fuchs, "Images of Love and War," 190, 194–195; Starr Sered, *What Makes Women Sick.*

prohibit acts of war but they also do not glorify them. The construction of Jewish masculinity, both human and (figuratively) divine, does as much to undermine as to support a militaristic stance. Just as there is no single, unchanging construction of Jewish masculinity, the differences and particularities in key periods in Jewish history make it impossible to isolate a single, unchanging attitude to war and violence or a single ideal of the Jewish warrior or man of peace—after all, even the Messiah himself has had both of these roles attributed to him.

8

Prisoner Abuse:
From Abu Ghraib to *The Passion of the Christ*

David Tombs

Gwyneth Leech, "Jesus is Stripped of His Garments,"
Stations of the Cross 10 (2005).

REVELATIONS FROM ABU GHRAIB DURING 2004 RAISED DISTURBING
questions on prisoner abuse and torture by U.S. forces in autumn 2003.[1]
This has been followed by further disclosures of abuses at Guantanamo
Bay in Cuba and Bagram airbase in Afghanistan, as well as concerns
over extraordinary "renditions" of prisoners for aggressive interrogation
in the post-9/11 era of a so-called "Global War on Terror." The ethical
challenges raised by prisoner abuse at Abu Ghraib and elsewhere are
especially pressing for Christians, since at the heart of Christian faith is
the horrific memory of prisoner abuse in the form of Christ's crucifixion. The cross on which Jesus of Nazareth died means Christians have
an especially poignant reason to be disturbed by what happened at Abu
Ghraib, and to seek to understand it more fully.[2] For this to happen,
Christians will need to resist the temptation to pass over "unspeakable
abuses" in silence, and find a way to address them more honestly.

The dramatic *Stations of the Cross* series by Gwyneth Leech picture
Christ as a prisoner in modern times.[3] Station 10, showing Jesus stripped
of his garments, echoes the famous photo of a naked prisoner cower-
ing from dogs at Abu Ghraib and is a helpful reminder of the crucial
link between the pictures of Abu Ghraib and the other most discussed
story of prisoner abuse during 2004—*The Passion of the Christ*.[4] The

1. Amongst the extensive media coverage on the Abu Ghraib photos and prisoner
abuse, the work of Mark Danner for the *New Yorker* is especially helpful; see especially
Danner, *Torture and Truth: America, Abu Ghraib and the War on Terror*. This book
includes his *New Yorker* articles, a collection of the torture photographs and the major
documents and official reports published on the abuse.

2. Whilst this wider discussion is beyond the scope of this chapter, some of the
different issues involved in this can be mentioned. These include: intentional policy
changes by the U.S. administration to limit the applicability of the Geneva Conventions
and universal human rights; the abusive practices in many domestic U.S. prisons; the
counter-insurgency techniques developed by military intelligence; the use of unac-
countable private contractors; and the moral failings of many of the individuals involved. It should also be noted that the images of Abu Ghraib fit well with the graphic
violence of modern pornography, and it is not just conservatives who argue that a close
relationship between the two is very likely. On the shifts in U.S. policy that led to Abu
Ghraib, see especially Hersh, *Chain of Command: The Road from 9/11 to Abu Ghraib*.

3. The project (2004–2005) was commissioned for St. Paul's Episcopal Church on
the Green, in East Norwalk, Connecticut and has been on public display since Lent
2005. The stations draw on Abu Ghraib and other scenes in the war on Iraq as well as
other contemporary conflicts such as Darfur.

4. See especially Plate, *Reviewing the Passion*; Corley and Webb, *Jesus and Mel
Gibson's The Passion of the Christ*; and Frediksen, *On The Passion of the Christ*.

controversy around Mel Gibson's film meant that it was one of the most discussed movie releases ever, yet little was done to link the two prison abuse stories together into a Christian understanding of crucifixion in the light of Abu Ghraib or vice-versa.[5]

Thus, whilst the film had striking similarities to violent pornography and seemed to rest on similar voyeuristic tendencies, the significance of this critique was not followed through.[6] What invariably went unnoticed in the discussion was that if *The Passion of the Christ* was at all successful in offering a graphic and realistic portrayal of crucifixion, then it should be no surprise if it looked like a pornographic movie. Crucifixion was sexually abusive torture drawing on similar dynamics of humiliation as those revealed in the photos at Abu Ghraib. What is surprising about *The Passion of the Christ* is not that at some points it comes close to pornography in its graphic violence, but that it completely avoids and in some places conceals the most obvious elements of sexual abuse that are explicit in the biblical narratives.

It is easy to read the bible without realizing that the sexual abuse we see in photos of Abu Ghraib is also what we read about in the New Testament. Stripping a prisoner naked is a deliberate form of abuse. What we see in the photos of naked men at Abu Ghraib we therefore rightly denounce as sexual humiliation. Strangely, however, the very similar treatment of Jesus of Nazareth seems to go unnoticed and un-remarked upon. Why is this? It was surely as shameful for the Romans to strip and display a Jewish man naked in first century Palestine as it is for U.S. forces to do this to Muslim prisoners in twenty-first century Iraq. If the bible is read carefully, and then taken seriously, the stripping of Jesus can be seen for what it really was, sexual humiliation as a form of sexual abuse and as part of a wider pattern of sexualized violence for prisoner abuse.

To explore the sexual dimension of prisoner abuse further, it is helpful to distinguish between sexual humiliation (such as enforced nudity, sexual mockery, and sexual insults) that stops short of physical violence, and sexual violence that extends to sexual assault (which involves forced sexual contact and ranges from molestation to penetration and

5. For my own attempt to do this in a radio interview, see Tombs, "Jesus and Abu Ghraib," *Sunday Sequence*, BBC Radio Ulster, 16 May 2004.

6. See for example, Camon, "American Torture, American Porn"; Davis, "The Bite of the Whip: Passion of the Christ in Abu Ghraib."

rape) and could be accompanied by extreme abuse such as castration or mutilation. The gospels clearly indicate that sexual humiliation was a prominent objective in the treatment of Jesus. However, beyond the obvious humiliation involved in Jesus's nakedness during flogging and crucifixion, I will argue that crucifixion symbolized physical violation in a way that was readily understood in gendered and sexualized terms. Furthermore, I will suggest that there is a clear possibility of sexual assaults on Jesus in the *praetorium* (governor's headquarters).[7] Taken together, these three strands suggest that Jesus's crucifixion should be read in terms of sexual humiliation, sexualized torture, and possibly sexual assault or other sexual violence.

Sexual Humiliation and Nakedness

Roman crucifixions are widely acknowledged as an extreme form of execution. Originally, it was a punishment reserved only for slaves.[8] However, under the Empire its use widened and crucifixions were used to punish brigands and others who committed serious crimes. Mass crucifixions were widely used to put down revolts and could even be used against Roman aristocrats in cases of treason.

It was for good reason that Seneca asked:

> Can anyone be found who would prefer wasting away in pain dying limb by limb, or letting out his life drop by drop, rather than expiring once for all? Can any man be found willing to be fastened to the accursed tree, long sickly, already deformed, swelling with ugly wounds on shoulders and chest, and drawing the breath of life amid long drawn-out agony? He would have many excuses for dying even before mounting the cross.[9]

Cicero referred to crucifixion as "the most cruel and disgusting punishment" (*crudelissimum taeterrimique supplicium*) and "the great-

---

7. In the absence of any way to know what really happened in the *praetorium,* this part of the argument must be seen as exploration of a possibility, and not as an assertion of fact. I want to do no more than draw attention to the question, and ask whether what has proved so common in recent torture practices cannot be entirely ruled out in the treatment of Jesus.

8. Cicero notes that it most commonly used for slaves; Cicero *Verr.* 2.5.169. Other writers also referred to it simply as slaves' punishment (*servile supplicium*); for example, Valerius Maximus *Facta.* 2.7.12.

9. Seneca *Dial.* 3:2.2.

est punishment" (*summum supplicium*).[10] The first-century Jewish historian Josephus called it "the most pitiable of deaths."[11] The North African theologian Origen (*c.* 185–*c.* 254) referred to it as "most vile death of the cross" (*mors turpissima crucis*).[12]

Modern scholars have done much to illuminate what can be known of Roman practice.[13] However, the extent to which crucifixions were intended to be a sustained attack on the "manliness" of the crucified victim has barely been noticed.[14] Flogging the victim in public whilst naked, which was routine practice in Roman times, was an important part of this. The custom was to strip the victim naked, tie the victim to a flogging pole and then flog the whole of their body.

According to William Fulco, who worked as a consultant scholar on the film *The Passion of the Christ*, Mel Gibson wanted the Jesus in his film to be a "macho" male who was in charge of his own crucifixion:

> Mel was very intent on having a macho Jesus in charge. He wanted to make sure that the Passion was something Jesus did, it was not something for which he was a victim.[15]

The Passion of the Christ portrays Jesus as suffering heroically and in an always manly way.[16] It shows how violent the floggings associated

10. Cicero *Verr.* 2.5.165 and 168.

11. Josephus *War* VII.203

12. See Origen *Commentary on Matthew* (on Matt 27:22 and following).

13. For useful overviews on Roman crucifixions, see Hengel, *Crucifixion in the Ancient World and the Folly of the Cross*; Kittel, *Theological Dictionary of the New Testament,* 7:572–84; O'Collins, "Crucifixion," I:1207–10; Sloyan, *The Crucifixion of Jesus: History, Myth, Faith*, 14–23. For a comprehensive account of the gospel narratives on crucifixion, and the historical scholarship surrounding them, see Brown, *Death of the Messiah*, including the exhaustive bibliography (885–87).

14. The fascinating work by Stephen D. Moore, *God's Beauty Parlour*, is highly unusual amongst biblical scholars in bringing out some of the violent gender dynamics in crucifixion.

15. Shepherd, "From Gospel to Gibson: An Interview with the Writers." Available from http://www.sbl-site.org/Article.aspx?ArticleId=406. This comment is just under 28 minutes into the interview.

16. Many writers have noted that there are parallels between this picture of Jesus and other heroes played by Gibson in movies like *Braveheart* and *Lethal Weapon*. For example, Benedict Fitzgerald (who co-scripted the film with Gibson) suggests that Gibson's belief that human suffering can have a redemptive value was a theme he had already explored in *Braveheart*, and reflected Gibson's own experiences in life; Shepherd, "From Gospel to Gibson: An Interview with the Writers."

with crucifixions would have been, but it misses one of the most important aspects to the punishment. To flog a victim was not just to hurt
them physically but also to shame and humiliate them by displaying
them naked. This may have gone against Gibson's understanding of a
macho Jesus, but Mark, Matthew, and John all imply that the flogging of
Jesus was no exception to this custom.[17]

Although Mark 15:15, Matt 27:26, and John 19:1 are not explicit
on this (and Luke does not mention a flogging), the sequence of events
they describe strongly suggests it.[18] Mark and Matthew, who have the
flogging at the end of the trial, and John, who has the flogging midway
through the trial, each report that immediately after the flogging Jesus
was handed over to the Roman soldiers to mock him. All three present the first act of mockery as the soldiers dressing Jesus in a crown
of thorns and a purple cloak (Mark 15:17), purple robe (John 19:2) or
scarlet cloak (Matt 27:28). There is no mention of needing to strip him
before doing so. By contrast, both Mark 15:20 and Matthew 27:31 explicitly state that after the mocking he is stripped of the garb and his
own clothes are put back on him for the procession to Golgotha.

In Jewish culture, nakedness in public—and especially the exposure of the genitals—was particularly shameful.[19] Thus Lamentations
1.8 uses the shame of nakedness to speak figuratively of the fall of
Jerusalem and the city's disgrace: "Jerusalem sinned grievously so she
has become a mockery; all who honored her despise her, for they have
seen her nakedness; she herself groans, and turns her face away."[20] The
Bible also refers to the practice of exposing male prisoners to public
shame and ridicule. In Isaiah 20:4, the prophet warns that "so shall the
king of Assyria lead away the Egyptians as captives and Ethiopians as
exiles, both the young and the old, naked and barefoot with buttocks
uncovered, to the shame of Egypt." For the Jews, this is an omen of what

17. Roman questioning of slaves and others of low status was also invariably conducted under torture, and the flogging that followed the sentencing may not have been
the first of the assaults or indignities that Jesus endured.

18. All Bible verses are from NRSV unless indicated otherwise.

19. See especially Edwardes, *Erotica Judaica: A Sexual History of the Jews*. For the
Romans, voluntary nudity was entirely acceptable in some contexts (such as the bath
house), but any coerced display of the naked body was deeply shameful and unmanly.

20. Cp. the warnings to Babylon (Isa 47:3) and Nineveh (Nah 3:5). There may be a
strong hint of latent sexual violence as well as humiliation in the language here.

they too can expect from the Assyrians. Likewise, 2 Samuel 10:4–5 describes how David's envoys were seized by Ha'nun and sent back with their beards half shaved and their garments cut off "in the middle at their hips."

Jewish sensitivity over the insulting exposure of nakedness is shown in a disaster that happened during the time that Cumanus was governor (48–52 CE). According to Josephus, a soldier on guard on the Temple colonnade during the Feast of Unleavened Bread sparked a fatal riot when he lifted his tunic and indecently exposed himself to the crowds below. In response to the commotion that followed, Cumanus sent for heavy infantry, but this triggered a panic. Josephus claims that 30,000 were crushed to death as they tried to escape. The nature of the insult is a little unclear because in Jospehus's *War* version of the story, the soldier exposed his backside and bent over whilst making indecent noises[21]; whereas in the *Antiquities* Josephus only refers to a soldier lifting his tunic, in which case he might have been exposing his penis.[22] However, whether the incident is understood as a straightforward toilet insult, an ironic offering of anal submission, an insulting display of a foreskinned penis in a sacred place, or an intentionally threatening display of phallic "virility," it illustrates both the power that insulting bodily gestures could have and the sensitivity around exposure of the private parts. [23]

The Roman practice of crucifying victims naked is attested by Artemidorus Daldianus.[24] Some commentators suggest that the Romans might have treated the Jews differently at crucifixion because of Jewish sensitivity on this.[25] However, it is equally plausible that since

21. Josephus *War* 2.223–27.

22. In general, *War* is seen as a stylistically superior but the *Antiquities* are seen as more historically reliable.

23. Allen Edwardes goes as far as to say that exposure of the genitalia or posterior was "an outrage Hebraically tantamount to sexual assault"; Edwardes, *Erotica Judaica*, 75.

24. Artemidorus Daldianus *Oneirocritika* 2.53.

25. For a careful review of the evidence, see Brown, *The Death of the Messiah*, 870 and 952–53. The basis for claiming that it might have been different in Jerusalem is the beheading of the tribune Celer, as described by Josephus. Josephus describes Celer as being dragged through the city and beheaded (*c.* 50CE) but makes no mention of him being disrobed or being naked; Josephus, *War* 2.12.7; idem., *Ant.* 20.6.3. Yet even if the inference that Celer was clothed is correct, and the explanation for it is rightly ascribed to special sensitivities in Jerusalem rather than to Celer's special status as a tribune, this

Jewish sensitivity was especially high, there might have been all the more reason to enforce the practice, to increase the sense of humiliation.[26] Certainly the Romans do not seem to have afforded the early Christians any concession along these lines. In the early fourth century, Phileas Bishop of Thmuis (Egypt) complained that the chief outrage to the Christian martyrs was that after torture, their disfigured and naked corpses were displayed in public.[27] In the absence of other evidence, there is no reason to think that Jesus or other Jews were given a special dispensation on this.[28]

As with flogging, to crucify victims naked was a ritualized form of public sexual humiliation. The gospels indicate that Jesus was stripped, flogged, insulted and then crucified and there is no good reason to think that Jesus would have been an exception to the rule that victims were crucified naked.[29] For example, Augustine assumes that Jesus was crucified naked, and reads Paul's reference to Christ being crucified in weakness (2 Cor 13:4) as a reference to his nakedness. It should also be remembered that the earliest images of Jesus's crucifixion—albeit from non-Christian sources—picture him as fully naked.[30] Furthermore, Christ's nakedness on the cross would explain why Christian artists who drew scenes from Jesus's life did not see Christ on the cross as

does not contradict the gospel accounts that imply that Jesus was paraded to execution whilst clothed, but crucified whilst naked (see n. 20 below).

26. Some commentators have suggested that the abuse at Abu Ghraib was designed to exploit Muslim sexual sensitivities and magnify the torture. It is not unrealistic to assume the Romans would have acted similar with respect to Jewish sensitivities. For one such commentary see Rejali, "Viewpoint: The Real Sahme of Abu Ghraib." Available from http://www.time.com/time/nation/article/0,8599,640375,00.html. I am grateful to Dylan Lee Lehrke for drawing my attention to Rajali's article.

27. See Eusebius *Hist. Eccl.* 8.10. Cited in Coleman, "Fatal Charades," 44–73 (49).

28. The surprising detail in the gospel accounts is not that Jesus was naked for flogging and crucifixion, but that he was not naked on his journey to Golgotha, since this too would have been Roman custom. For example, Dionysius of Halicarnassus, records how a slave had his arms fastened to a crossbeam and was then marched naked through the city for execution. The lash of the whips on his back made him cry out in pain and forced his body into indecent movements; Dionysius of Halicarnassus *Rom. Ant.* VII.69.2. It may be that sensitivity over nakedness within the Holy City, especially at Passover, was the reason for this (see fn. 18 above).

29. Furthermore, Augustine links Noah's shameful nakedness when asleep drunk (Gen 9:20–25), to Christ's humiliation in the Passion; Augustine *City of God* 16.2.2.

30. See the discussion of the amber gemstone and Palatine Palace drawing below.

appropriate subject for art. The first Christian images of Christ on the cross come from the fifth century, at least sixty years after Constantine had prohibited crucifixion as a punishment in 337 CE.[31]

The gospel of John also gives important support for the belief that Jesus was crucified naked. John 19:23–24 records that after putting Jesus on the cross, the soldiers took his clothes to divide amongst themselves and that these included his undergarment, for which they cast lots so as not to tear. The synoptic gospels (Mark 15:24, Matt 27:35, and Luke 23:34) are less clear on this (they simply refer to the division of his clothes by lots) but they do not contradict John's account. It is only the medieval apocryphal Gospel of Nicodemus that attests to Jesus being left with a loincloth.[32]

The belief that Jesus would have kept his loincloth while on the cross is more likely to be a result of how Christian artists have pictured Christ than what the texts suggest. The strong likelihood is that, in this case, art is drawing a veil over the historical reality, and this temptation remains strong even today, as evidenced in *The Passion of the Christ*. This veiling of the naked body hides an integral dimension of crucifixion. Crucifixion was intended to be more than the ending of life. Prior to actual death it sought to reduce the victim to something less than human in the eyes of society. Displaying the victim to onlookers during public floggings and crucifixions was part of ritualized torture that needs to be understood in gendered and sexualized terms set in the cultural context of Roman imperial power and Roman sexual politics.

The Sexualized Symbolism of Crucifixion

Crucifixion is usually seen as originating with the Persians, who used it to display both living and dead victims.[33] Later, crucifixion was used by the Greeks and Carthaginians, and the Romans possibly learnt cru-

---

31. See Harries, *The Passion in Art*, 11. Prior to this, Christian artists had shown only an empty cross, or a cross with the Greek letters X (chi) and R (rho) incorporated into the cross as symbols for Christ; ibid., 4.

32. See Wijngaards, "Naked without Shame," 12–13.

33. See Herodotus *Hist.* 1:128.2; 3:125.3; 3:132.2; 3:159.1. Herodotus used the verb *anaskolopizein* for living victims and *anastauroun* for corpses, however, after Herodotus the verbs become synonymous; See O'Collins, "Crucifixion," 1207; Hengel, *Crucifixion in the Ancient World and the Folly of the Cross*, 24.

cifixion from the Carthaginians during the Punic Wars.[34] Yet, although crucifixions were common in Roman times, Roman historians and other writers do not dwell on them.[35] It appears that there was significant variety in how crucifixions might be carried out and some of the historical details on Roman practice remain open to debate. Analysis of crucifixion is complicated by the close relationship between crucifixion, impalement, and the hanging of bodies.[36] Victims could be tied or nailed to stakes or trees (with or without crossbeams) as well as crosses, and the readiness of New Testament writers to move between crucifixion and hanging on a tree suggests that there were not always clear boundaries between them (Gal 3:13 and Acts 5:30 and 10:39).

When the Romans first adopted crucifixion, it was used primarily to humiliate and punish slaves, and did not necessarily result in death. It was only from the first century BCE onwards that the Romans started to use it as an aggravated form of execution.[37] In time, in addition to punishing slaves, it was also used against rebels, bandits, and insurgents.[38] After suppressing revolts, mass crucifixions were an effective means of state terror that reminded conquered subjects of the cost of opposition to Rome. For example, Josephus describes how Varus (Governor of Syria) responded to the upheaval caused by the inept rule of Herod's son Archelaus with the crucifixion of 2,000 "ringleaders" of the troubles in 4 BCE.[39]

34. Hengel, *Crucifixion in the Ancient World and the Folly of the Cross*, 22–23.

35. For example, Gerald O'Collins points out that Tacitus' *Historiae* does not mention the many crucifixions in Palestine (Tacitus *Hist.* 5.8.13); O'Collins, "Crucifixion," 1208. Likewise Tacitus offers little on Jesus's crucifixion, he refers simply to Jesus as someone who "suffered the extreme penalty under Pontius Pilate during the reign of Tiberius"; Tacitus *Ann.* 15.44. Regrettably, the Jewish historian Josephus also has very little to say about Jesus's crucifixion. Josephus only reports that when Pilate heard high-standing Jews were accusing Jesus, Pilate condemned Jesus to be crucified; Josephus *Ant.* 18.63.

36. See esp. the short note Thornton, "Trees, Gibbets and Crosses," 130–31; Tzaferis, "Crucifixion: The Archaeological Evidence," 44–53.

37. See Tzaferis, "Crucifixion: The Archaeological Evidence," 47–48.

38. Because of the disgrace crucifixion involved, it was very rare for it to have been used against Roman citizens, though there were exceptions to this especially if charges for treason were involved; see Hengel, *Crucifixion in the Ancient World and the Folly of the Cross*, 39–46.

39. Josephus *War* 2.69–79. The census revolt of 6 CE, when Quirinius was Governor of Syria (6–7 CE) and Coponius Procurator of Judea (6–9 CE), also met with widespread reprisals; Josephus, *War* II.117–18; idem., *Ant.* 18.1–10.

The gospels provide the fullest description of a Roman crucifixion in ancient literature. It is likely that wooden crosses were used for more formal executions when part of the punishment was for the victim to carry their own crossbeam (*patibulum*) to the point of public execution, where it would be erected on the upright (*stauros*). The crossbeam was then fixed a little down from the top of the upright to make the familiar Latin † shape (*crux immissa*), or at the top of the upright to make a tau T shape (*crux commissa*).[40] For more *ad hoc* punishments during military campaigns, victims might be nailed or tied to any available tree, with or without a crossbeam.

Victims were usually either tied or nailed at their wrists and ankles.[41] Roman practice might include a small support peg or block on which the victim could sit (*sedile*) or stand (*suppedaneum*), depending on its position.[42] This extra support was likely to drag the torture out for longer, meaning that rather than two to four hours, crucifixion might last two to four days. Crucifixion brought death through hypovolemic shock (because of the loss of blood) or through asphyxiation (because the victim's position eventually made it impossible to breathe).[43] Asphyxiation could be a protracted affair. The struggle to breathe would force victims to constantly try and take their weight onto their arms and shoulders to relieve the pressure on their chests and allow their lungs to breathe. Eventually they would exhaust their strength for this struggle

40. See O'Collins, "Crucifixion," 1207. The *crux immissa* lent itself to the addition of a small board (*titulus*) above the head of the victim, describing why the prisoner was crucified; See Matt 27:37; Mark 15:26; Luke 23:38; and John 19:19–22.

41. The nails had to go through the wrist-area (rather than the hands) otherwise the hands would just tear, especially if the nails had to support the body's weight.

42. The Early Church writers Irenaeus and Justin Martyr both speak of a cross as having five points, with the *sedile* affixed to the *stauros* as the fifth point. Their arguments suggest that they understood that this was also the case for Jesus's cross (though neither explicitly state this), and that the *sedile* was more like a strong peg than a wood block or small block. Irenaeus, says "The very form of the cross, too, has five end points, two in length, two in breadth, and one in the middle, on which the person rests who is fixed by the nails"; Irenaeus *Adversus Haereses* II.24.4. Justin says "And the part which is fixed in the centre, on which are suspended those who are crucified, also stands out like a horn"; Justin Martyr *Dialogue contra Trypho* §91. The gospel texts make no mention of either a *sedile* or a *suppedaneum* but they do not categorically exclude it either. The *suppedaneum* became common in later Christian art, though some doubt it would have been used at the time.

43. For a medical assessments of the cross, see Edwards, "On the Physical Death of Jesus Christ," 1455–63.

but it could last for days. The more support that the body had the longer it would take. The Romans normally left the bodies to hang for days but breaking the victims' legs could ensure a relatively speedy death if this was necessary. There is evidence of this from the bones discovered at Givat ha-Mivtar in 1968, which are believed to be of a first-century victim of crucifixion called Yehohanan, the son of Hagakol.[44] John 19:31 refers to Jewish concerns that bodies not be left overnight and the Romans may have given them a special dispensation on this.

In any case, death by crucifixion was a sustained attack on the dignity of the human spirit as well as the physical body. Displaying the cross in public was to maximize the victim's public humiliation. The shame for Jews was further heightened by the belief that "anyone hung on a tree is under a curse" (Deut 21:23), a curse that Paul refers to in relation to Jesus's crucifixion in Gal 3:13.

Hebrews 12:2 refers to the "shame of the cross" and to appreciate just how shameful crucifixion was, it is necessary to understand crucifixion in terms of Roman and Jewish attitudes towards the body. For the Romans, crucifixion carried heavily sexual overtones because it involved public penetration of the body. As Craig Williams and others writing on Roman sexual politics have argued, sexual relations were regulated by who might penetrate whom. A real man—i.e. a Roman man—was one who might penetrate his social inferiors (women, slaves, or non-Roman men, and boys) but would never allow himself to be penetrated by them. To the Romans any form of bodily penetration could readily be understood in sexual terms and nailing a body to the cross would inevitably have carried this significance. The physical and symbolic penetration of the victim when flogged and then nailed or tied to the cross should be understood against this background.

In both flogging and crucifixion, the victim was held up as a symbol of penetration that served as a warning to all. Furthermore, on top of this physical violation, the penetrative gaze of onlookers may have been an equally significant part of sexualized humiliation. In any

---

44. The expedition was led by Vassilios Tzaferis; see Tzaferis, "Crucifixion: The Archaeological Evidence," 52. See also Charlesworth, "Jesus and Jehohanan: An Archaeological Note on Crucifixion." Tzaferis argues that it was likely that Yehohanan was nailed to the cross with his legs in a bent double position and his knees positioned to the left side, forcing him to twist his body from the waist up into a forced and unnatural position, supported by a *sedile* wood block under his left buttock.

patriarchal society, where men compete against each other to display virility in terms of sexual power over others, the public display of the naked victim in this way carried the message of shameful vulnerability.[45] In the ancient world, to penetrate with the eyes was even more likely to be seen as akin to physical penetration, as is suggested in the story of Noah's shame.[46] The way that crosses held their victims—framing them vertically and horizontally—added to the visual sense of the victim's penetration. To those familiar with the symbolic importance of penetration, the upright and the crossbeam would have been readily understood in sexual terms of phallic violation.

If the vulnerable body was left to hang, it might suffer further penetrative violence when it attracted carrion birds. Reference to this possibility is made in Genesis 40, where the baker imprisoned with Joseph tells of a dream in which he has three baskets of baked goods on his heads and birds eat from the top basket that was meant for Pharaoh (Gen 40:16–17). Joseph's interpretation of the dream is that "within three days Pharaoh will lift up your head—from you!—and hang you on a pole; and the birds will eat the flesh from you" (Gen 40:19).[47] Josephus says that "He (Joseph) told him that the baskets meant three days, and that on the third day he would be crucified and devoured by birds, being unable to defend himself.[48] By adding the detail that the baker would be unable to

45. As evidenced in the photos from Abu Ghraib, and in many of the lynchings under Jim Crow laws in the United States, where victims were often left to hang naked.

46. The story of Noah's disgrace, where his youngest son Ham is said to "see the nakedness" of his father (Gen 9:22), is interpreted by some Jewish commentators as castration and/or sexual abuse; see Edwardes, *Erotica Judaica*, 45. In support of this interpretation, Noah's enraged reaction when he wakes certainly seems to suggest that Ham did more than just catch a glance of him sleeping naked. The words "When Noah awoke from his wine and knew what his youngest son *had done to him*" (verse 24, emphasis added) are suggestive of a more physical act than just seeing him, or at the very least it is indicative of how closely visual penetration and physical penetration were associated.

47. The denouement to the story confirms Joseph's interpretation (Gen 40:20–22). However, there is some ambiguity as to whether Joseph's interpretation of the dream is that the baker would be beheaded, and the head separately impaled (perhaps whilst the rest of the body was hung up), or whether the reference to lifting up the head simply describes the way a head is jerked up in a hanging. Genesis 40:20–22 preserves this ambiguity with a reference to lifting up the head in verse 20 and to hanging in verse 22.

48. Josephus *Ant.* 2. 72. Since Josephus is writing for a Roman audience it is not surprising that he refers to this hanging or impalement as "crucifixion." As noted above, the distinctions between these forms of execution were not hard and fast. A further

defend himself against the birds, Josephus may be revealing that he was familiar with crucifixions where victims could not defend themselves against the birds even when they were still alive.[49] Crucifixions could therefore involve mutilations of the genital area of the corpse—or even the still-living body—by carrion birds.[50] If the victim was placed close enough to the ground, the body could be mutilated by other beasts as well. This may help to explain why the Jews—who saw human beings as created in the image of God—viewed hanging as a particular curse (Deut 21:22–23) and sought to avoid bodies left hanging after death.[51] This would have been especially the case on the eve to a Sabbath and would add to the sense of urgency that prompted Jesus's followers to press for the body to be taken down (see John 19:31).

Some forms of crucifixion put the victim into positions that high-lighted the vulnerability of the genital area by separating the legs. A *sedile* could be used to splay the legs apart as well as to support the body, as suggested by the image of crucifixion engraved on the Pereia amber gemstone (dating to c. 200 CE).[52] Other positions may have been even more inventive and humiliating.[53] This may be what Josephus is

---

example of this is Josephus's account of the punishment of Big'than and Te'resh in the Esther story (Est 2.23); Josephus *Ant.* XI.208.

49. See also Horace's reference to slaves "feeding crows on the cross," Horace *Epist.* 1.16.46–48; Cited in O'Collins, "Crucifixion," 1208.

50. Reports on abuses committed by security forces in El Salvador and Guatemala during the 1980s suggest that the areas of a victim's body that carrion birds were most likely to attack first were the soft areas of the face (especially the eyes and the lips) and the genital region.

51. See especially Josephus, *War* 4.310.

52. The gemstone shows a victim with spread legs, presumably supported by a *sedile* peg; see Smith, *Jesus the Magician*, 61. Along with the Palace wall drawing described below, this gemstone is one of the earliest images of Jesus's crucifixion and like the Palace wall drawing is assumed to have been made by someone who was unsympathetic to Christianity. The visual impression of the *sedile* may explain why it is rarely pictured in Christian art, and why the *suppedaneum*, which has the opposite effect, is strongly preferred. For a wider discussion of the treatment of Jesus nakedness and sexuality by Christian artists, see especially Steinberg, *The Sexuality of Christ in Renaissance Art and in Modern Oblivion*; for a discussion with reference to the cross in particular, see Trexler, "Gendering Jesus Crucified," 107–19.

53. Nico Hass, who headed the medical team which examined bones at Giv'at ha-Mivtar, has argued that they are consistent with the usual view that the heel bones were nailed onto the upright of the cross by a single nail; Hass, "Anthropological Observations on the Skeletal Remains from Giv'at ha-Mivtar," 38–59. However, Yitzak Yadin has

referring to when he says that during the siege of Jerusalem the soldiers sometimes experimented with different types of crucifixion as a "grim joke" on the victims. In his words:

> The soldiers themselves through rage and bitterness nailed up their victims in various attitudes as a grim joke, till owing to the vast numbers there was no room for the crosses, and no crosses for the bodies.[54]

Alternatively, Josephus might be referring to crucifixions that involved actual genital mutilation or impalement. The Roman historian Seneca the Younger (4 BCE–65 CE) offers conclusive evidence that the gendered violence of crucifixion could go beyond symbolism to actual genital penetration. Reporting from a campaign he witnessed in Bithynia, he remarks:

> I see crosses there, not just of one kind but fashioned in many ways: some have their victims with head down toward the ground; some impale their private parts; others stretch out their arms on their crossbeam.[55]

When crucifixion took the form of actual impalement, the element of sexual violence would have been unavoidable. In the novel *Bridge Over the Drina* (1945), the Nobel Laureate Ivo Andrić describes an impalement set in the sixteenth century.[56] Amongst other things, his description of this violent punishment brings out how a knife could be used in an overtly sexual manner to prepare the body for the stake:

> Without another word the peasant (Radisav) lay down as he had been ordered, face downward . . . Merdjan placed the stake on

---

suggested—from both the inscription and the skeletal remains—that the soles of the feet were attached bow-legged together and then the legs were looped over the top of the cross for the victim to hang upside down; see Yadin, "Epigraphy and Crucifixion," 18–22. If Yadin is right about the bow-legged method, whether the victim was upside down or not, the exposure of the genitals would have been particularly pronounced. See the two re-construction drawings in "Crucifixion, Method of" in *The Interpreter's Dictionary of the Bible Supplementary Volume*, 199–200, which bring out the display of the genitals in the second position although this is disguised by the loincloth.

54. Josephus *War* 5.446–452.

55. Seneca *To Marcia on Consolation* 20.3; cited in Hengel, *Crucifixion in the Ancient World and the Folly of the Cross*, 25.

56. Andrić, *The Bridge Over the Drina*. I am grateful to Ruth Gidley of the Guatemala Solidarity Network for first drawing my attention to this passage.

two small chocks so that it pointed between the peasant's legs. Then he took from his belt a short broad knife, knelt beside the stretched-out man and leant over him to cut away the cloth of his trousers and to widen the opening through which the stake would enter the body. This most terrible part of the bloody task was, luckily, invisible to the onlookers. They could only see the bound body shudder at the short and unexpected prick of the knife, then half rise as if it were going to stand up, only to fall back again at once, striking dully against the planks.[57]

There is insufficient evidence to judge whether any of the many crucifixions in Roman Palestine involved impalement or genital mutilation.[58] The possibility that this was the case, in at least some crucifixions, cannot be ruled out. A second-century drawing on a wall discovered at the Imperial Palace on the Palatine, pictures a man looking up at a crucifixion, with the victim of the crucifixion seen from behind the cross. The victim's arms are outstretched but his feet rest on a small beam allowing him to stand. A notable feature of the image is that although the body of the victim is human, the head is a donkey's.[59] A misspelled

57. Andrić, *The Bridge Over the Drina*, 48–49. On the influence of this story on Serb social memory and their attitudes to rape, see Boose, "Crossing the River Drina: Bosnian Rape Camps, Turkish Impalement, and Serb Cultural Memory," 91–96 (esp. 81–85). Boose graphically describes Andrić's account as "a four-hour rape scene" and argues for its importance at an unconscious level in Serb attitudes to rape, which contributed to atrocities committed in the 1990s.

58. Seneca's observations above carry weight, but he refers to his experiences elsewhere and suggests that they are exceptional. Josephus is not explicit, and in any case he is describing events that took place forty years after Jesus's crucifixion. Although Josephus implies something particularly brutal he leaves the nature of the grim joke unclear. Josephus's coyness in alluding only indirectly to the atrocity might suggest a sexual element to the violence but in the absence of other evidence it is not possible to determine this for certain. Equally, it is unclear whether Seneca's reference to impalement refers to impalement by the upright (presumably something akin to the passage from Andrić) or whether it might have been a protrusion from the main upright. An appropriately angled *sedile* could certainly serve this purpose, and could be set to repeatedly penetrate the victim as they struggled to rise up on their arms to breathe and then sagged back down on the peg.

59. This may reflect special crucifixions in Rome where animal skins or heads were placed on the victims to add to their humiliation. For example, Tacitus records that Nero's persecution of Christians in Rome had included covering some in animal skins to be torn apart by dogs, whilst others were fastened on crosses and burned at night; Tacitus *Ann.* 15.44.4.

note on the wall reads, "Alexamenos worships his God."[60] Because of
the inscription (and assuming the figure looking up is Alexamenos),
the drawing is usually understood as a mocking reference to Christ's
crucifixion. If so, it is probably the earliest image of Jesus's crucifixion
currently available and, although not historically reliable, it is intrigu-
ing that the victim seems to be at least partly impaled with the upright
emerging in his lower back.

The gospel texts (Mark 15:24, Matt 27:35, Lk 23:33, and John 19:18)
do not give a clear picture of how Jesus was attached to the cross. John
20:25 suggests that Jesus was nailed through his hands, though as noted
above, if his wrists were not tied as well, the hands would tear trying to
support the body on their own.[61] It is therefore more likely that Jesus
was nailed to the cross through his wrists, or that he was first tied at
the wrists and then nailed through the hands.[62] In any case, there is no
textual evidence to suggest that Jesus's crucifixion involved impalement
or physical penetration of the genital area. Nonetheless, even though it
is fair to assume that this was not the case, it is still very likely that the
association of crucifixion with sexual violence would have been much
more readily appreciated at the time than it is now.[63] The symbolism
involved in any penetration of the body carried a sexual message whatever form the crucifixion took. Unmanning the victim in the eyes of
the public was an intentional element of the punishment and a powerful warning to others.[64] Because of this, crucifixion has to be seen as a
sexualized form of torture.

60. Morton Smith suggests that the donkey's head was a slur, that mocked the faith
of the victim's followers in believing him to be divine by picturing him as the Egyptian
God Seth (for whom the donkey was the sacred animal); see Smith, *Jesus the Magician*,
62.

61. It is possible that John 20.25 might be translated as "arms" rather than "hands."

62. Tzaferis argues that Yehonahan was nailed through his wrists not hands;
Tzaferis, "Crucifixion: The Archaeological Evidence," 52.

63. This would have been all the more the case if crucifixion and impalement were
seen as closely related.

64. A passage from Josephus on the Hasmonean ruler Alexander Janneus (104–78
BCE) implies the sadistic sexual pleasures that some might actually enjoy in these spec-
tacles; see Josephus, *War* 1.97; idem., *Ant.* 13, 320. According to Josephus: "Eight hundred of the prisoners he impaled (crucified) in the middle of the City, then butchered
their wives and children before their eyes; meanwhile cup in hand he reclined amidst
his concubines and enjoyed the spectacle"; Josephus *War* 1.97. Josephus says that crucifying the men and killing their families in this way frightened those who opposed

The Unanswered Questions from the Praetorium

On the basis of the above, there is good reason to recognize the element of sexual humiliation involved in the Roman practice of flogging and crucifying victims naked, and to understand the penetrative element of crucifixion itself as sexualized torture. There is, however, still a further question about direct sexual violence.

Plato's description of tortures associated with crucifixion of a good man in the *Republic*, pictures the victim as being scourged, fettered, blinded, and finally, after the most extreme suffering, crucified.[65] In the *Gorgias* (473c), Plato also refers in a seemingly off-hand way to castration as a prelude to crucifixion, when he mentions it in his hypothetical example of the punishment of a tyrant.[66] In the Greco-Roman world, crucifixion could be readily linked to other extreme acts, and this raises questions about what further abuse Jesus might have suffered prior to crucifixion.

All the gospels, apart from Luke, report that when Jesus was handed over to the Roman soldiers they mocked him by placing a crown of thorns on his head (Mark 15:17, Matt 27:29, and John 19:2) and clothing him in a purple (Mark 15:17 and John 19:2) or scarlet (Matt 27:28) garment.[67] The texts also mention that the soldiers spat at Jesus (Mark 15:19 and Matt 27:30), struck him with a reed (Mark 15:19 and Matt 27:30), and mocked him with verbal taunts (calling him "King," Mark 15:18, Matt 27:29, and John 19:3) and symbolic homage (kneeling

---

Alexander so much that 8,000 fled in terror. This event has been central to discussion of whether the Jews themselves practised crucifixion in cases of high treason; see Hengel, *Crucifixion in the Ancient World and the Folly of the Cross*, 84–85.

65. Plato *Republic* 361e–362a.

66. Cited in Sloyan, *The Crucifixion of Jesus*, 16.

67. Luke places the mocking of Jesus earlier in the story at a point that is unlikely to have involved Roman soldiers. According to Luke 22:63–64, the mockery takes place prior to the trial before the Jewish elders. The mocking, beating, blindfolding, and challenges to prophesy (Luke makes no mention of spitting) were carried out by the men who were holding Jesus overnight before the trial before the Council. Presumably these were members of "the crowd" mentioned as capturing him in Luke 22:47, Mark 15:18–19, and Matt 26:67–68 also report that Jesus was spat at, struck, and challenged to prophesy, but both place this immediately after the Council had condemned him, rather than before, and say it was carried out by members of the Council themselves. John does not mention any parallel treatment associated with the questioning by the High Priest (John 18:19–24).

before him, Mark 15:19, Matt 27:29, and John 19:2).[68] The privacy of the *praetorium* (whether Pilate's palace or the Antonia fortress) means that the details of what transpired inside are inevitably circumstantial and would probably not have been known even at the time. However, there are a number of indications that suggest an important part of the picture would be left out if the possibility that sexual violence was used is not confronted.

Both Matthew and Mark describe Jesus as being handed over weakened and naked—already a condemned man without any recourse to justice—to soldiers who took him inside the *praetorium* and assembled the other troops.[69] Mark 15:16 states:

> Then the soldiers led him into the courtyard of the palace (that is the governor's headquarters); and they called together the whole cohort.[70]

Both gospels explicitly state that it was the whole cohort (*speira*) of Roman soldiers (between six hundred and one thousand men) that was assembled together to witness and participate in the "mockery." This probably included a significant number of Syrian auxiliaries who might have viewed their Jewish neighbors with particular hostility.[71] This detail of overwhelming and hostile military power sounds a particularly disturbing note, especially when considered in the light of testimonies from prisoners at Abu Ghraib who have claimed that in addition to well-known photos of abuse there were also cases of male rape.[72]

68. In addition, Matt 27:29 also mentions placing the reed in Jesus's right hand prior to striking him and although John makes no mention of a reed, John 19:3 records Jesus being struck in the face.

69. Luke does not refer to mistreatment in the *praetorium* but states that Jesus was mocked, beaten, blindfolded, and told to prophesy when in the High Priests house (Luke 22:63–65). He also includes a questioning before Herod and reports: "Even Herod with his soldiers treated him with contempt and mocked him; then he put an elegant robe on him, and sent him back to Pilate (Luke 23:11)."

70. Cp. Matt 27:27: "Then the soldiers of the governor took Jesus into the governor's headquarters, and they gathered the whole cohort around him."

71. Josephus suggests that, at least whilst Felix was procurator (52–60 CE), the majority of the Roman garrison in Caesarea were raised in Syria and they readily sided with the Syrian inhabitants of Caesarea in a civil dispute against its Jewish citizens; Josephus, *War* 2.266–270 [268].

72. For a sustained discussion of how some type of sexual violence go unreported— even by official truth commissions—see Tombs, "Unspeakable Violence: The Truth Commissions in El Salvador and Guatemala," 55–84.

Rape of male prisoners is a relatively common but frequently under-reported abuse during military conflicts.[73] In the bible, it is a fate that Saul understands when, after a military defeat, he begs his own sword-bearer to kill him. First Samuel 31:4 records:

> Then Saul said to his armor-bearer, 'Draw your sword and thrust through me with it, so that these uncircumcised may not come and thrust me through, and make sport of me.'[74]

King Zedekiah speaks of a similar fear when he rejects Jeremiah's demand that he end the doomed revolt against Nebuchadnezzar (Jer 37–39). He says: "I am afraid of the Judeans who have deserted to the Chaldeans (Babylonians), for I might be handed over to them and they would abuse me." The same word *ghalal* (meaning "to thrust in") is used in both verses and although not absolutely explicit is highly suggestive that Saul and Zedekiah both feared male rape.[75] Saul's reference to the "uncircumcised" suggests particular Jewish sensitivity in this matter, a concern that some of their enemies might have delighted in exploiting.

It is possible that Pilate deliberately handed Jesus over to be sexually assaulted or otherwise abused by his soldiers as part of his punishment. A "festive offering" of this sort to the troops would probably have strengthened rather than weakened his popularity.[76] Furthermore, it allowed Pilate to demonstrate his status as triumphant lord, able to display his manly prowess through the actions of his underlings. When members of all-male institutions like the military are kept from contact with women it often encourages men who are able to impose their will on men of inferior rank and/or status to force them to serve as "women" for them. One writer claimed: "bad army officers and wicked tyrants are

73. For example, Anna Politkovskaya (one of Russia's most respected journalists), reports from Chechnya: "The junior officers who interrogated them (Chechen men) told them that they had nice butts, and raped them. And they added as an excuse: 'Your women wouldn't let us fuck them'"; Politkovskaya, "Crisis in Chechnya."

74. I am grateful to John Jarick, St. Stephen's House, Oxford, for originally drawing my attention to this.

75. Edwardes notes that the Babylonian Talmud preserves a tradition that after the fall of the city Nebuchadnezzar violated all the Jewish leaders but was unable to violate Zedekiah; Edwardes, *Erotica Judaica*, 98–99.

76. Iris Chang reports on the rape of Nanking that: "Chinese men were often sodomized or forced to perform a variety of repulsive sexual acts in front of laughing Japanese soldiers"; Chang, *The Rape of Nanking: The Forgotten Holocaust of World War II*, 95.

the main sources of rapes of young men."[77] If this was common in the treatment of low-ranking soldiers, it was probably all the more likely in the treatment of prisoners.[78] Thus, despite the attempts of the Gospels to excuse Pilate from blame over the treatment of Jesus, if an assault did take place in the *praetorium*, presumably it would have done so only with Pilate's positive approval or at least his knowing indifference.

If this is plausible, perhaps even the widely held assumption that the soldiers forced Jesus to wear scarlet/purple clothing for the purposes of political mockery might be reconsidered. Richard Trexler points out that dressing a male victim in bright clothing was sometimes a prelude to sexual assault.[79] Clement of Alexandria's discussion in *Paidagogos* is particularly interesting in this regard. Clement encourages women to ward-off compliments about their looks by wearing a veil across their faces. However, he warns against using a purple veil:

> If I could but wring the purple out of all the veils, that passers-by might not turn to catch a glimpse of the face behind it! Yet, such women, who weave almost the whole ensemble of their wardrobe, make everything purple to inflame lusts.[80]

77. Cited in Richlin, *The Garden of Priapus: Sexuality and Aggression in Roman Humour*, 225; Cp. Trexler, *Sex and Conquest: Gendered Violence, Political Order, and the European Conquest of the Americas*, 34. On the rites of sexual humiliation that are often part of military training in the British army; see Burke, "Sex Fear of Army Teens." A U.S. Defence Department survey of female graduates from the Air Force Academy indicated that 1 in 8 of cadets experienced rape or attempted rape during training; see Schemo, "Rate of Rape at Academy is put at 12% in Survey," A12.

78. The high level of male rape in U.S. prisons indicates that male rape is much more common when men's opportunities to express power and dominance over women are limited. Soldiers in an all-male institution like the army may behave the same way, especially if they have little contact with women. In the first and second centuries CE, Roman soldiers were not allowed to marry during military service. This rule probably originated with Augustus and seems to have remained in force until Septimus Severus abolished it in 197 CE; see Campbell, *The Roman Army: 31 BC–AD 337 A Sourcebook*, 151–60. Despite this, some soldiers in the more permanent bases and garrisons seem to have formed unions with women who lived in nearby settlements known as *canabae*, see Davies, *Service in the Roman Army*, esp. 67. Depending on the posting there might also be access to brothels and/or camp prostitutes. However, whether there was a Roman *canabae* in Palestine is unknown. Likewise, how easily Roman soldiers might visit—or be visited by—a prostitute is also unclear.

79. At very least it could have been intended as a sexual insult, perhaps akin to the photos of male prisoners in Abu Ghraib with women's underwear over their heads.

80. Clement of Alexandria *Paid.* 2.10.114. I am grateful to Michel Desjardins for drawing this to my attention.

A little later Clement warns:

> For the sake of this purple, Tyre and Sidon and the shores of the Laconian Sea are sedulously cultivated . . . Affected women and men who are effeminate in their self indulgence have become insanely covetous of these artificial dyes to color their fine woven robes . . .[81]

If some form of sexual assault occurred in the *praetorium*, it would be simplistic to suppose that it could only have been penile rape, or even that this would have been most likely. Williams notes that the social stigma of effeminacy was even stronger for men who fellated (and who were thereby orally penetrated) than for men who were anally penetrated. This led some Roman writers to suggest that forced fellation might be an even more severe punishment than anal rape.[82]

Alternatively, within the *praetorium* the soldiers might have used knives, stakes, or other "foreign objects" to carry out a bodily violation or mutilation. In Ivo Andrić's account of the preparation for impalement (above), it is notable that what he refers to as "the most terrible part" was widening the anal opening with a knife so that it could receive the stake. Presumably the same step was involved in Roman impalements and Roman soldiers who were used to this might even have humiliated a victim in this way even if it was not directly required for the form of crucifixion that was to be used.[83]

A biblical suggestion of something similar to this is offered in Numbers 25, where Moses is told to punish the unfaithful Israelites by impaling the ringleaders in the sun (Num 25:4).[84] Just as Moses is relating this instruction to his faithful followers they see an Israelite

81. Clement of Alexandria *Paid.* 2.10.115. It should also be noted that the Romans especially associated soft effeminate men (*cinaedi*) with the East.

82. Williams, *Roman Homosexuality*, 197–203 (esp. 201). On reports of sexual intimidation of Iraqi prisoners, in which Iraqi prisoners were forced to kneel in front of trouser-less British soldiers that pre-date the Abu Ghraib scandal, see Burke, "Sex Fear of Army Teens."

83. In the case of castration, the soldiers might even have been aware of the specific cultural implications of their actions. The prohibition against eunuchs in Deut 23:1 is phrased as "No one whose testicles are crushed or whose penis is cut off shall be admitted to the assembly of the Lord." (However, this is subsequently contradicted by Isa 56:3–4.).

84. According to Num 25:1, the Israelites had been unfaithful by having sexual relations with the women of Moab and yoking themselves to the Baal of Peor.

man (Zim'ri son of Salu) take a Moabite woman (Coz'bi) into his tent. At this point Phin'ehas takes his spear, goes into the tent, and is said to pierce both Zim'ri and Coz'bi in one stroke (Num 25.8). Although not absolutely explicit there is a suggestion of sexual violence in the language here and at least some rabbinic commentators understood the spear as going through the sexual organs.[85] However, the suggestion of sexual violence is easily lost in translation and most English translations are more circumspect. The RSV says he pierced them "through the body" and the NRSV "through the belly." Others, like the RNEB, do not mention which part of the body, only stating that, "he transfixed the two of them, the Israelite and the woman, pinning them together." The Jerusalem Bible is an exception to this because it says the thrust was "right through the groin" and the Vulgate is even more frank in its reference to *in locis genitalibus*.

Along the same lines, Suetonius refers to a new torture introduced by Domitian (81–96 CE) that applied fire to the private parts of victims.[86] If Suetonius is right that this was a new torture, then it could not have been practiced in Jesus's day, at least in this form. However, Josephus's account of the siege of Jerusalem[87] suggests that there were a wide variety of cruel sexual tortures available. In his description of the way that Jewish militants inside Jerusalem mistreated the civilian population he writes:

> They stuffed bitter vetch up the genital passages of their victims, and drove sharp stakes into their seats.[88]

Given the political and gendered symbolism of such violations, there is no need to suppose that they were intended to give sexual pleasure as such.[89] Making sport of the victim and adding to his pain and shame is sufficient reason for sexual torture of this type. If the soldiers

---

85. See *Midrash Rabbâh* and *Neziqîn: Sanhedrin*; cited in Edwardes, *Erotica Judaica*, 17–18.

86. Suetonius *Dom.*, 10.

87. Josephus *War* 5.420–572.

88. Josephus *War* 5.435.

89. For further discussion of these dynamics in a contemporary context, see Tombs, "Honour, Shame and Conquest: Male Identity, Sexual Violence and the Body Politic," 21–40.

had been aware of Jesus's reputation as a religious teacher this might have added to their amusement.[90]

There will never be a clear answer to the question of what happened inside the *praetorium*. Nonetheless, the suspicions raised by the experiences of those who have suffered in torture centers in more recent times suggest that a question mark needs to be put against the completeness of the gospel narratives at this point. Testimonies of sexual violence and humiliations in modern torture centers are not direct evidence for what happened in first-century Palestine. They are nonetheless highly suggestive of the types of abuse that can take place within closed walls, and alongside other evidence of Roman practices they raise important questions as to what may have happened in the *praetorium*.

Whereas the gospel texts offer clear indications of sexual humiliation as part of flogging and crucifixion—in the enforced nakedness and symbolism of penetration—the possibility of sexual assault in the *praetorium* can be based only on silence, circumstance, and the conventions of the day. However, it should be remembered that although a distinction in sexual abuse between humiliation and assault is helpful, there can also be considerable overlap between them and the two tend to go together. In sexual torture, sexual assault is also a form of sexual humiliation. Conversely, sexual humiliation often rests on the threat or fact of physical or sexual assault. What form of sexual assault—if any— might actually have taken place may be impossible to determine, but the possibility needs to be recognized and confronted more honestly than has happened so far. It is disturbing but possible that the fraternal and respectful kiss of greeting in the Garden of Gethsemane might have set in motion the events that led to some form of sexual assault in the *praetorium*.

Conclusion

The extensive media coverage of Abu Ghraib has generated a new iconic image of torture in a hooded prisoner standing on a box with arms outstretched like Christ, and wires attached to his fingers, toes, and

---

90. Iris Chang suggests that Japanese soldiers took particular delight in forcing Buddhist monks (and others who had taken religious vows of celibacy) to engage in sexual acts; Chang, *The Rape of Nanking*, 95. If this was the case for Jesus, normal Jewish sensitivities over the privacy of sexual activity might have added to the soldiers' sense of delight; see Boyarin, *Carnal Israel: Reading Sex in Talmudic Culture*, 125.

penis.[91] Yet the revelations from Abu Ghraib have not yet prompted Christians to re-read the story of Christ's crucifixion with attention to the sexual dimension that is so common in torture practices.

Reading the gospels with an awareness of how sexual humiliation was used against prisoners at Abu Ghraib highlights aspects of the text that are otherwise easily passed over. Prior to crucifixion, Jesus was handed over to a cohort of Roman soldiers to be further humiliated by being undressed, dressed and undressed again (Mark 15:16–20, Matt 27:28–31, and John 19:1–5).[92] Based on what the gospel texts themselves indicate, the sexual humiliation in this treatment is unavoidable. An adult man was stripped naked for flogging, then dressed in an insulting way to be mocked, struck, and spat at by a multitude of soldiers before being stripped again (at least in Mark 15:19 and Matt 27:30) and re-clothed for his journey through the city—already too weak to carry his own cross—only to be stripped again (a third time) and left naked to die in front of a mocking crowd. When the textual presentation is stated like this, the sexual element of the humiliation becomes clear.[93] If this assertion is controversial, it is not because it is not supported by the text but because the implications of stripping a defenseless prisoner naked at least three times in a short space of time are too disturbing and it is usually easier to pass over it in silence.

Beyond this, it is also necessary to appreciate that in its cultural context the penetrative aspects of crucifixion had a readily sexual significance, and that this was an intentional part of the torture practice. Crucifixions could include violent penetrations of the genital areas as documented in Roman sources and confirmed in crucifixions from other historical periods. Furthermore, in Roman times, even where the body was penetrated in places not usually seen as sexual, the symbolism of penetration would nonetheless always have been understood as

---

91. See Danner, *Torture and Truth*, 8.

92. For Mark and Matthew this happens at the end of the trial and both mention it taking place in the *praetorium*. For John the mockery takes place during the trial within Pilate's headquarters (John 18:28).

93. Whilst the focus here has been on how the gospel texts present events without necessarily pressing behind beyond this to ask about historicity, the picture of abuse they present is historically plausible. Furthermore, given the shame and embarrassment that would have been associated with sexual abuse, it is unlikely that the gospels would have introduced it into the narrative unless it had some historical foundation.

having a sexual edge. The shape of the cross itself would have been seen in this context.

Finally, whilst by no means conclusive, there is a clear possibility that the abuse in the *praetorium* may have included further forms of sexual humiliations or even some form of male rape. At the very least, it needs to be recognized that such things were common practice, that they fit the general picture of crucifixion that the gospels offer, and that could have easily been part of what Jesus suffered.

It is striking that there is no acknowledgment of this side of Christ's suffering in *The Passion of the Christ*. Despite its graphic portrayal of physical pain, the movie hides the full cruelty of crucifixion. It is as if sexual humiliation is a taboo that prevents the full-story from being told, as if it is too much for Christ to suffer. To picture Jesus as naked and powerless before the resurrection would have gone against Gibson's understanding of Christ's power, manliness, and sanctity. It is signifi-cant that in *The Passion of the Christ* it is only in the very last scene, where Jesus is witnessed rising triumphant from death, that he is briefly glimpsed as naked, and his garments left behind. It seems that it is only when Jesus is risen and glorious is it safe to picture him as naked.[94]

Yet, whilst acknowledging the challenges that thinking of crucifix-ion as sexually abusive may bring up for Christian faith, it should also be stressed that understanding the extent of Jesus's torture gives a more authentic insight into his real humanity. Jesus was a real person who suffered as other people suffer. Jesus didn't live in sanitized isolation. It is wrong to sanitize the historical record to suggest that he did. He faced the same evils as others of his day would have faced, and as others have faced since. However, naming this abuse and raising further ques-tions about it is not intended to valorize the cross. Nor is it to suggest that there is something admirable about Jesus's suffering that is to be imitated today. On the contrary, it helps to show why such abuse should never be permitted.

First, the cross is a reminder that torture is often not about gather-ing intelligence. Attempts to justify torture in these terms are often a smokescreen. Torture is an exercise in power and is used to convey the

---

94. See the reference to the linen wrappings left behind with the rising of the body, Luke 24:12 and John 20:5–7. Benedict Fitzgerald says the scene is based on a painting he saw in Florence by Andrea del Sarto (1486–1531) showing Jesus staring at his hands in the tomb; see Shepherd, "From Gospel to Gibson: An Interview with the Writers."

apparent omnipotence of the torturer. Whether the victim has any intelligence information to give, and whether this information is reliable or not, is beside the point. The real purpose of torture is to humiliate and dehumanize the victim in ways that will terrorize others as well. Roman crucifixions were used to intimidate whole populations. In the same way, the pictures of torture at Abu Ghraib were used to frighten new prisoners into compliance and obedience.

Second, understanding the reality of the cross makes clear that Christians should do all they can to protest all such abuses today. The first and most compelling reason not to use torture is that it is unethical to treat any human being in this way. If Christians recognize in the abuses at Abu Ghraib the same abuses that were endured by Christ, they have even more reason to make sure that international laws on torture and the treatment of prisoners are respected. Political leaders, especially political leaders who espouse Christian faith, need to be called to account when they seek ways to set these laws aside.

9

Islam, Women, and the Politics of Violence: Illustrations from the Middle East

Haleh Afshar

THERE IS A TENDENCY FOR OBSERVERS TO BRAND ISLAM AS A FAITH TO be intrinsically violent both to its women and on the world stage. Such discussions imagine Muslim women as silent obedient victims hidden in the cloak of the *hijab* awaiting the return of their men to the home and the brave warriors to the hearth. It is the contention of this paper that such imaginings, though sometimes encouraged by some Muslim men, remain far from the truth. These ascribed identities are perhaps better understood in the context of the history of Orientalism rather than Islam.

As violence in the Middle East escalates, so does Islamaphobic propaganda, creating a climate of fear and distrust that makes interfaith understanding between "Islam and the rest" about the complexities of culture and faith extremely difficult. This chapter endeavors to highlight some of the misconceptions about Islam brought about by this climate. In particular, it demonstrates that violence against any human being is abhorrent to Islamic teachings, but when it comes to defending the nation or the cause of justice, Muslims, be they male or female, like people the world over, are likely to resort to violence. To begin, some of the general arguments about Islam and violence will be explored, focusing more specifically on questions relating to violence against women. Consideration will then be given to the argument that Muslim women are as a matter of history, culture, and practice secluded and in need of men's protection. In reality, such imaginings echo the traditions of

Orientalists who branded an entire region as exotic but unintelligent and hidebound in need of Western assistance to become politically and socially civilized. The chapter will conclude by considering some of the recent struggles of Muslim women who, in the name of their faith, have argued for different pathways to peace.

Orientalism

It may be argued that many commentators, firmly anchored in the West, have returned to the historical perspectives constructed by the Orientalists to Otherize an entire faith and its followers. Edward Said coined the word Orientalism to analyze the way that Western scholarship reflected a distorted image of the East. He argued that the work of imperialists, though rigorous in many ways, was rooted in the limitations of their experiences of the East. They used these narrow experiences to construct "an accepted grid for filtering through the Orient into Western consciousness."[1] As a result, the Orient was seen as essentially ancient, exotic, and absurd; a land of despots and mystics; populated by a backward population of supine men and subordinated, silent women. Life experiences in general and those of women in particular were assumed to be fundamentally different, not only in terms of faith and culture but specifically in terms of intellectual caliber. It was assumed that the Oriental mind was distinct and different from that of the Occident.

The Oriental was understood as being inferior and uncivilized, and the Oriental woman was assumed to be alluring, be-witching, and extremely dangerous.[2] Often these understandings were constructed by scholars and painters who had no access to the lives of women and chose to present their own fantasies as true images. This Otherizing, in turn, resulted in a deeply rooted belief that the Orientals could only progress, within their limited abilities, if they looked to the Occident. Over the decades, scholars have considered the ways that this process of Otherization has misrepresented and caricaturized the Oriental Other in terms of sex, gender, race, ethnicity, and religion.[3] Most attribute the

1. Said, *Orientalism: Western Conceptions of the Orient*, 5–6.

2. Stott, *The Fabrication of the late-Victorian Femme Fatale: The Kiss of Death*.

3. Albet-Mas, "Voices from the Margins: Gendered Images of 'Otherness' in Colonial Morocco"; Amstutz, *Interpreting Amida: History and Orientalism in the Study of Pure Land Buddhism;* Jeyifo, "On Mazrui's 'Black Orientalism': A Cautionary Critique"; Kahani-Hopkins, "'Representing' British Muslims: the Strategic Dimension to

labeling of the entire Orient as the Other a direct result of the power of imperialists to frame the scholarship and understanding of the West about the rest. Many argue that the disparity of power that existed between the scholars of those they were analyzing was central in this process of Otherization.[4]

The vast Orientalist literature simply ignored the dynamic millennial interactions between the Orient and the West that then, as now, impacted on, shaped, and reshaped the ideas, philosophies, art, and literature of both.[5] Those who were labeled Oriental were categorized as members of "a subject race"[6] that had to be ruled for their own good, but also only to the level of their limited intellectual capacity. The static torpor of the East had to be conquered by the dynamism of Western modernity to benefit the West and perhaps edge the Orient towards Occidental levels of civilization. The problem was the unwillingness of the Oriental subjects to yield to this project. This resistance was merely projected as yet more evidence of their inability to grasp Western concepts and meanings.

Islamaphobia

Orientalism is not merely part of a forgotten past; it remains very much at the core of the current Western conceptions of race and gender in Islam and attitudes on the various conflicts in the Middle East. Islamaphobia is an "unfounded hostility towards Islam, and therefore fear or dislike of all or most Muslims." A report by the Commission on British Muslims and Islamophobia noted that Islamaphobia defines Islam as being monolithic, separate, and Other; without any common values with other cultures; and essentially barbaric and sexist. Muslims

Identity Construction"; Lewis, *Gendering Orientalism: Race, Femininity and Representation;* Mazrui, "Black Orientalism? Further Reflections on 'Wonders of the African World'"; Prasch, "Orientalism's Other, Other Orientalisms: Women in the Scheme of Empire"; Zubaida, "Is there a Muslim Society? Ernest Gellner's Sociology of Islam."

4. Minear, "Orientalism and the Study of Japan"; Musallam, "Power and Knowledge."

5. Akhavi, "Islam and the West in World History"; Moallem, *Between Warrior Brother and Veiled Sister: Islamic Fundamentalism and the Politics of Patriarchy in Iran;* Najmabadi, *Women with Mustaches and Men without Beards: Gender and Sexual identities of Iranian Modernity.*

6. Said, *Orientalism: Western Conceptions of the Orient,* 206–7.

are therefore imagined as being fundamentally uncivilized and unwilling to conform to the values of the West.[7] It is therefore assumed that there must be a "clash of civilizations" between Muslims and the West that could only harm the latter.[8] It is the contention of this chapter that this assumption is rooted in the perception of the Oriental as the Other.

Muslims are often denounced the as the enemy within, often from the pages of major circulation newspapers. This was the case even before 9/11. One opinion piece from *The Daily Express* (circulation about 800,000 daily) in 1995 stated that:

> they (Muslims) are backward and evil, and if it is being racist to say so then I must be and happy and proud to be so.[9]

After 9/11, the language only intensified. An opinion piece in November 2001 in *The Sunday Times* (with a circulation of 1.3 million once a week, making it the dominant Sunday broadsheet), claimed:

> We have a fifth column in our midst . . . Thousands of alienated young Muslims, most of them born and bred here but who regard themselves as an army within, are waiting for an opportunity to help to destroy the society that sustains them. We now stare into the abyss, aghast.[10]

The Islamophobia expressed in the above statements, and many others, inflamed the already tense situation post 9/11. The resultant climate of hatred would have severe repercussions. Perhaps one of the most prophetic reports on this subject was that of the above-mentioned Commission on British Muslims and Islamophobia. In June 2004, prior to the 7/7 attacks on the London Underground, it warned that Islamophobia in the United Kingdom, including increased attacks against individuals and mosques, was resulting in bitterness that created violent "time-bombs."[11] The commission was concerned that

7. Commission on British Muslims and Islamophobia, *Islamophobia: A Challenge for Us All.*

8. Huntington, "The Clash of Civilizations."

9. Kilroy-Silk, *The Daily Express*, January 15, 1995.

10. Phillips, *The Sunday Times*, November 4, 2001.

11. Casciani, "Islamophobia pervades UK—report." Available from http://news .bbc.co.uk/2/hi/uk_news/3768327.stm.

previous suggestions for dealing with Islamaphobia had not been taken and as a result:

> The cumulative effect of Islamophobia's various features . . . is that Muslims are made to feel that they do not truly belong here—they feel that they are not truly accepted, let alone welcomed, as full members of British society. On the contrary, they are seen as "an enemy within" or "a fifth column" and they feel that they are under constant siege. This is bad for society as well as for Muslims themselves. Moreover, time-bombs are being primed that are likely to explode in the future—both Muslim and non-Muslim commentators have pointed out that a young generation of British Muslims is developing that feels increasingly disaffected, alienated and bitter.[12]

The report recommended that Islamophobia be "rigorously challenged, reduced and removed." However, the advice was not heeded and one year after the report came out, on July 7, 2005, the "time bombs" went off. The 7/7 attacks on the London underground exacerbated the situation and the language of war flourished.

Perhaps the clearest pathological statement was that made in *The Sunday Telegraph* (circulation about 680,000) by Harry (Will) Cummins, who was a senior press officer with the British Council (the UK's public diplomacy and cultural organization) at the time he wrote:

> All Muslims, like all dogs, share certain characteristics. A dog is not the same animal as a cat just because both species are comprised of different breeds. An extreme Christian believes that the Garden of Eden really existed; an extreme Muslim flies planes into buildings—there's a big difference.[13]

According to the leader of the opposition in the UK, David Cameron, the threat from extremist Islamist terrorism would have to be countered at all costs:

> we can and should try to understand the nature of the force that we need to defeat. The driving force behind today's terrorist threat is Islamist fundamentalism. The struggle we are engaged in is, at root, ideological. During the last century, a strain of

12. Commission on British Muslims and Islamophobia, *Islamophobia: Issues, Challenges and Action,* 9. Available from www.insted.co.uk/islam.html.

13. Cummins, "Muslims are a threat to our way of life." Available from http://www.telegraph.co.uk/opinion/main.jhtml?xml=/opinion/2004/07/25/do2504.xml.

Islamist thinking has developed which, like other totalitarianisms, such as Nazism and Communism, offers its followers a form of redemption through violence.[14]

Cameron's comparisons between Islamist fundamentalists and Nazis continued. This depiction of the world as black and white, with the West being pure good and the Other being evil, was not new. Back in 2004 world leaders such as George Bush were already declaring that there is:

> no neutral ground in the fight between civilization and terror . . . because there is no neutral ground between good and evil, freedom and slavery, and life and death.[15]

"Good" was intended to serve as a synonym for "American" and "evil" meant to mean "Other." By using this broad brush, the term "evil" could be applied to specific people, regimes, or peoples.[16] The lack of a middle ground left little place for most Muslims, who are loath to support Western versions of civilization but also not necessarily supporters of some terrorist tactics. Thus, Muslims in general and in the Middle East in particular were burdened with the labels of terrorism, evilness, and enslavement; the latter is particularly interesting since, despite the myth of white slavery, enslavement has been a very specific feature of North American economic development.

The division of the world between Orient and Occident has led some commentators, such as columnist and Author Melanie Phillips, to express a fear of being overrun:

> from the 1990s, Islamist radicals had been given free rein in Britain in a "gentlemen's agreement" that if they were left alone, they would not turn on the country that was so generously nurturing them. The result was "Londonistan," as Britain became the hub of al-Qaeda in Europe . . . no fewer than 1,200 Islamist terrorists are biding their time within British suburbs . . . Trained "Afghan Arab" warriors made their way instead to Britain, attracted, they said, by its "traditions of democracy and justice."

14. Cameron, "Full text, David Cameron's speech." Available from http://education .guardian.co.uk/faithschools/story/0,13882,1555406,00.html.

15. For text of Bush's speech see http://www.sfgate.com/cgi-bin/article.cgi?file=/ c/a/2004/03/20/MNG355OKV91.DTL

16. For a discussion on the language used to create the identity of "evil" terrorists and "good" America see Jackson, *Writing the War on Terrorism*, 66–70.

> But they had now been trained to be killers. They had discov-
> ered jihad. And the radical ideology they brought with them
> found many echoes in the Islamism and seething resentments
> that, by now, were entrenched in British Muslim institutions.[17]

Embedded in these statements is the assumption that the West and its warriors must rush to bomb the Middle East to democracy and liberate the Muslim woman from the chains imposed on her by her faith. Such an analysis, by its very nature, makes the *mohajebeh*, women who cover, into objects of pity; they have been forced to cover and therefore must be liberated, in the West as well as in the East; even if this has to be done at the expense of closing the doors of schools to them. The few who can imagine that the very act of veiling may imply that she would chose to publicly label herself as Muslim, see this very action not only as "threatening to the very fabric of society"[18] but also as an act of desperation and thus a dangerous deed.[19]

Nor is Islamaphobia limited to the U.S. and the UK. As Ziauddin Sardar notes:

> from Germany to the Netherlands, onwards to Belgium and fi-
> nally into France—the object of much recent attention—I meet
> people all too ready to describe Muslims in the colours of dark-
> ness. Islamophobia is not a British disease: it is a common, if
> diverse, European phenomenon. It is the singular rock against
> which the tide of European liberalism crashes.[20]

It is clear that in the wake the 9/11 attacks Islamaphobia has gained a momentum of its own, creating a ravine between Muslims and non-Muslims in the West. The Otherization of the Orient has contributed to a belief in an inevitable clash of civilization and this has subsequently been reified.

Islam, Women, and Violence

The condemnation of Islam as a faith that is intolerant, violent in general, and specifically cruel to its women has become an almost favorite pastime with many Muslims and non Muslims in the West. In the

17. Phillips, *The Observer*, May 28, 2006.

18. Barry, "Democracy Needs Dialogue and Deliberation—Not Political Blocs," 26.

19. Moore, "Dutch Convert to Islam: Veiled and Viewed as a 'Traitor.'"

20. Sardar, *The Listener*, December 5, 2005.

United States, Syrian born Wafa Sultan denounced the teachings and practice of Islam as "barbaric" and "medieval."[21] The Somali-born Dutch politician Ayaan Hirsi Ali blames the practice of female circumcision in Muslim North Africa on her faith rather than the culture of the region. And Irshad Manji, a Canadian of Pakistani descent, attacks Islam for intolerance and violence against women.[22] This cacophony is echoed by non-Muslims.

In this discourse of hate, covered women are singled out as the living example of backwardness and fearful subordination. Islam is considered to have defined itself "through disgust for women's bodies."[23] Polly Toynbee, in fact, lashed out announcing that that the veil arouses lasciviousness:

> More moderate versions of the garb—dull, uniform coat to the ground and the plain headscarf—have much the same effect, inspiring lascivious thoughts they are designed to stifle.

Toynbee suggests that Islam defines itself, "through disgust for women's bodies."[24] A collection of leading ladies in the West have already proclaimed their grave concern over the dress code of Afghan women and their intention liberate them at all costs.[25]

These beliefs about Islam are rooted in a superficial understanding of the faith and an inability to engage with the vibrant discussions initiated by Muslim women. Over the past century and a half, women have contested many of the misinterpretations of the Qur'an that had become part and parcel of the thirteen centuries of interpretation and instruction by men about the lives of women. At the core of the contestations has been the question of violence against women.

Oft quoted Qur'anic injunctions have been misinterpreted as giving men authority over women (IV:25) and permitting them to beat their disobedient wives (IV:34). Some male and many women scholars have addressed these misinterpretations, demonstrating quite clearly

---

21. Sultan, *The Sunday Times,* March 19, 2006.

22. Manji, *The Trouble with Islam Today: A Wakeup Call for Honesty and Change.*

23. Toynbee, *The Guardian*, September 28, 2001.

24. Ibid.

25. For one example, see Laura Bush's November 19, 2001 radio address available at http://www.whitehouse.gov/news/releases/2001/11/20011117.html.

that many prevalent cultural conceptions are incorrect.[26] The veil however remains highly contested.[27]

The process of deconstruction and reconstruction of the Qur'an has been multi-dimensional. Some scholars have argued that, in essence, Islam is egalitarian and to understand it as such sheds a light on the Qur'an that enables believers to understand the fundamental respect Islam has for equality amongst all. Others demand that the textual specificities of the Qur'an be respected and not extended. Thus, for example, where the Qur'an states that two women's evidence is equal to that of one man, the faithful must note that this stipulation applies only to a particular transaction concerning negotiation for a debt (II:282); it cannot be extended to all other activities. Similarly, when the Qur'an gives an injunctions to the believers not to marry more than one wife (IV:3) they should act accordingly.

Some scholars argue that Qur'anic text has different forms of narrative as far as the believers are concerned: the descriptive and illustrative, the advisory and the prescriptive. The descriptive describes a historical situation without condoning it. Often the Qur'an may even suggest that such situations could be improved. Thus, for example, when the text states that men beat their disobedient wives (IV:34), this merely describes what happened at the time; it is not an injunction demanding that men should beat up their wives. Similarly, the statement that good women are obedient can be seen as merely illustrative. Other verses are advisory, such as the one cited above that suggests good men marry only one wife. There are parts of the Qur'an that delineate contractual obligations and procedures, like a marriage contract where the certain prescribed individuals are allowed to determine the terms. Finally there are the injunctions that are addressed to the believers and must be obeyed. The injunctions, which are few, are on the whole commandments demanding that the believers behave with honesty and integrity, pray regularly, and not disinherit their dependents.

26. Afshar, *Islam and Feminisms: an Iranian Case Study;* Ahmed, *Women and Gender in Islam;* Engineer, *The Rights of Women in Islam;* Hassan, "Made from Adam's Rib: The Woman's Creation Question"; Mir-Hosseini, *Islam and Gender: The Religious Debate in Contemporary Iran.*

27. Mernissi, *Beyond the Veil;* Milani, *Veils and Words: The Emerging Voids of Iranian Women Writers;* Shaarawi, *Harem Years: The Memoirs of an Egyptian Feminist (1879-1924);* Shirazi, *The Veil Unveiled: Hijab in Modern Culture;* Williams, "A Return to the Veil in Egypt."

Defending this interpretative approach the scholar Mohsen Qaeni states that in the discourse of *fiqh*, Islamic jurisprudence,[28] there is a question about the importance of Qur'anic dictum and its application to the lives of those who have not been directly addressed by the relevant verse. The question is whether it is possible to find a rationale for extending stipulations addressed to a particular individual or group to the community of Muslims as a whole? Qaeni is of the opinion that since God is almighty, Qur'anic statements would have included everyone if that had been his wish:

> Why has the Qur'an not stated categorically 'Good women, obey the men' . . . why has it not done so, as it has in the case of *namaz* prayers and *ruzeh*, fast? . . . Why has it not issued a direct commandment? This is because it is how things were at the time. But it was common practice in this as in the case of marriage, the situations are a matter of contract and agreement by the signatories.[29]

Women Warriors

Persian Women in War

A second unfortunate trend in the combination of Islamaphobia and Orientalism that obscures reality is the stereotypical representation of Muslim women as submissive, covered, hidden, and absent from the public domain. Historically women in the Middle East have had far greater influence on the destiny of their nations than appears in the Western accounts. Throughout the ages, they have been active participants in wars, not only as camp followers, caregivers, and providers, but also as generals and combatants.

If we take Iran as a case study, we can see that women were present in the public sphere and at the battlefronts at the inception of the Persian Empire. High-profile women headed the army and navy. The Commander of the Immortal Guards of Cyrus the Great, who came to power in 559 BCE, was a woman called Panthea. Similarly, Darius the Great's army was led by a woman called Artunis. Pari Satis, the wife

---

28. *Fiqh* is often considered at expansion of *Sharia* to include legal rulings (*fatawa*) by scholars.

29. Qaeni, *Zanan*.

of Darius the second, was a field marshal and his daughter, Amestris, was a commander of the army. The powerful Grand Admiral and leader of the Persian navy during Xerxes reign was a woman called Artemis. At the end of the era, a woman called Youtab who was commander Achaemenids's Army fought the Greeks and Macedonians to the death (480 BCE). Some women warriors such as Artemis and Youtab became legends in her own time. The Ashkanid and subsequently the Sassanid dynasties continued this tradition. At the invasion of the Arabs (651 CE), the forces of Emperor Yadgar III were led by the legendry woman Apranik. Though Persia was eventually defeated, women warriors such as Negan and Banu continued to lead the resistance movement. Sadly Orientalist literature does not look back at this long history of civilization in Persia that, from its inception, included women in command positions.

Islamic Women in Wars and the Public Sphere

Though the faith in Iran changed to Islam, women remained important in the destiny of their nation; the Caliph Al Ma'mun (813 CE) appointed a woman, Buran, as his *vazir* (advisor). This was possible because Islam at its inception was far from misogynistic and had powerful women shaping its destiny. The first convert to Islam was the Prophet's wife Khadijeh, who was powerful and wealthy enough to offer him economic security and political protection. After her death, the Prophet migrated from Mecca to Medina. In the subsequent wars he waged, the Prophet was often accompanied by women. His wife Ayisha played a pivotal part in the future of Islam. She was a close friend and companion of the Prophet and he called on the faithful to recognize her as the mother of all Muslims. She related more than 2,000 sayings of the Prophet Mohamad; 170 of these have been approved by the strict Islamic scholar Bukhari who himself included 54 of the sayings in his treaties.[30]

After the Prophet's death, Ayisha was instrumental in the selection of the first caliph. She called on the eldest companions of the Prophet to meet and come to a decision about the next caliph; this process of consultation, *ijma*, has remained important in Islamic politics ever since. The Libyan Jamahiriya system, which demands of every citizen to participate in decision-making meetings, is rooted in this

---

30. Husayn, *Shahirat al-nisaalam al-islamiyya*. 33.

precedent.[31] Ayisha's father, Abu Bakre, was selected as the next caliph and the subsequent caliphs, Omar and Othman, also enjoyed her support. However, when the Prophet's cousin and son-in-law, Ali, was selected as the fourth Caliph, Ayisha raised an army and went into battle against him. Although she was defeated, she returned to her home with respect. This may well be seen as one of the early points at which Muslim male leaders began distrusting women in the public sphere.

Nevertheless, Muslim women continued to participate in wars and struggles across the centuries. To take Iran as an example again, the long history of women's participation in wars, protests, revolutions, and rebellions continued. In Iran, revolutions prove they have real and extensive popular support when women take to the streets. In the late nineteenth century, veiled women led riots demanding cheaper bread. Their presence convinced the Qajar king that he needed to respond positively to that demand. In another instance, early in the reign of the Qajar king Nasseredin Shah, the price of copper imported from Britain spiraled, which had a crippling effect on artisans in the bazaars. In Isfahan, the wives and female relatives of the guildsmen organized a public demonstration; attacking the British consulate there. The consulate reported the event to the ambassador in Tehran and he immediately ordered the price of copper be halved.[32]

Similarly, women played an important role in the tobacco revolution of 1881. When Nasseredin Shah granted a tobacco monopoly to a British company, allowing them to control the industry from the point of production to consumption, women protested. The handing over of such a lucrative industry to a foreign company met with intense opposition among the merchant classes and their close allies in the religious establishment. As a result, the eminent Shiia leader Haj Mirza Hassan Shirazi issued a *fatwa*, or religious order, banning the use of tobacco. The entire nation obeyed. Women of all classes, including the royal entourage, felt so outraged that they broke their water pipes and gave up smoking. When the Shah smoked a water pipe (*qualyan*), in the presence of his favorite wives and ordered them to follow his example, they refused pointing out that they would not touch alcohol because it was forbidden by Islam and: 'Right now tobacco has been forbidden

---

31. Hajjar, "The Jamahiriya Experiment in Libya: Qadhafi and Rousseau."

32. Ravandi, *Tarikheh Ejtmayieh Iran* (Social History of Iran), 729.

by the senior religious leader. (Thus) It cannot be made licit for us by the monarch's command."[33] The king subsequently revoked the tobacco concession.

The 1906–11 constitutional revolution had women participants at all levels. Of the 44 members of the first revolutionary committee, 20 were women.[34] They also had an important presence in the demonstrations. As the historian Ahmad Kasravi notes:

> One of the disturbing features of this revolutionary movement is the disturbance amongst women. These covered up creatures of the harem who should not have been even heard by outsiders, have now come forth to the battle fields. We see them participating, and effectively so, in the public demonstrations . . . They grapple with soldiers . . . take food and water to those who are besieged in mosques. They have been so successful that Eiynedolleh has ordered the armed forces to prevent them from taking to the streets and demonstrating.[35]

Similarly, Morgan Shuster has written:

> It is not too much to say that without the powerful moral force of the so-called chattels of the oriental lords of creation . . . the revolutionary movement, however well conducted by Persian men, would have early paled into a mere disorganised protest. The women did much to the spirit of liberty alive.[36]

When the king ordered the arrest of a number of religious leaders who were central to the revolution, veiled women mobbed the royal carriage:

> Yelling and screaming and crying they said: we want our masters and religious leaders . . . They have ratified our marriage contracts, they are the ones who act on our behalf and let out our houses . . . all our worldly and other worldly affairs are in the hands of these gentlemen . . . Oh Shah of the Muslims do not denigrate or undermine the leaders of Islam! Oh Shah of Islam,

---

33. Ibid., 719.

34. Kermani, *Tarikheh Bidaryeh Iranian* (The History of the Awakening of Iranians), 21.

35. Kasravi, *Khaharan va Dokhtaraneh ma* (Our Sisters and Daughters), 17–19.

36. Shuster, *The Strangling of Persia*, 195.

should Russia or England come to you these leaders could order 60,000 Iranians to fight a *jihad* against them.[37]

There were even some redoubtable tribal women who took up arms against the king's forces and beat them in battle. During the 1906 revolution a woman called Qezi, who was the daughter of a Bakhtiari chieftain, is reported to have:

> chased a hundred men on horseback who had been sent to catch her husband. . . . She chased these riders for about a *farsakh* (mile), killed eight and chased the rest away.[38]

During the revolution, she wrote to the constitutional leader Modir al Islam to congratulate him on its success. At the same time she warned him about taking her and her tribe on:

> Even if you took an army with all the usual equipment to fight us, it would be useless. . . . We have proved this and it is unnecessary to repeat it.[39]

Later in the century, Iranian women continued to play their part. They were active in resisting the military occupation that ravaged the country during World War II, and in the revolutions of 1953 and 1979. In 1979, the presence of veiled women by the millions in anti-Shah demonstrations spelt the downfall of the Pahlavi rule in Iran. Even in the post-revolutionary period under the Islamification laws, women continued to play a role in preserving the nation. During the war against Iraq, women served as nurses, cooks, and washerwomen behind the frontlines. At the same time there were rafts of photographs and posters of women covered in the full-length chador, carrying rifles on parade. Though the presence of armed women at the frontline and in army processions may have been merely a propaganda ploy, nevertheless, it indicated a necessity for the post revolutionary government in Iran to demonstrate that women were actively participating in the war.

Even when women are not present in direct combat, they continue to play important roles in supporting the cause. Usually they operate

37. Kasravi, *Takhireh Mashroutiat Iran* (History of the Iranian Constitutional Revolution), 77.

38. Kermani, *Tarikheh Bidaryeh Iranian* (The History of the Awakening of Iranians), 306.

39. Ibid., 309.

within their traditional frameworks, providing men with vital support and backup. For many, the Islamic cover proved a useful tool of battle; Iranian women carried arm under their all-covering chador in Tehran. During the Algerian war of resistance, it was well known that women used the cover of the veil to carry arms to the resistance fighters.

In the post-revolutionary era in Iran, while Massoud Rajavi, the Iranian resistance leader of the Islamic Mujahedin, worked in exile, his wife, Ashraf Rabiee, stayed behind to continue the fight to the death. After Rabiee's death, Rajavi married Maryam, the wife of his second in command. In 1985 she became the leader of the Mujahedin in exile.

Women in Recent Struggles

When nations live under military occupation, be it by foreign or by coercive internal forces, the traditional divides between feminine and masculine roles and spaces are blurred. During both the first and second *Intifada* in Palestine, for example, women confronted Israeli soldiers in their homes and neighborhoods more often than men did during the day:

> Usually soldiers come each day in the morning . . . this is the usual routine: the soldiers come, enter some houses without knocking and take the men and boys away.[40]

In Palestine, women belonging to Amal and Hezbollah have been partially liberated by the war. They have shed their invisible domestic roles to participate actively in the public sphere, albeit veiled and segregated. They may not join the military, but they have been and remain an integral part of the resistance movement. They smuggle food and keep watch, but of late have expanded their role. Two recent events are illustrative of the strategies used by women to defend their nation, navigating a middle pathway between the role of warrior and peacemaker. On November 3, 2006, about 3,000 protestors, mostly women, shielded at least a dozen Palestinian gunmen who had taken refuge in a mosque, enabling them to escape. At least one woman was killed.[41]

40. 'Adi, "Fifty-three Days' Curfew in Kufr Malek," 124.

41. http://www.cnsnews.com/news/viewstory.asp?Page=/ForeignBureaus/archive/200611/INT20061103b.html.

An instance two weeks later was groundbreaking, the first time Palestinians were able to prevent an Israeli airstrike by forming a human shield. The event took place after a local leader of the Popular Resistance Committees was informed by the Israeli army that his house would be bombed. People began to gather around the house immediately and by the next afternoon about two dozen women were camped on the leader's roof. Israel was forced to call of the airstrike.[42]

But unfortunately this concern for civilian deaths seems limited and rare. In the attacks on Palestine, and more recently Lebanon, civilians, women, children entire communities are flattened with little concern, or so it would seem, for human life or human rights, let alone age and gender.

The attacks and destruction of camps and villages in the 2002 Israeli invasion of the West Bank further obliterated any notion of divide between home and war fronts or any gender divide in terms of death and destruction. Rita Giacaman, Professor of Public Health at Birzeit University, reported "rampant" stealing of people's belongings and valuables and the stealing of food from stores by the army as a matter of everyday experience.[43] Homes were bulldozed and there were reports of mass graves.[44] At such times and in such battles, men, women, and children are be labeled as "terrorists" and murdered indiscriminately. Children as young as four were accused of terrorism and murdered with apparent impunity.[45]

Human Right's Double Standards

Perhaps, instead of faith and gender, we could consider an explanation in terms of nomenclature, labeling, and the differentiated understandings of the application of human rights provisions. The term "terrorist" appears to many to have a color and a creed. When suicide bombers engage in heinous attacks and murders of civilians, they are labeled as terrorists. However, when civilians are attacked, bombed, murdered, and massacred in Afghanistan, Iraq, Palestine, and Lebanon, the per-

42. http://www.cbsnews.com/stories/2006/11/19/world/main2199420.shtml.

43. Reported in her e-mails of April 11 and 15, 2002, among many more.

44. *The Guardian*, April 16, 2002.

45. Interview with an Israeli squadron leader on the BBC Radio Four *Today* program April 16, 2002.

petrators are not labeled terrorists but more often branded as liberators and heroes. This double standard is pervasive in the conflicts between the Occident and Orient.

Those killed lose their humanity and are too often labeled "collateral damage." It is this loss of humanness that needs closer scrutiny. The 1948 Universal Declaration of Human Rights and the raft of subsequent conventions and UN resolutions are not the exclusive right of some privileged groups. Even though in some languages the translation refers to the "rights of men," most people the world over have accepted the terms of the declaration. Islamic nations too have endorsed the declaration, which in its own way endeavors to deliver the very kind of peace, justice and equality that the Qur'an calls for. Yet in practice, there seems to be different rules for different nationalities that create tensions, un-peace, and eventually wars. This is not caused by a "clash of civilizations"[46] but rather a clash of powers; some people are considered to be more human and entitled to more rights than others. It seems to many that some people are entitled to more defense, more support, and more understanding than others. Many in the Middle East, both Muslim and non Muslim, have realized that in the real world, the UN and the declarations concerning human rights do not necessarily protect them.

For eight years the world stood by while as many as one million Iranians were killed by missiles and chemical weapons propelled from Iraq.[47] There was no humanitarian assistance, no mention of weapons of mass destruction, even though these were surely used, and no condemnation. When the Iraqis were attacking the Kurds in Halabcheh, including with chemical weapons, the world did not rise as one and call it terrorism. Although an Iraqi plane accidentally attacked an American warship, killing 37, United States focused its aggressive efforts on Iran, bombing Iranian oil installations, skirmishing with Iranian forces, and destroying Iranian naval ships. When an American warship destroyed an Iranian civil airliner on a scheduled flight over the Persian Gulf, the world did not cry our terrorism. As a matter of fact, the captain of the warship was given a medal for his "exceptionally meritorious conduct in

---

46. Huntington, "Clash of Civilizations."

47. As is usually the case in such long, intense wars, the casualty figures are highly debated. However, even the lower estimates place Iranian losses at about 500,000.

the performance of outstanding service as commanding officer."[48] The Iranians were dehumanized and the deaths of the Iranian passengers were seen as "collateral damage."

The occupation of Palestine and its long war of independence provide similar examples. The imbalance between the Israeli and Palestinian forces is not often questioned. Nor are the repeated failures of Israel to follow international guidelines.

The rules of an occupying power are laid down in the Fourth Geneva Convention relative to the Protection of Civilian Persons in Time of War (1949), to which Israel is a High Contracting Party. Yet in April 2002, Israeli forces caused havoc in Jenine for more than ten days: They destroyed homes, burned, and pillaged with impunity.[49] Destruction of property in occupied territories is forbidden under Article 53 of the Fourth Geneva Convention. It further constitutes extra-judicial punishment and arbitrary interference in home and property. The Fourth Geneva Convention states in Article 47 that:

> protected persons who are in occupied territory shall not be deprived, in any case or in any manner whatsoever of the benefits of the present Convention by any change introduced, as the result of the occupation of a territory, into the institutions or government of the said territory, nor by any agreement concluded between the authorities of the occupied territories and the Occupying Power, nor by any annexation by the latter of the whole or part of the occupied territory.

But this is not adhered to. Palestinians were and continue to be targeted for assassination even though willful killing is prohibited under Article 147 of the Fourth Geneva Convention. These activities amount to grave breaches, which under Article 8 of the Rome Statute of the International Criminal Court and Protocol One to the Fourth Geneva Conventions (neither of which Israel is a signatory) are defined as war crimes. Article 148 of the Fourth Geneva states that:

> no High Contracting Party shall be allowed to absolve itself or any other High Contracting Party of any liability incurred by itself or by any other High Contracting Party....

---

48. Omid, *Islam and the Post Revolutionary State in Iran.*
49. *The Palestine Monitor,* June 21, 2002.

Israel's ongoing human rights violations and its refusal to allow the immediate deployment of an international protection presence to prevent violations of the Fourth Geneva Convention and protect Palestinian persons within the Occupied Palestinian Territories further illustrates the imbalance between the rights afforded to Palestinian and those to Israeli citizens.

There is a similar disregard for international conventions in the recent attacks by Israel on Lebanon. According to Jan Egeland, the UN Under-Secretary-General for Humanitarian Affairs:

> The civilian population . . . have been the biggest losers in this senseless cycle of violence that is now exactly one month old . . . Civilians were supposed to be spared and in this conflict they are not.[50]

Amnesty International and the United Nations Office for the Coordination of Humanitarian Affairs reported that across the country villages came under artillery fire. In some cases cluster bombs were used and homes were singled out for precision-guided missile attacks.[51] In addition to the human toll—an estimated 1,183 fatalities, about one third of who have been children[52]—two government hospitals, in Bint Jbeil and in Meis al-Jebel, were completely destroyed in Israeli attacks and three others were seriously damaged. In a country of fewer than four million inhabitants, more than 25 percent of them took to the roads as displaced persons. An estimated 500,000 people sought shelter in Beirut alone, many of them in parks and public spaces, without water or washing facilities. The Catholic charity Caritas reported that:

> The Israeli Army is making the situation even worse for Lebanese civilians by targeting warehouses and factories. In fact, food storage houses in particular have become the target.[53]

---

50. Amnesty International, "Israel/Lebanon: Deliberate destruction or 'collateral damage'? Israeli attacks on civilian infrastructure."

51. *Los Angeles Times*, August 13, 2006.

52. UNICEF. *Middle East Crisis UNICEF Situation Report No. 26* (August 18 2006). Available from http://www.reliefweb.int/rw/rwb.nsf/db900SID/HMYT-6SSLUF?Open Document&rc=3&emid=SODA-6RT2S7.

53. http://www.caritas.org/jumpNews.asp?idChannel=3&idLang=ENG&idUser=0 &idNews=4264.

What Middle Easterners as well as journalists and observers, of all religions and none, found surprising was that these unwarranted attacks continued without any formal condemnations. As Robert Fisk noted in the first days of the onslaught:

> European politicians have talked about Israel's "disproportionate" response to Wednesday's capture of its soldiers. They are wrong. What I am now watching in Lebanon is an outrage. How can there be any excuse for the 73 dead Lebanese blown apart these past three days?[54]

As a matter of fact, the bombardment of Lebanon by the Israeli armed forces lasted more than a month. The country's infrastructure was destroyed. Entire families were killed in air strikes on their homes or in their vehicles while fleeing the aerial assaults on their villages. The Red Cross and other rescue workers were prevented from accessing the areas by continuing Israeli strikes. The Israeli Air Force launched more than 15,000 sorties to attack about 7,000 targets in Lebanon between 12 July and 14 August, while the Navy conducted 2,500 bombardments of targets.[55]

Yet the world dragged its heels, looked to condemn, Iran, Syria, Lebanon, Hamas, Hezbollah—the "terrorists"—anyone but Israel. Perhaps it is time to address this question of inequality and disproportionality rather than focusing on Islam as the culprit in the current crisis in the Middle East.

54. *The Independent*, http://news.independent.co.uk/world/fisk/article1178636.ece.

55. Israeli Defence Force report, quoted in Amnesty International "Lebanon: Deliberate Destruction or Collatoral Damage?" www.amnesty.org/en/library/asset/MDE18/007/2006/en/dom-MDE180072006en.html.

Bibliography

'Adi, Suha. "Fifty-three Days' Curfew in Kufr Malek." In *Palestinian Women: Identity and Experience,* edited by Ebba Augustin, 131–141. London: Zed, 1993.

Abu-Odeh, Lama. "The Case for Binationalism." *Boston Review* (December 2001/January 2002).

Aeschylus. *The Oresteia.* Translated by Robert Fagles. Introduction by W. B. Stanford. New York: Bantam, 1977.

Afshar, Haleh. *Islam and Feminisms: an Iranian Case Study.* New York: St. Martin's, 1998.

Ahmed, Leila. *Women and Gender in Islam.* New Haven: Yale University Press, 1992.

Ahmed, Rashid. *Jihad.* New Haven: Yale University Press, 2002.

Akhavi, Shahrough. "Islam and the West in World History." *Third World Quarterly* 24 (2003) 545–62.

al-`Awaji, Muhsin. Interview by Al Jazeera television. July 10, 2002. Translated by Middle East Media Research Institute as "Saudi Opposition Sheikhs on America, Bin Laden, and Jihad." Special Dispatch Series No. 400. July 18, 2002. Available from http://memri.org/bin/articles.cgi?Page=archives&Area=sd&ID=SP40002.

Al-Faraj, Muhammad. *Al-Faridah Al-Ghaibah.* Translated by Johannes J. G. Jansen as *The Neglected Duty.* New York: Macmillan, 1986.

Al-Shafi`I, Muhammad Ibn Idris. *Al-Risala.* Translated by Majid Khadduri as *Islamic Jurisprudence: Shafi`i's Risala.* Baltimore: Johns Hopkins University Press, 1961.

Al-Shaybani, Muhammad Al-Hasan. *Kitab Al-Siyar.* Translated and edited by Majid Khadduri as *The Islamic Law of Nations: Shaybani's Siyar.* Baltimore: Johns Hopkins University Press, 1966.

Albet-Mas, Abel, et al. "Voices from the Margins: Gendered Images of 'Otherness' in Colonial Morocco." *Gender Place & Culture: A Journal of Feminist Geography* 5:3 (1998) 229–40.

Amnesty International. "Israel/Lebanon: Deliberate destruction or 'collateral damage'? Israeli attacks on civilian infrastructure." *AI Index: MDE 18/007/2006* (August 23, 2006). Available from http://web.amnesty.org/library/index/engmde180072006.

Amstutz, G. Interpreting Amida: History and Orientalism in the Study of Pure Land Buddhism. Albany: SUNY Press, 1997.

Anderson, Benedict. *Imagined Communities: Reflections on the Origin and Spread of Nationalism.* London: Verso, 1983.

Andrić, Ivo *The Bridge Over the Drina.* Translated by Lovett F. Edwards. London: Harvill, 1995.

Anselm. "Cur Deus Homo." In *St. Anselm: Basic Writings.* Translated by S. N. Deane. La Salle, IL: Open Court, 1979.

Aquinas, Thomas. *Summa Theologiae.* Translated by the Fathers of the English Dominican Province. 61 vols. Cambridge: Cambridge University Press, 2006.

Aquino, María Pilar, and Deitmar Mieth, editors. *The Return of the Just War.* Concilium 2001/2. London: SCM 2001.

Artemidorus Daldianus, *Oneirocritika.*

Augustine. *The City of God.* Translated by Henry Bettenson. Harmondsworth: Penguin, 1977.

Avineri, Shlomo. *Hegel's Theory of the Modern State.* London: Cambridge University Press, 1972.

Balthasar, Hans Urs von. *Martin Buber and Christianity: A Dialogue between Israel and the Church.* Translated by Alexander Dru. London: Harvill, 1961.

Baron, Salo. "Ghetto and Emancipation: Shall we revise the traditional view?" *The Menorah Journal* 14 (1928) 513–26.

Barry, Brian. "Democracy Needs Dialogue and Deliberation—not Political Blocs." In *Democracy and Islam,* by Haleh Afshar. London: Hansard Society, 2006. Available from www.hansard-society.org.uk/blogs/downloads/archive/2007/08/29/democracy-and-islam-may-2006.aspx.

Barstow, Anne Llewellyn, editor. *War's Dirty Secret: Rape, Prostitution, and Other Crimes against Women.* Cleveland: Pilgrim, 2000.

Barth, Karl. *Church Dogmatics.* Vol. 1, part 2. Translated by G. T. Thompson and Harold Knight. Edinburgh: T. & T. Clark, 1956.

———. *The Humanity of God.* Richmond: John Knox, 1960.

Bartov, Omer. *Mirrors of Destruction: War, Genocide and Modern Identity.* New York: Oxford University Press, 2000.

Bauer, Yehuda. *The Jewish Emergence from Powerlessness.* London: Macmillan, 1980

Beaumont, Peter. "Israel Outraged as EU Poll Names It a Threat to Peace." *Observer* (November 2, 2003).

Beauvoir, Simone de. *The Second Sex.* New York: Bantam, 1961.

Beckman, Morris. *The Jewish Brigade: An Army With Two Masters, 1944–45.* New York: Sarpedon, 1999.

Beestermöller, Gerard. "Eurocentricity in the Perception of Wars." *Concilium* (2001/2) 33–42.

Beisel, David R. "The Group Fantasy of German Nationalism, 1800–1815." *Journal of Psychohistory* 8 (1980) 1–19.

Ben-Yehuda, Nachman. *The Masada Myth: Collective Memory and Mythmaking in Israel.* Madison: University of Wisconsin Press, 1995.

Benedict XVI, Pope. "Faith, Reason and the University: Memories and Reflections," available at www.guardian.co.uk/world/2006/sep/15/religion.uk accessed on June 21 2007.

Benjamin, Jessica. *The Bonds of Love: Psychoanalysis, Feminism and the Problem of Domination.* New York: Random House, 1988.

Berger, Peter. *The Sacred Canopy.* Garden City, NY: Doubleday, 1969.

Berkovits, Eliezer. *With God in Hell: Judaism in the Ghettos and Death Camps.* New York: Sanhedrin, 1979.

Berrigan, Daniel. *Uncommon Prayer: A Book of Psalms.* New York: Seabury, 1978.

Biale, David. *Power and Powerlessness in Jewish History.* New York: Schocken, 1986.

Bion, W. R. *Experiences in Groups and Other Papers.* New York: Basic, 1961.

Black, Jeremy. *War: Past, Present, and Future.* New York: St. Martin's, 2000.

Blankenhorn, David, et al., editors. *The Islam/West Debate.* Lanham, MD: Rowman & Littlefield, 2005.

Bleich, J. David. "Preemptive War in Jewish Law." *Tradition* 21 (1983) 3–41.

Boose, L. E. "Crossing the River Drina: Bosnian Rape Camps, Turkish Impalement, and Serb Cultural Memory." *Signs: Journal of Women in Culture and Society* 28 (2002) 91–96.

Boothby, Richard. *Death and Desire: Psychoanalytic Theory in Lacan's Return to Freud.* London: Routledge, 1991.

Bowker, John, editor. *The Oxford Dictionary of World Religions.* Oxford: Oxford University Press, 1997.

Boyarin, Daniel. *Carnal Israel: Reading Sex in Talmudic Culture.* Berkeley: University of California Press, 1993.

———. "Justify My Love." In *Judaism since Gender,* edited by Miriam Peskowitz and Laura Levitt, 131–37. New York: Routledge, 1997.

———. *Unheroic Conduct: The Rise of Heterosexuality and the Invention of the Jewish Man.* Berkeley: University of California Press, 1997.

Brann, Ross. *Power in the Portrayal: Representations of Jews and Muslims in Eleventh and Twelfth-Century Islamic Spain.* Princeton and Oxford: Princeton University Press, 2002.

Bregman, Ahron. *Israel's Wars: 1948–1993.* London: Routledge, 2000.

Brennan, Teresa. *Exhausting Modernity: Grounds for a New Economy.* London: Routledge, 2000.

———. *The Transmission of Affect.* Ithaca, NY: Cornell University Press, 2004.

Brenner, Michael. *The Renaissance of Jewish Culture in Weimar Germany.* New Haven: Yale University Press, 1996.

Brod, Harry, editor. *A Mensch Among Men: Explorations in Jewish Masculinity.* Freedom, CA: Crossing, 1988.

Brown, Hunter. *William James: On Radical Empiricism and Religion.* Toronto: University of Toronto Press, 2000.

Brown, Raymond E. *Death of the Messiah.* 2 vols. Anchor Bible Reference Library. New York: Doubleday, 1994.

Brownmiller, Susan. *Against Our Will: Men, Women, and Rape.* Harmondsworth: Penguin, 1976.

Broyde, Michael. "Fighting the War and the Peace." Available from www.jlaw.com/Articles/war1.html.

Buber, Martin. *I and Thou.* Translated by Walter Kaufmann. New York: Scribners, 1970.

———. *Israel and the World.* New York: Schocken, 1948.

———. *On Zion: The History of an Idea.* Translated by Stanley Godman. New York: Schocken, 1973.

———. *Paths in Utopia.* Translated by R. F. C. Hull. London: Routledge & Kegan Paul, 1949.

Bulliett, Richard. "The Crisis within Islam." *Wilson Quarterly* 26 (2002) 11–19.

Burke, Jason. "Sex Fear of Army Teens." *Observer* (8 June 2003).

Bush, Laura. Radio Address. November 19, 2001. Available from http://www.whitehouse.gov/news/releases/2001/11/20011117.html.

Caillois, Roger. *Man and the Sacred*. Translated by Meyer Barash. Glencoe, IL: Free Press, 1959.

Cameron, David. "Full text, David Cameron's speech." *Guardian Unlimited* (August 24, 2005). Available from http://education.guardian.co.uk/faithschools/story/0,13882,1555406,00.html.

Camon, Alessandro. "American Torture, American Porn." www.salon.com (7 June 2004).

Campbell, Brian. *The Roman Army: 31BC–AD 337 A Sourcebook*. London: Routledge, 1993.

Casciani, Dominic. "Islamophobia Pervades UK—report." June 2, 2004. Available from http://news.bbc.co.uk/2/hi/uk_news/3768327.stm.

Cassirer, Ernst. *The Myth of the State*. New Haven: Yale University Press, 1946.

Chang, Iris. *The Rape of Nanking: The Forgotten Holocaust of World War II*. New York: Basic, 1997.

Charlesworth, J. H. "Jesus and Jehohanan: An Archaeological Note on Crucifixion." *Expository Times* 84 (February 1973) 147–50.

Childress, James F. *Moral Responsibility in Conflicts*. Baton Rouge: Louisiana State University, 1980.

———. "Scripture and Christian Ethics: Some Reflections on the Role of Scripture in Moral Deliberation and Justification." *Interpretation* 34 (1980) 371–80.

Cohen, Jeremy. *Dear Chief Rabbi: From the Correspondence of Chief Rabbi Immanuel Jakobovits*. Hoboken NJ: Ktav, 1995.

Cohen, Mark R. *Under Crescent and Cross: The Jews in the Middle Ages*. Princeton: Princeton University Press: 1994.

Cohn, Norman. *Warrant for Genocide: The Myth of the Jewish World-Conspiracy and the Protocols of the Elders of Zion*. London: Penguin, 1967.

Coleman, Michael. "Fatal Charades." *Journal of Roman Studies* 80 (1990) 44–73.

Commission on British Muslims and Islamophobia. Islamophobia: A Challenge for Us All. *London: The Runnymede Trust, 1997*. Summary available from http://www.runnymedetrust.org/publications/currentPublications.html#islamophobia.

Commission on British Muslims and Islamophobia. *Islamophobia: Issues, Challenges and Action*. 2004. Available from www.insted.co.uk/islam.html.

Condren, Mary. "Mercy Not Sacrifice: Toward a Celtic Theology." *Feminist Theology* 15 (1997) 31–54.

———. *The Serpent and the Goddess: Women, Religion and Power in Celtic Ireland*. 1989. Reprinted, Dublin: New Island, 2002.

———. "War, Religion, Gender and Psyche: An Irish Perspective." In *Holy War and Gender: 'Gotteskrieg' und Geschlecht Violence in Religious Discourses. Gewaltdiskurse in der Religion*, edited by Christina von Braun et al., 143–77. New Brunswick, NJ: Transaction, 2006.

Corbett, Sara. "The Permanent Scars of Iraq." *The New York Times Magazine,* February 15, 2004, 34–66.

Corley, Kathleen E., and Robert L. Webb, editors. *Jesus and Mel Gibson's The Passion of the Christ: The Film, the Gospels and the Claims of History*. New York: Continuum, 2004.

Cummins, Will. "Muslims are a threat to our way of life." *The Sunday Telegraph* (July 25, 2004). Available from http://www.telegraph.co.uk/opinion/main.jhtml?xml=/opinion/2004/07/25/do2504.xml.

Danner, Mark. *Torture and Truth: America, Abu Ghraib and the War on Terror.* New York: New York Review of Books, 2004.

Davies, Roy W. *Service in the Roman Army.* Edited by David Breeze and Valerie A. Maxfield. Edinburgh: Edinburgh University Press, 1989.

Davis, Walter A. "The Bite of the Whip: Passion of the Christ in Abu Ghraib." Counterpunch (19/20 June 2004). Available from http://www.counterpunch.org/davis06192004.html.

"Declaration on the Question of Admission of Women to the Ministerial Priesthood." Sacred Congregation for the Doctrine of the Faith. Vatican City, 1976.

Dionysius of Halicarnassus, *Roman Antiquities.*

Doubrawa, Erhard. "Martin Buber, the Anarchist." Available at http://ourworld.compuserve.com/homepages/gik_gestalt/doubrawa.html.

Draculic, Slavenka. "The War on People—and on the Truth—in Croatia." *The Chronicle of Higher Education* (June 11, 2004).

Durkheim, Emile. *The Elementary Forms of Religious Life.* Translated by Joseph Ward Swain. 1915. Reprinted, New York: Free, 1965.

Edrei, Arye. "Divine Spirit and Physical Power: Rabbi Shlomo Goren and the Military Ethic of the Israel Defense Forces." *Theoretical Inquiries in Law* 7 (2006) 255–97. Available from www.bepress.com/cgi/viewcontent.cgi?article=1124&context=til.

———. "Law, Interpretation, and Ideology: The Renewal of the Jewish Laws of War in the State of Israel," *Cardozo Law Review* (2006) 187–227.

Edwardes, Allen. *Erotica Judaica: A Sexual History of the Jews.* New York: Julian, 1967.

Edwards, William D. "On the Physical Death of Jesus Christ." *Journal of the American Medical Association* 255 (1986) 1455–63.

Eilberg-Schwartz, Howard. *God's Phallus and Other Problems for Men and Monotheism.* Boston: Beacon, 1994.

Elman, Pearl. "Deuteronomy 21:10–14: The Beautiful Captive Woman." *Women in Judaism* 1 (1997) 1–18. Available from www.utoronto.ca/wjudaism/journal/vol1n1/v1n1elma.htm.

Elshtain, Jean Bethke. *Women and War.* New York: Basic Books, 1987.

Enayat, Hamid. *Modern Islamic Political Thought.* Austin: University of Texas Press, 1982.

Engels, Friedrich. *The Origin of the Family, Private Property and the State.* Harmondsworth: Penguin, 1985.

Engineer, Asghar Ali. *The Rights of Women in Islam.* Hurst: London, 1992.

Eshel, David. *Bravery in Battle: Stories from the Front Line.* London: Brockhampton, 1997.

Ettinger, Bracha. "Transgressing with-in-to the Feminine." *Women's Philosophy Review* 25 (2000) 56–85.

Falwell, Jerry. *Listen, America!* Garden City, NY: Doubleday, 1980.

Fein, Helen. "Genocide and Gender: the Uses of Women and Group Destiny." *Journal of Genocide Research* 1 (1999) 43–63.

Feinstein, Edward. "God's Four Questions." Sermon for Yom Kippur 1993. Available from http://www.vbs.org/rabbi/rabfeins/divre/kiteztze.htm

Flohr, Paul R. "The Road to 'I and Thou': An Inquiry into Buber's Transition from Mysticism to Dialogue." In *Texts and Responses: Studies Presented to Nahum N. Glatzer on the Occasion of His Seventieth Birthday by His Students*, edited by Michael A. Fishbane and Paul R. Flohr, 201–25. Leiden: Brill, 1975.

Fornari, Franco. *The Psychoanalysis of War*. Bloomington: Indiana University Press, 1975.

Fox, Marvin. *Modern Jewish Ethics, Theory and Practice*. Columbus: Ohio State University Press, 1975.

Frank, Daniel H. *Commandment and Community: New Essays in Jewish Legal and Political Philosophy*. Albany, NY: SUNY Press, 1995.

Frantzen, Allen. *Bloody Good: Chivalry, Sacrifice, and the Great War*. Chicago: University of Chicago Press, 2004.

Frediksen, Paula, editor. *On The Passion of the Christ: Exploring the Issues Raised by the Controversial Movie*. Berkeley: University of California Press, 2005.

Freud, Sigmund. "Beyond the Pleasure Principle." (1924) In *The Standard Edition of the Complete Psychological Works of Sigmund Freud*. Vol. 18. Edited and translated by James Strachey. London: Hogarth, 1951–1973.

———. "Moses and Monotheism." (1939) In *The Standard Edition of the Complete Psychological Works of Sigmund Freud*. Vol. 23. Edited and translated by James Strachey. London: Hogarth, 1951–1973.

———. *Totem and Taboo: Some Points of Agreement between the Mental Lives of Savages and Neurotics*. Translated by James Strachey. London: Routledge & Kegan Paul, 1918.

———. "Why War?" Sigmund Freud to Albert Einstein and League of Nations. In *Civilisation, War and Death: Sigmund Freud*. Edited by John Rickman. London: Hogarth, 1932.

Friedman, Maurice. "Martin Buber's Encounter with Mysticism." *Human Inquiry: Review of Existential Psychology and Psychiatry* 10 (1970) 43–81.

Fuchs, Esther. "Images of Love and War in Contemporary Israeli Fiction: Toward a Feminist Revision." *Modern Judaism* 6 (1986) 189–96.

Fuchs, Jo-Ann Pilardi. "On the War Path and Beyond: Hegel, Freud and Feminist Theory." *Women Studies International Forum* 6 (1983) 565–52.

Galbraith, Peter. "How to Get Out of Iraq." *The New York Review of Books* 51:8 (May 13, 2004).

Gallant, Christine. *Tabooed Jung: Marginality as Power*. London: Macmillan, 1996.

Galloway, Joseph. "Combat in Iraq: What's It Really Like?" *Durham Herald-Sun* (June 27, 2004) A13.

Gendler, Everett E. "Zionism and Judaism." In *The Challenge of Shalom: The Jewish Tradition of Peace and Justice,* edited by Murray Polner and Naomi Goodman, 87–90. Philadelphia: New Society, 1994.

George, Lloyd. *The Truth about the Peace Treaties*. Vol. II. London: Gollancz, 1938.

Gertz, Nurith. *Myths in Israeli Culture: Captives of a Dream*. Portland, OR: Valentine-Mitchell, 2000.

Ghayth, Abu. "In the Shadow of the Lances." Translated by Middle East Media Research Institute as "'Why We Fight America': Al-Qa'ida Spokesman Explains September

11 and Declares Intentions to Kill 4 Million Americans with Weapons of Mass Destruction." Special Dispatch Series No. 388. June 12, 2002. Available from http://memri.org/bin/articles.cgi?Page=archives&Area=sd&ID=SP38802.

Giddens, Anthony. *The Nation-State and Violence*. Cambridge: Polity, 1985.

Gilman, Sander L. *Franz Kafka: The Jewish Patient*. New York: Routledge, 1995.

———. *The Jew's Body*. New York: Routledge, 1991.

Girard, René. *The Scapegoat*. Translated by Yvonne Freccero. Baltimore: Johns Hopkins University Press. Originally published as *Le Bouc Emissaire*. Paris: Grasset & Fasquelle, 1982, 1986.

———. *Violence and the Sacred*. Translated by Patrick Gregory. Baltimore and London: Johns Hopkins University Press, 1977. Originally published as *La Violence et le sacré*. Paris: Grasset, 1972, 1977.

Goldhagen, Daniel Jonah. *Hitler's Willing Executioners: Ordinary Germans and the Holocaust*. London: Little Brown, 1996.

Goldman, Eliezer. *Yeshayahu Leibowitz: Judaism, Human Values, and the Jewish State*. Cambridge: Harvard University Press, 1992.

Goldman, Emma. "Preparedness: The Road to Universal Slaughter." *Mother Earth* (December 1915). Reprinted in *Instead of Violence: Writings by the Great Advocates of Peace and Nonviolence Throughout History*, edited by Arthur and Lila Weinberg. 277–81. New York: Grossman, 1963.

Goldstein, Joshua S. *War and Gender*. Cambridge: Cambridge University Press, 2001.

Gopin, Marc. *Between Eden and Armageddon: The Future of World Religions, Violence, and Peacemaking*. New York: Oxford University Press, 2000.

Goren, Arthur, editor. *Dissenter in Zion: From the Writings of Judah L. Magnes*. Cambridge: Harvard University Press, 1982.

Gray, J. Glen. *The Warriors: Reflections on Men In Battle*. New York: Harper, 1967.

Grenn, Deacon Stan. "Letter." *Jesus Journal* 88 (Spring 2004).

Groner, Tzvi. "A Response to the Halakhic Ruling Against the Return of Territory." Oz V'shalom – Netivot Shalom (Strength and Peace—Paths of Peace). Available from www.netivot-shalom.org.il/judaism/halter.php.

Grossman, Dave. *On Killing: The Psychological Cost of Learning to Kill in War and Society*. Boston: Little Brown, 1995.

Grossman, Nosson Zeev. "The Danger of Secular Control of Eretz Yisroel." *Dei'ah ve-Dibur* (May 31, 2000).

Gustafson, James M. *Theocentric Ethics*, 2 vols. Chicago: University of Chicago, 1981, 1984.

Habermas, Jürgen, *Religion and Rationality*. Edited by Eduardo Mendieta. Cambridge: MIT Press, 2002.

Hajjar, Sami. "The Jamahiriya Experiment in Libya: Qadhafi and Rousseau." *Journal of Modern African Studies* 18:2 (1980) 181–200.

Halpérin, Jean, and Georges Levitte. *La conscience juive face à la guerre: données et débats*. Paris: Presses Universitaires de France, 1976.

Hamas, *Charter*. Translated by M. Maqdsi. Dallas: Islamic Association for Palestine, 1990.

Hanf, Theodor. "Reducing Conflict through Cultural Autonomy: Karl Renner's Contribution." In *State and Nation in Multi-Ethnic Societies: The Breakup of*

Multinational States, edited by Uri Ra'anan et al., 33–52. Manchester: Manchester University Press, 1991.

Häring, Bernard. *The Law of Christ*. New York: Paulist, 1969.

Harries, Richard. *The Passion in Art*. Aldershot: Ashgate, 2004.

Hartsock, Nancy. "The Barracks Community in Western Thought: A Prologemonena to a Feminist Critique of War and Politics." *Women's Studies International Forum* 5:3–4 (1982) 283–86.

———. *Money, Sex and Power: Toward a Feminist Historical Materialism*. Boston: Northeastern University Press, 1985.

Hass, Nico. "Anthropological Observations on the Skeletal Remains from Giv'at ha-Mivtar." *Israel Exploration Journal* 20 (1970) 38–59.

Hassan, Riffat. "Made from Adam's Rib: The Woman's Creation Question." *Al-Mushir* 27:3 (Autumn 1985) 124–25

Hattis, Susan Lee. *The Bi-national Idea in Palestine During Mandatory Times*. Haifa: Shikmona, 1970.

Hauerwas, Stanley. "Can a Pacifist Think About War?" In *Dispatches From the Front: Theological Engagements With the Secular*. Durham, NC: Duke University Press, 1994.

———. *Cross-Shattered Christ*. Grand Rapids: Brazos, 2005.

———. "In a Time of War: An Exchange." *First Things* 120 (February 2002).

———. *Performing the Faith: Bonhoeffer and the Practice of Nonviolence*. Grand Rapids: Brazos, 2004.

———. "Reflections on the 'Appeal to Abolish War' or What Being a Friend of Enda's Got Me Into." In *Between Poetry and Politics: Essays in Honour of Enda McDonagh*, edited by Linda Hogan and Barbara FitzGerald, 135–47. Dublin: Columba, 2003.

———. "Should War Be Eliminated?" In *Against the Nations: War and Survival in a Liberal Society*. Notre Dame: University of Notre Dame Press, 1992.

Hawthorne, Susan, and Bronwyn Winter, editors. *September 11, 2001: Feminist Perspectives*. Melbourne: Spinifex, 2002.

Heaney, Seamus. *Opened Ground, Poems 1966–1996*. London: Faber & Faber, 1998.

Hedges, Chris. *War is a Force That Give Us Meaning*. New York: Public Affairs, 2002.

Hegel, G. W. F. *Phenomenology of Mind*. Translated by J. B. Baillie. New York: Harper & Row, 1967.

———. *Philosophy of Nature*. Translated by A. V. Miller. Oxford: Clarendon, 1970.

Hengel, Martin. *Crucifixion in the Ancient World and the Folly of the Cross*. Translated by John Bowden. Philadelphia: Fortress, 1977.

Herodotus, *History*.

Hersh, Seymour M. *Chain of Command: The Road from 9/11 to Abu Ghraib*. New York: HarperCollins, 2004.

Hertzberg, Arthur, editor. *The Zionist Idea: A Historical Analysis and Reader*. New York: Atheneum, 1973.

Heschel, Abraham Joshua. "The Moral Outrage of Vietnam." In *Vietnam: Crisis of Conscience*, Robert McAfee Brown et al., 48–61. New York: Behrman, 1967.

Hirsch, Samson Raphael. *Terumath Zvi: The Pentateuch*. Edited by E. Oratz. New York: Judaica, 1986.

Hirschfeld, Hartwig. *Judah Hallevi's Kitab al Khazari*. London: Routledge, 1905.

Homer. *The Iliad*. Translated by Richard Lattimore. Chicago: University of Chicago Press, 1962.

Horowitz, George. *The Spirit of Jewish Law*. New York: Central, 1953.

Hourani, Albert. *Arabic Thought in the Liberal Age*. Cambridge: Cambridge University, 1983.

Housman, A. E. *A Shropshire Lad*. Portland, ME: Mosher, 1913.

Hubert, Henri, and Marcel Mauss. "Essai sur la Nature et la Fonction du Sacrifice." *L'Année Sociologique* 2 (1898). Translated by W. D. Halls as *Sacrifice: Its Nature and Function*. Chicago: University of Chicago Press, 1964.

Huntington, Samuel P. "Clash of Civilizations." *Foreign Affairs* 72:3 (1993) 22–28.

Husayn, Qadariyya. *Shahirat al-nisaalam al-islamiyya*. Translated by Turkish by Abdol Aziz Amin al-Khanji as *Famous Women in the Muslim World*. Cairo: Matba'at al'Sa'adeh, 1924.

Huston, Nancy. "Tales of War and Tears of Women." In *Women's Studies International Forum* 5 (1982) 271–82.

Ibn Kathir. *Tafsir*. Translated by Adbul Malik Mujahid as *Tafsir Ibn Kathir*. New York: Darussalam, 2000.

Idziak, Janine Marie, ed. *Divine Command Morality*. New York: Mellen, 1979.

Irigaray, Luce. *Sexes et Parentés*. Paris: Minuit, 1987. Translated by Gillian C. Gill as *Sexes and Genealogies*. New York: Columbia University Press, 1993.

———. *Speculum of the Other Woman*. Translated by Gillian C. Gill. Ithaca: Cornell University Press, 1985.

———. *This Sex Which is Not One*. Translated by Catherine Porter with Carolyn Burke, NY. Ithaca: Cornell University Press, 1985.

Israeli Defence Force report, quoted in Amnesty International "Lebanon: Deliberate Destruction or Collatoral Damage?" www.amnesty.org/en/library/asset/MDE18/007/2006/en/dom-MDE180072006en.html.

Jackson, Richard. *Writing the War on Terrorism: Language Politics and Counter-terrorism*. Manchester: Manchester University Press, 2005.

James, William. "The Moral Equivalent of War." In *The Moral Equivalent of War and Other Essays*, edited by John Roth, 3–16. New York: Harper, 1971.

Jantzen, Grace. *Foundations of Violence* London: Routledge, 2004.

Jay, Nancy. *Throughout Your Generations Forever: Sacrifice, Religion, and Paternity*. Chicago: University of Chicago Press, 1992.

Jeyifo, Biodun. "On Mazrui's 'Black Orientalism': A Cautionary Critique." *The Black Scholar* 30 (2000) 19–22.

John Kelsay. *Islam and War: A Study in Comparative Ethics*. Louisville: Westminster John Knox, 1993.

Johnson, James Turner "Aquinas and Luther on War and Peace: Sovereign Authority and the Use of Armed Force." *Journal of Religious Ethics* 31 (2003) 3–22.

———. "The Broken Tradition." *The National Interest* (Fall 1996) 30.

———. *The Holy War Idea in Western and Islamic Traditions*. University Park: Pennsylvania State University Press, 1997.

———. *Just War Tradition and the Restraint of War*. Princeton: Princeton University Press, 1981.

———. *Morality and Contemporary Warfare*. New Haven: Yale University, 2001.

————. *The War to Oust Saddam Hussein: The Context, the Debate, the War, and the Future.* Lanham, MD: Rowman & Littlefield, 2005.

Johnstone, Brian, "Political Assassination and Tyrannicide: Traditions and Contemporary Conflicts." *Studia moralia* 41 (2003) 25–40 .

————. "Pope John Paul and the War in Iraq." *Studia moralia* 41 (2003) 309–30.

————. "The War on Terrorism: A Just War?" *Studia moralia* 40 (2002) 39–61.

Jones, Ernest. *Psycho-Myth, Psycho-History: Essays in Applied Psycho-Analysis.* 2 vols. New York: Hillstone, 1974.

Judt, Tony. "Israel: The Alternative." *The New York Review of Books* (23 October 2003).

Kadish, Sharman. *Bolsheviks and British Jews: The Anglo-Jewish Community, Britain, and the Russian Revolution.* London: Cass, 1992.

Kahane, Meir. "What Will the Goyim Say?" Jan. 19, 1968. Available from http://www.living-martyr.org/doc4.html.

Kahani-Hopkins, Vered, and Nick Hopkins. "'Representing' British Muslims: the strategic dimension to identity construction." *Ethnic and Racial Studies* 25 (2002) 288–309.

Kasravi, Ahmad. *Khaharan va Dokhtaraneh ma* (Our Sisters and Daughters). Tehran, 1944.

————. *Takhireh Mashroutiat Iran* (History of the Iranian Constitutional Revolution). Tehran, 1940.

Katz, Steven. *Frontiers of Jewish Thought.* Washington, DC: B'nai B'rith, 1992.

Keegan, John. *A Brief History of Warfare: Past, Present, Future.* Southampton: University of Southhampton, 1994.

Kelsay, John. "Arguments Concerning Resistance in Contemporary Islam." In *The Ethics of War*, edited by Richard Sorabji and David Rodin, 61–91. Aldershot: Ashgate, 2006.

————. "Democratic Virtue, Comparative Ethics, and Contemporary Islam." *Journal of Religious Ethics* 33.4 (December 2005) 697–708.

————. "Islam, Politics, and War." *Sewanee Theological Review* 47 (2003) 11–19.

————. "Islamic Tradition and the Justice of War." In *The Ethics of War in Asian Civilizations,* edited by Torkel Brekke, 81–110. New York: Routledge, 2006.

————. *Islam and War: A Study in Comparative Ethics*, Louisville: Westminster John Knox, 1993.

————. *Islam and War: A Study in Comparative Ethics.* Louisville: Westminster John Knox, 1993.

————. "The New Jihad and Islamic Tradition." *Foreign Policy Research Institute WIRE* 11.3 (2003). Available from http://www.fpri.org/fpriwire/1103.200310.kelsay.newjihad.html.

Keren, Michael. *Ben-Gurion and the Intellectuals: Power, Knowledge and Charisma.* Dekalb: Northern Illinois University Press, 1983.

Kermani, Nezim al-Islam. *Tarikheh Bidaryeh Iranian* (The history of the awakening of Iranians). Vol. 1, Tehran: Bondyadeh Farhangeh, 1972.

Khalidi, Ahmad. "A One-State Solution." *Guardian* (29 September 2003).

Kimelman, Reuven. "Abravanel and the Jewish Republican Ethos," In *Commandment and Community: New Essays in Jewish Legal and Political Philosophy*, edited by Daniel Frank. Albany, NY, 1995, 201–11.

————. "Non-Violence in the Talmud." *Judaism* 17 (1968) 316–334.

Kittel, Gerhard, editor. *Theological Dictionary of the New Testament.* Translated and edited by Geoffrey W. Bromiley. Grand Rapids: Eerdmans, 1964–76.

Klein, Melanie. "Envy and Gratitude." (1957) In *Envy and Gratitude and Other Works 1946–1963.* London: Virago, 1988.

————. "Some Reflections on the *Oresteia.*" (1963) In *Envy and Gratitude and Other Works 1946–1963.* London: Virago, 1988.

Kraemer, Joel. *Perspectives on Maimonides: Philosophical and Historical Studies.* Oxford: Littman, 1996.

Kristeva, Julia. *Melanie Klein.* Translated by Ross Guberman. New York: Columbia University Press, 2001.

————. *Powers of Horror.* Translated by Leon Roudiez. New York: Columbia University Press, 1982.

————. *Revolution in Poetic Language.* Translated by Margaret Waller. New York: Columbia University Press, 1984.

————. "Woman's Time." In *Kristeva Reader,* edited by Toril Moi. New York: Columbia University Press, 1986.

Kurzman, Dan. *The Bravest Battle.* Los Angeles: Pinnacle, 1978.

Lappin, Shalom. "Israel/Palestine: Is There a Case for Bi-nationalism?" *Dissent* (Winter 2004).

Lavsky, Hagit. *Before Catastrophe: The Distinctive Path of German Zionism.* Detroit: Wayne State University Press, 1996.

Lazare, Daniel. "The One-State Solution." *The Nation* (3 November 2003).

Leech, Gwyneth. "Jesus Is Stripped of His Garments," Stations of the Cross 10 (2005). The project (2004–2005) was commissioned for St. Paul's Episcopal Church on the Green, in East Norwalk, Connecticut and publicly displayed in Lent 2005.

Leed, Eric J. *No Man's Land: Combat and Identity in World War I.* Cambridge: Cambridge University Press, 1979.

Leibowitz, Yeshayahu. "Heroism." In *Contemporary Jewish Religious Thought: Original Essays on Critical Concepts, Movements and Beliefs,* edited by Arthur A. Cohen and Paul Mendes-Flohr. New York: Free, 1987.

Lentin, Ronit. *Israel and the Daughters of Shoah.* New York: Berghahn, 2000.

Levene, Mark. "Going against the Grain: Two Jewish Memoirs of War and Anti-War 1914–18." In *Forging Modern Jewish Identities: Public Faces and Private Struggles,* edited by Michael Berkowitz, et al., 96–101. Portland, OR: Vallentine-Mitchell, 2003.

Lévinas, Emmanuel. "Les dommages causés par le feu: Leçon talmudique." In *La conscience juive face à la guerre,* edited by J. Halpérin and G. Lévitte, 13–26. Paris: Presses Universitaires de France, 1976.

Lewis, Reina. *Gendering Orientalism: Race, Femininity and Representation.* London: Routledge, 1996.

Lichtenstein, Aharon. "Protecting the Stranger." *Parshat Naso* 5755. Available from http://www.vbm-torah.org/archive/ral5-na2.htm.

Linenthal, Edward Tabor. *Changing Images of the Warrior in America: A History of Popular Symbolism.* Vol. 6, *Studies in American Religion.* New York: Mellen, 1982.

Liulevicius, Vejas Gabriel. *War Land on the Eastern Front: Culture, National Identity and German Occupation in World War 1.* New York: Cambridge University Press, 2000.

Lowy, Michael. *Redemption and Utopia: Jewish Libertarian Thought in Central Europe, A Study in Elective Affinity.* Translated by Hope Heaney. London: Athlone, 1992.

Lubarsky, Sandra. "Reconstructing Divine Power: Post-Holocaust Jewish Theology, Feminism, and Process Philosophy." In *Women and Gender in Jewish Philosophy*, edited by Hava Tirosh-Samuelson. Bloomington: Indiana University Press, 2004.

Maimonides, Moses. *The Guide of the Perplexed.* Translated by Shlomo Pines. Chicago: University of Chicago Press, 1963.

———. "*Mishneh Torah*, Laws of Kings and Their Wars." In *Kings, Their Wars and the Messiah: From the Mishneh Torah of Maimonides*, trans. H. M. Russell and J. Weinberg, chapter 5. Edinburgh: Royal College of Physicians of Edinburgh, 1987.

Manchester, William. *Goodbye, Darkness: A Memoir of the Pacific War.* Boston: Little, Brown, 2002.

Magnes, Judah L. *Arab-Jewish Unity: Testimony before the Anglo-American Inquiry Commission for the Ihud (Union,) by Judah Magnes and Martin Buber.* London: Gollancz, 1947.

Manji, Irshad. *The Trouble with Islam Today: A Wakeup Call for Honesty and Change.* Toronto: Vintage Canada, 2005.

Marvin, Carolyn, and David Ingle. *Blood Sacrifice and the Nation: Totem Rituals and the American Flag.* Cambridge: Cambridge University Press, 1999.

Mazali, Rela. "'And What about the Girls?': What a Culture of War Genders Out of View." *Nashim: A Journal of Jewish Women's Studies and Gender Issues* 6 (2003) 44–47.

Mazrui, A. A. "Black Orientalism? Further Reflections on 'Wonders of the African World.'" *The Black Scholar* 30 (2000) 15–18.

McClendon, James. *Systematic Theology: Ethics.* Vol. 1. Nashville: Abingdon, 1986.

Mead, Margaret. *Male and Female.* New York: New American Library, 1959.

Meed, Vladka. *On Both Sides of the Wall: Memoirs from the Warsaw Ghetto.* Translated by Steven Meed. New York: Holocaust Library, 1993.

Menand, Louis. *The Metaphysical Club: A Story of Idea in America.* New York: Farrar, Straus, and Giroux, 2001.

Mendes-Flohr, Paul R. *A Land of Two Peoples: Martin Buber on Jews and Arabs.* New York: Oxford University Press, 1983.

———, and Jehuda Reinharz. *The Jew in the Modern World: A Documentary History.* New York: Oxford University Press, 1980.

Mernissi, Fatima. *Beyond the Veil.* New York: Wiley, 1975.

Meyer, Aubrey. "Contraction and Convergence." Available from http://www.gci.org.uk.

Midrash Rabbâh. Translated and edited under the direction of H. Freedman and Maurice Simon. London: Soncino, 1939.

Milani, Farzaneh. *Veils and Words: The Emerging Voids of Iranian Women Writers.* London: Tauris, 1993.

Miller, David. *Dreams of the Burning Child: Sacrificial Sons and the Father's Witness.* Ithaca: Cornell University Press, 2003.

Miller, Rory. "J. L. Magnes and the Promotion of Bi-nationalism in Palestine." *Jewish Journal of Sociology* 48 (2006) 50–68.

Minear, Richard H. "Orientalism and the Study of Japan." *Journal of Asian Studies* 39 (1980) 507–17.

Mir-Hosseini, Ziba. *Islam and Gender: The Religious Debate in Contemporary Iran.* Princeton: Princeton University Press, 1999.

Moallem, Minoo. *Between Warrior Brother and Veiled Sister: Islamic Fundamentalism and the Politics of Patriarchy in Iran.* Berkeley: University of California Press, 2005.

Money-Kyrle, Roger. E. *Psychoanalysis and Politics: A Contribution to the Psychology of Politics and Morals.* London: Duckworth, 1951.

Moore, Molly. "Dutch Convert to Islam: Veiled and Viewed as a 'Traitor.'" *Washington Post Foreign Service* (March 19, 2006) A21.

Moore, Stephen D. *God's Beauty Parlour: And Other Queer Spaces in and around the Bible.* Stanford: Stanford University Press, 2001.

Mosse, George L. *Germans and Jews: The Right, the Left, and the Search for a "Third Force" in pre-Nazi Germany.* New York: Fertig, 1970.

Muhammad, Shaykh ʾUmar Bakri. *Jihad: The Method for Khilafah?*

Musallam, Basim. "Power and Knowledge." *Middle East Research and Information Project* 9:6 (1979) 19–26.

Musrahi, Robert. "Essai d'analyse philosophique de la guerre," 11–26.

Naert, Frederik. "The Impact of the Fight against Terrorism on the *ius ad bellum*." *Ethical Perspectives* 11 (2004) 144–61.

Najmabadi, Afsaneh. *Women with Mustaches and Men without Beards: Gender and Sexual Identities of Iranian Modernity.* Berkeley: University of California Press, 2005.

National Conference of Catholic Bishops. *The Challenge of Peace: God's Promise and Our Response.* Washington, DC: U.S. Conference of Catholic Bishops, 1983.

Niditch, Susan. *War in the Hebrew Bible: A Study in the Ethics of Violence.* New York: Oxford University Press, 1993.

Nietzsche, Friedrich. *Thus Spoke Zarathustra: A Book for Everyone and No One.* Translated by R. J. Hillingdale. Middlesex: Penguin, 1969.

Novak, David. "Buber and Tillich." *Journal of Ecumenical Studies* 29 (1992) 159–74.

———. *The Image of the Non-Jew in Judaism: An Historical and Constructive Study of the Noahide Laws.* Lewiston, NY: Mellen, 1983.

Novikova, Irina. "Lessons from the Anatomy of War: Svetlana Alexievich's Zinky Boys." In *War Discourse, Women's Discourse Essays and Case-studies from Yugoslavia and Russia,* edited by Svetlana Slapšak, 99–116. Ljubljana: TOPOS, 2000.

O'Collins, Gerald. "Crucifixion." In *The Anchor Bible Dictionary,* edited by David Noel Feedman. Vol. 1. New York: Doubleday, 1992.

O'Donovan, Oliver. *The Just War Revisited.* New York: Cambridge University Press, 2003.

Omar, Rashied. "Pope Benedict XVI's Comments on Islam in Regensburg: A Muslim Response." Panel Discussion Pope Benedict in Regensburg: The Catholic Church and Islam: Allies or Adversaries, University of Notre Dame, September 28, 2006, at http://www.wcc-coe.org/wcc/what/interreligious/cd48-04.html (consulted on June 14th 2007).

Omid, Homa. *Islam and the Post Revolutionary State in Iran*. Basingstoke: Palgrave Macmillan, 1994.

Orrmont, Arthur. *Requiem for War: The Life of Wilfrid Owen*. New York: Four Winds, 1974.

Perry, Anne. *Shoulder the Sky*. New York: Ballantine, 2004.

Petchesky, Rosalind P. "Phantom Towers: Feminist Reflections on the Battle between Global Capitalism and Fundamentalist Terrorism." In *September 11, 2001: Feminist Perspectives*, edited by Susan Hawthorne and Bronwyn Winter, 316–30. Victoria: Spinifex, 2002.

Pew Forum on Religion and Public Life. "Iraq and Just War: A Symposium." Washington DC, September 2002. Transcript available at http://pewforum.org/events/index.php?EventID=36.

Plaskow, Judith. "The Sexuality of God." Sherman Lectures. Center for Jewish Studies, Department of Religions and Theology, University of Manchester. Manchester. 2000.

Plate, S. Brent, editor. *Reviewing the Passion: Mel Gibson's Film and its Critics*. New York: Palgrave Macmillan, 2004.

Politkovskaya, Anna. "Crisis in Chechnya." *Guardian* (27 February 2001).

"Potential Sanhedrin." Available from http://www.chayas.com/sanhed.htm#launch.

Prasch, Thomas J. "Orientalism's Other, Other Orientalisms: Women in the Scheme of Empire." *Journal of Women's History* 7:4 (1995) 174–88.

Qaeni, Mohsen. *Zanan* 3:18 (1994).

Qutb, Sayyid. *In the Shade of the Qur'an*, Translated and edited by Adil Salahi and Ashur Shamis. Markfield: Islamic Foundation, 2001.

Rackman, Emanuel. *Modern Halakhah for Our Time*. Hoboken, NJ: Ktav, 1995.

Rad, Gerhard von. *Holy War in the Old Testament*. Translated by Marva J. Dawn. Grand Rapids: Eerdmans, 1991.

Ragland-Sullivan, Ellie. *Essays on the Pleasures of Death*. London: Routledge, 1993.

Ramsey, Paul. *Speak Up for Just War or Pacifism*. University Park: Pennsylvania State University, 1988.

Raphael, Melissa. "The Face of God in Every Generation: Jewish Feminist Spirituality and the Legend of the Thirty-Six Hidden Saints." In *Spirituality and Society in the New Millennium*, edited by Ursula King, 234–46. Brighton: Sussex Academic Press, 2001.

———. *The Female Face of God in Auschwitz: A Jewish Feminist Theology of the Holocaust*. London and New York: Routledge, 2003.

Rapoport-Adler, Ada, editor. *Hasidism Reappraised*. London: Littman Library of Jewish Civilisation, 1996.

Ratzabi, Shalom. *Between Zionism and Judaism: The Radical Circle in Brith Shalom, 1925–1933*. Leiden: Brill, 2002.

Ravandi, Morteza. *Tarikheh Ejtmayieh Iran* (Social History of Iran) Vol. 3, 2nd edition. Tehran: Amir Kabir, 1957.

Ravitsky, Aviezer. *Messianism, Zionism and Jewish Religious Radicalism*. Chicago: University of Chicago Press Press, 1997.

Rejali, Darius. "Viewpoint: The Real Sahme of Abu Ghraib." *Time* (May 20, 2004). Available from http://www.time.com/time/nation/article/0,8599,640375,00. html.

Rich, Adrienne Cecile. *The Arts of the Possible: Essays and Conversations.* New York: Norton, 2001.

———. *The Arts of the Possible.* New York: Norton.

Richlin, Amy. *The Garden of Priapus: Sexuality and Aggression in Roman Humour.* New Haven: Yale University Press, 1983.

Ricoeur, Freud. *Freud and Philosophy: an Essay in Interpretation.* Translated by Denis Savage. New Haven: Yale University Press, 1970.

Ricoeur, Paul. "The Critique of Religion." In *The Philosophy of Paul Ricoeur: An Anthology of His Work,* edited by C. Reagan and D. Stewart. Boston: Beacon, 1978.

Ringold Spitzer, Julie. *When Love is not Enough: Spousal Abuse in Rabbinic and Contemporary Judaism.* New York: Women of Reform Judaism, Federation of Temple Sisterhoods, 1995.

Riskin, Shlomo, "Shabbat Shalom: Parshiot Acharei Mot—Kedoshim Leviticus 16:1– 20:27." *OHR Online* (Apr. 20, 2001). Available from www.ohrtorahstone.org.il/ parsha/5762/achareimot_kedoshim62.htm.

Rizzuto, Ana-Maria, et al. *The Dynamics of Human Aggression: Theoretical Foundations and Clinical Applications.* New York: Brunner-Routledge, 2004.

Robinson, Paul A. *Just War in Comparative Perspective.* Aldershot: Ashgate, 2003.

Rose, Jacqueline. *Why War?—Psychoanalysis, Politics, and the Return of Melanie Klein.* Oxford: Blackwell, 1993.

Rushdoony, R.J. *Institutes of Biblical Law.* Nutley, NJ: Craig, 1973.

Russell Baker, "In Bush's Washington." *The New York Review of Books* 51:8 (May 13, 2004).

Said, Edward W. *Orientalism: Western Conceptions of the Orient.* London: Penguin, 1995.

Sanday, Peggy. *Divine Hunger: Cannibalism as a Cultural System.* Cambridge: Cambridge University Press, 1986.

———. *Female Power and Male Dominance: On the Origins of Sexual Inequality.* Cambridge: Cambridge University Press, 1981.

Schemo, Diana J. "Rate of Rape at Academy is Put at 12% in Survey." *The New York Times* (29 August 2003) A12.

Schilpp, Paul, and Maurice Friedman, editors. *The Philosophy of Martin Buber.* La Salle, IL: Open Court, 1967.

Schindler, Pesach. *Hasidic Responses to the Holocaust in the Light of Hasidic Thought.* Hoboken, NJ: Ktav, 1990.

Schmitt, Carl. *Roman Catholicism and Political Form.* Westport, CT: Greenwood, 1996.

Schwartz-Bart, André. *The Last of the Just.* Translated by Stephen Becker. London: Secker & Warburg, 1962.

Scodie, Mark. "Israel is 'least beautiful country.'" *Jewish Chronicle* (January 7, 2005).

Segev, Tom. *The Seventh Million: The Israelis and the Holocaust.* Translated by Haim Watzman. New York: Hill & Wang, 1993.

Segre, Dan V. "The Emancipation of Jews in Italy." In *Paths of Emancipation: Jews, States and Citizenship*, edited by Pierre Birnbaum and Ira Katznelson, 227–37. Princeton, NJ: Princeton University Press, 1995.

Shaarawi, Hodda. *Harem Years: The Memoirs of an Egyptian Feminist (1879–1924)*. Translated and edited by Margot Badran. London: Virago, 1986.

Shapira, Anita. *Land and Power: The Zionist Resort to Force, 1881–1948*. Oxford: Oxford University Press, 1992.

Shapra, Avraham. "Buber's Attachment to Herder and German 'Volkism.'" *Studies in Zionism* 14 (1993) 1–30

Shavit, Yaacov. *Jabotinsky and the Revisionist Movement 1925–1948*. London: Frank Cass, 1988.

Shepherd, David. "From Gospel to Gibson: An Interview with the Writers." Society of Biblical Literature Annual Meeting, San Antonio 2004. Available from http://www.sbl-site.org/Article.aspx?ArticleId=406.

Shirazi, Faegheh. *The Veil Unveiled: Hijab in Modern Culture*. Gainesville: University Press of Florida, 2001.

Shuster, Morgan. *The Strangling of Persia*. New York: Century, 1968.

Sinclair, Daniel B. "Jewish Law in the State of Israel." *Jewish Law Annual* 9 (1991) 154–67.

Sloyan, Gerard S. *The Crucifixion of Jesus: History, Myth, Faith*. Minneapolis: Fortress, 1995.

Smith, Morton. *Jesus the Magician*. London: Gollancz, 1978.

Solomon, Norman, "The Ethics of War: Judaism." In *The Ethics of War*, edited by Richard Sorabji and David Rodin, 108–37. Aldershot: Ashgate, 2006.

Soloveitchik, Joseph B. "Insights." Lecture, Jan. 6, 1979. Notes available from http://www.613.org/rav/ravnotes2.html#jan0679.

Starr Jordan, David. *War and the Breed*. Boston: Beacon, 1915.

Starr Sered, Susan. *What Makes Women Sick: Maternity, Modesty, and Militarism in Israeli Society*. Hanover: University Press of New England, 2000.

"Statue of Liberty." Kansas City: Lillenas, 1974.

Stein, Ruth. "Fundamentalism, Father and Son and Vertical Desire." *Psychoanalytic Review* 93 (2006) 201–30.

Steinberg, Leo. *The Sexuality of Christ in Renaissance Art and in Modern Oblivion*. London: Faber & Faber, 1984.

Stott, Rebecca. *The Fabrication of the late-Victorian Femme Fatale: The Kiss of Death*. Basingstoke: Palgrave Macmillan, 1992.

Strange, James F. "Crucifixion, Method of." In *The Interpreter's Dictionary of the Bible. Supplementary Volume*, edited by Keith Crim, 199–200. Nashville: Abingdon, 1976.

Strenski, Ivan. *Contesting Sacrifice: Religion, Nationalism, and Social Thought in France*. Chicago: University of Chicago Press, 2002.

Stromberg, Roland N. *Redemption by War: The Intellectual and 1914*. Lawrence: Regent's Kansas, 1982.

Taylor, Diana. "Spectacular Bodies: Gender, Terror, and Argentina's 'Dirty War.'" In *Gendering War Talk*, edited by Miriam Cooke and Angela Woollacott. Princeton: Princeton University Press, 1993.

Taylor, Sandra C. *Vietnamese Women at War: Fighting for Ho Chi Minh and the Revolution*. Lawrence: University Press of Kansas, 1999.

Tec, Nachamah. *Resilience and Courage: Women, Men, and the Holocaust*. New Haven: Yale University Press, 2003.

———. "Women among the Forest Partisans." In *Women in the Holocaust*, edited by Dalia Ofer and Lenore J. Weitzman, 223–64. New Haven: Yale University Press, 1998.

Tendler, Mordecai. "Exchanging Territories for Peace." Lecture, Yeshiva University, New York City, March 2, 2000. Available from www.yu.edu/faculty/emayer/riets_notes/notes_pages/contemphalakha_sp00.doc.

The White House. *The National Security Strategy of the United States of America*. 2002. http://www.whitehouse.gov/nsc/nss.pdf.

Thornton, T. C. G. "Trees, Gibbets and Crosses." *Journal of Theological Studies* 23 (1972) 130–31.

Tombs, David. "Unspeakable Violence: The Truth Commissions in El Salvador and Guatemala." In *Reconciliation: Nations and Churches in Latin America*, edited by Iain Maclean, 55–84. Aldershot: Ashgate, 2006.

———. "Crucifixion, State Terror and Sexual Abuse." *Union Seminary Quarterly Review* 53 (1999) 89–108.

———. "Honour, Shame and Conquest: Male Identity, Sexual Violence and the Body Politic." *Journal of Hispanic/Latino Theology* 9.4 (2002) 21–40.

Tracy, David. *Plurality and Ambiguity: Hermeneutics, Religion, Hope*. San Francisco: Harper & Row, 1987.

Trexler, Richard C. "Gendering Jesus Crucified." In *Iconography at the Crossroads*, edited by Brendan Cassidy, 107–19. Princeton: Index of Christian Art, Department of Art and Archaeology, Princeton University, 1993.

———. *Sex and Conquest: Gendered Violence, Political Order, and the European Conquest of the Americas*. Cambridge: Polity, 1995.

Tropper, Amram. "Yohanan ben Zakkai, Amicus Caesaris: A Jewish Hero in Rabbinic Eyes." *Jewish Studies, an Internet Journal* 2 (2005) 1–17.

Tzaferis, Vassilios. "Crucifixion: The Archaeological Evidence." *Biblical Archaeology Review* 11 (1985) 44–53.

UNICEF. *Middle East Crisis UNICEF Situation Report No. 26* (August 18 2006). Available from http://www.reliefweb.int/rw/rwb.nsf/db900SID/HMYT-6SSLU F?OpenDocument&rc=3&emid=SODA-6RT2S7.

United Methodist Church Council of Bishops. *In Defense of Creation: The Nuclear Crisis and a Just Peace*. Nashville: Graded, 1986.

Usama bin Laden to "America," November 24, 2002. Available from www.observer.co.uk/worldview/story/0,11581,845725,00.html.

Valadier, Paul. "La barbarie dans la civilization: Réflexions sur le terrorisme international." *Revue théologique de Louvain* 34 (2003) 457–72.

van Iersel, Fred. "Stopping the Murdering Martyr: Just War Tradition and the Confrontation with Ethical Asymmetry in Warfare." In *Just War and Terrorism*, edited by Wim Smit, 165–90. Leuven: Peeters, 2005.

Vernant, Jean Pierre, and Pierre Vidal-Naquet. *Tragedy and Myth in Ancient Greece*. Sussex: Harvest, 1981.

Wallace, Andy. "Reason, Society and Religion: Reflections on September 11th from a Habermasian Perspective." *Philosophy and Social Criticism* 29 (2003) 491–515.

Walzer, Michael. *Arguing about War*. New Haven: Yale University Press, 2004.

———. *Just and Unjust Wars: A Moral Argument with Historical Illustrations*. New York: Basic Books, 1977.

Warner, Marina. *Alone of All Her Sex: The Myth and the Cult of the Virgin Mary*. New York: Wallaby, 1976.

Weigel, George. "World Order: What Catholics Forgot." *First Things* 143 (May, 2004) 31–38.

Weil, Simone. "The Iliad or the Poem of Force." In *Revisions: Changing Perspectives in Moral Philosophy*, edited by Stanley Hauerwas and Alasdair MacIntyre, 222–48. Notre Dame: University of Notre Dame, 1983.

Weise, Christian. "Struggling for Normality: The Apologetics of *Wissenschaft des Judentums* in Wilhelmine Germany as an Anti-colonial Intellectual Revolt against the Protestant Construction of Judaism." In *Towards Normality? Acculturation and Modern German Jewry*, edited by Rainer Liedtke and David Rechter. Tübingen: Mohr/Siebeck, 2003.

Weiss-Rosmarin, Trude. "Martin Buber." *Jewish Spectator* (September 1965) 3–5.

Weiss, Yfaat. "Central European Ethnonationalism and Zionist Binationalism." *Jewish Social Studies* 11 (2004) 94.

Wijngaards, John. "Naked without Shame." *Mission Today* (Summer 1995) 12–13.

Wilcock, Evelyn. *Pacifism and the Jews*. Stroud: Hawthorn, 1994.

Williams, J. A. "A Return to the Veil in Egypt." *Middle East Review* 11:3 (1979) 49–54.

Wittenberg, Jonathan. "Hope amid Flames." *Jewish Chronicle* (August 4, 2006).

Wittgenstein, Ludwig. *Tractatus logico-philosophicus*. Translated by D. F. Pears and B. F. Mcguinness. London: Routledge & Kegan Paul, 1921.

World Islamic Front. *Jihad against Jews and Crusaders*. Statement, February 23, 1998. Available from http://www.fas.org/irp/world/para/docs/980223-fatwa.htm.

Yadin, Y. "Epigraphy and Crucifixion." *Israel Exploration Journal* 23 (1973) 18–22.

Yoder, John Howard. *He Came Preaching Peace*. Eugene, OR: Wipf & Stock Publishers, 1998.

———. *Nevertheless: The Varieties and Shortcomings of Religious Pacifism*. Scottsdale, PA: Herald, 1992.

———. *When War Is Unjust: Being Honest in Just-War Thinking*. Minneapolis: Augsburg, 1984.

Yosef, Ovadia. "Ceding Territory of the Land of Israel in Order to Save Lives." *Crossroads* 3 (1990) 11–28.

Yuchtman-Yaar, Ephraim. "Shas: the Haredi-dovish Image in a Changing Reality." *Israel Studies* 5:2 (2000) 32–77.

Zoar, Noam J. "Morality and War: A Critique of Bleich's Oracular Halakha." In *Commandment and Community: New Essays in Jewish Legal and Political Philosophy*, edited by D. H. Frank, 245–58. Albany, NY: SUNY Press, 1995.

Zubaida, Sami. "Is there a Muslim society? Ernest Gellner's Sociology of Islam." *Economy and Society* 24:2 (1995) 151–88.